This is New Jersey

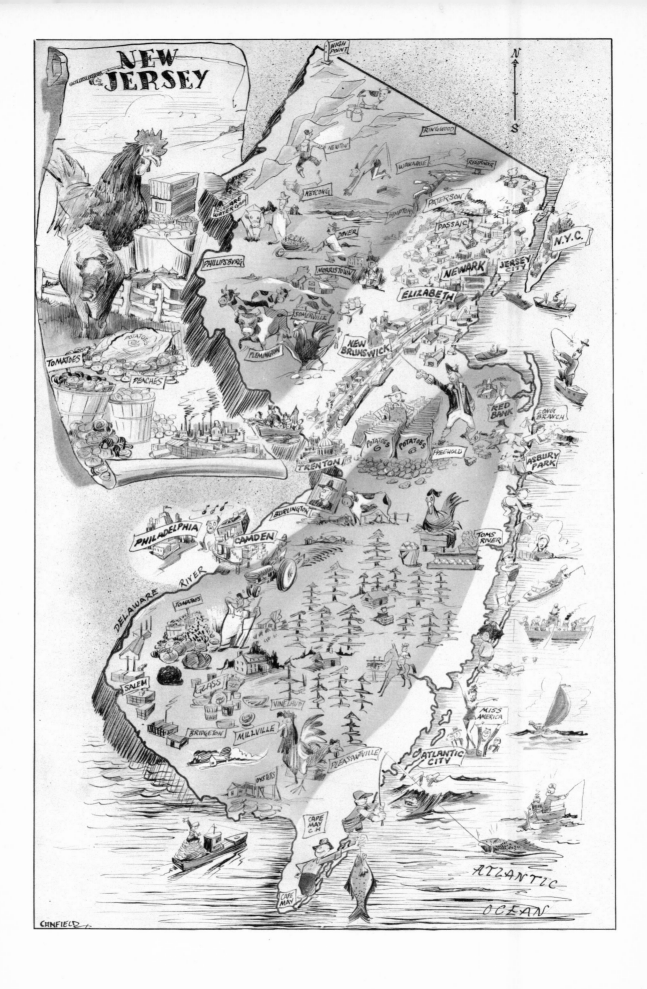

This
is
NEW JERSEY

from High Point

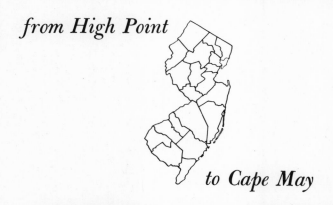

to Cape May

John T. Cunningham
MAPS BY WILLIAM M. CANFIELD

1953

Rutgers University Press

NEW BRUNSWICK   NEW JERSEY

FOR
Jay and Ruth

Foreword

This book is an outgrowth of the enthusiasm for New Jersey held by Richard B. Scudder, publisher, and Lloyd M. Felmly, editor, of *The Newark News*. Most of the material in these pages appeared originally in *The News*, and the entire project was planned and developed by *The News* after a conference with several leading New Jersey historians and the author.

Recognizing that the principal dedication of the paper must be to present news as it happens each day, Mr. Felmly nevertheless believes that *The News* should pause at times and take stock of what has gone before. Thus, the paper has brought its readership several highly interesting and authentic series dealing with New Jersey's heritage.

These have ranged through many topics—Indians, inventors, governors of the state, sketches of old Newark, the development of railroading in New Jersey, intriguing places for summer motorists to explore and, finally, the series on the 21 counties.

The News has been cited for these series by the State of New Jersey and by the American Association for State and Local History. It has earned the high regard and sincere appreciation of teachers, historians, publicists and others intimately concerned with bringing to many people a knowledge of New Jersey. Possibly most important of all, however, is the fact that *The News* has proved that by telling the story of New Jersey's absorbing background it has heightened the general reader's interest in the Jersey scene.

RICHARD P. McCORMICK

Rutgers University

New Brunswick, 1953

Acknowledgments

It is clear that no one could prepare a state-wide study without the cooperation of many people. The difficulty comes in paying sufficient tribute to those who saw the merit of *This Is New Jersey* and contributed freely of their time, information and advice.

Particular appreciation is expressed to Lloyd M. Felmly, editor of *The News*, who conceived the idea of this work and accorded me complete editorial freedom in preparing the material. His willingness to permit publication of the manuscript by Rutgers University Press is deeply appreciated.

Richard P. McCormick, Rutgers University history professor; Roger McDonough, state librarian; Miriam Studley, New Jersey librarian at Newark Public Library, and Joseph T. Scarry of *The News* helped in the initial planning of the work. I am especially grateful to Arlene R. Sayre of the State Department of Conservation and Economic Development for her patient, careful reading of the entire manuscript and for her many useful suggestions. Miss Studley and Miriam Ball of Newark Library assisted often in gathering information and pictures.

The list of people who aided in individual studies in each county is long, and I hope they know that without their aid the project would have been much ·more difficult. These included Edwin L. Gerber, Fannie T. Taber, Hiram B. D. Blauvelt, Nathaniel R. Ewan, Karl A. Dickinson, J. Meade Landis, Emma V. Duffield, Harvey B. Nelson, Hiram E. Deats, Donald A. Sinclair, Edward N. Feltus, Grace J. Vogt, Jack Lamping, D. Stanton Hammond, Harry A. Crispin, Dr. David R. Evans, Joseph Valler, Dr. A. L. Johnson and Robert E. Frederick. These are the "grass roots" authorities, all of whom are intrigued by local history and vitally concerned with keeping it alive.

The advice and editing of the material by Robert T. Taylor, feature editor of *The News*, and Edward S. Hipp and Joseph Taddeo of *The News* tightened the original manuscript considerably. I am also grateful to Harold N. Munger, Jr., former director of Rutgers University Press, for believing in the work, and to David Grinnell and Alan James of the Press for their work on the book. Page Spencer, who edited *This Is New Jersey*, has earned my respect and gratitude for a conscientious, capable job.

Many of the pictures in the book are from the picture files of *The Newark News*, where Bert Hunt, Stanley Grupy and Albert Orr aided in securing them. Credits for pictures go also to Newark Public Library, the State Library at Trenton, State Department of Conservation and Economic Development, New Jersey Department of Agriculture, Southern New Jersey Development Council, Standard Oil Company of New Jersey, Middlesex County Industrial Commission, New Jersey Bell Telephone Company, Union County Park Commission, Campbell's Soup Company, Rutgers University, Atlantic City Electric Company, Port of New York Authority, Palisades Interstate Park Commission, South Jersey Port Commission, Delaware River Port Authority and Atlantic City Convention Bureau.

Thanks go, too, to the staff photographers of *The News*, who worked closely with the author in preparing illustrative matter; to Bruce Owen Nett of Madison, for assistance in gathering supplemental illustrative material, and to Elizabeth G. Brophy and Dorothy P. Gulgun of the State Department of Conservation and Economic Development for helping me find needed pictures.

The maps, which excited a great deal of interest and contributed materially to the success of the series as it appeared originally, are all reproduced in their warm detail. They are the work of Bill Canfield, talented staff artist of *The News*.

Naturally I am grateful to the many people who have offered me pictures, books and suggestions for the manuscript. Such material often filled in blank spots in the work, and, above all, offered me proof that the project had the firm support of many people.

Finally—and obviously not the least important—

I am in deep debt to my wife Dot, and our Jay and Ruth, who patiently waited for the long, long hours of work on *This Is New Jersey* to end. They ask, quite rightly, "Is it time now for *us* to enjoy New Jersey too?" The answer is, "Yes, it's time!"

JOHN T. CUNNINGHAM

Florham Park
June, 1953

Contents

The Spirit of Jersey

You watch the moon cut a silver path across Lake Hopatcong or you climb Sunrise Mountain in Stokes State Forest to look at sun-bathed Kittatinny Valley. You watch cattle picking at grass on rocky slopes in Northwest Jersey or you stop to see a maple tree tapped for syrup at Newfoundland.

. . . and a vaudeville comedian can get a laugh by mentioning that he's from "Joisey."

You wake up in a Bridgeton hotel on a beautiful August morning, and the delightful aroma of spices seeping through the window tells you forcibly that it's catsup time again in South Jersey.

. . . and all over America people think New Jersey smells like the Secaucus meadows.

The wind whistles through stunted trees as you shuffle across the sand beneath old Barnegat Lighthouse, and dark clouds scudding overhead foretell an impending October seaside storm, one of nature's most impelling spectacles.

. . . and millions of people think the Jersey shore is just a long boardwalk or acres of burning skin.

You look at dozens of 200-year-old houses in old Salem or you see the charm of the old churches at Tennant, Shrewsbury and Middletown. You sit on the fishing docks along the canals in Sea Isle City or you watch the oyster fleet come in at Bivalve.

. . . and wonder why all roads lead to New England.

Climbing a fire tower in Lebanon State Forest to look out over hundreds of square miles of almost unbroken pine lands, you contrast this vast wilderness with the view off Eagle Rock, where the eye encompasses the most densely settled section of America.

. . . and you're glad you know New Jersey.

Familiarity with New Jersey breeds respect, because here there is diversity; here there is contrast.

There are windmills by the Millstone River, factories by the Passaic; rugged grandeur in the Palisades, handsome hills in Somerset; vegetables in the fields of South Jersey, railroad patterns in Hudson; chickens on Hunterdon's hillsides and Miss America in Atlantic City.

Truly New Jersey is a paradox; its location astride the main transportation routes of the East has made it both tremendously vital and relatively unadmired. The rising sun throws New York's shadow over the state, the setting sun bathes Jersey in the shade of Philadelphia. Caught between these two great cities, New Jersey has been thought of largely as a path—or, as Benjamin Franklin said, "like a barrel tapped at both ends."

But beside that Philadelphia-New York path there is intriguing variance, so much that it makes knowing New Jersey difficult. Statistics can prepare the way to knowing the state, although they can't reveal the charm—any more than a tape measure can reflect Miss America's personality.

Jersey is small, as every one knows—45th in size in the country—in fact, so small that if all states were the size of New Jersey, the American flag would have 370 rather than 48 stars. Yet within this small space are living 4,800,000 people, most of them so jammed in the "city belt" between Hudson County and Camden that 84 per cent of the state's acreage is still either farmland or forestland.

A Garden State? Well, yes and no.

Yes, to the extent that its 25,000 farms have an annual gross income of close to $400,000,000 and a national standing of first in value of farm income per acre. No, to the extent that New Jersey's industries rank sixth in value of manufactured goods, ranging from silk to petroleum.

All work and no play? Hardly. The lakelands in

North Jersey and the famed beaches in South Jersey add up to an annual multi-billion dollar enterprise, ranked third in the nation.

But statistics do not necessarily engender pride or deepen a heritage. Those require the focusing of attention on the home lot, on the twenty-one counties which comprise New Jersey. The reward far transcends mere provincialism, because in New Jersey are found all the elements which have combined to change a new world into the United States in less than three centuries.

The Dutch, Swedes and Finns first settled New Jersey, but they found no difficulty in living with their English conquerors. Dutch, Swedes, Finns, English, Irish, Scotch, in turn, found room for Germans who came early in the eighteenth century to farm the fields of Hunterdon or to work in Salem County glassworks or in Passaic County iron mines.

Later, in the nineteenth century, masses of Irish who fled the potato famine came to build the state's railroads. Germans who fled political persecution came to breathe freely in New Jersey. The state found room for Italians who came at the time of the Civil War to help create Vineland and Hammonton in the South Jersey pines.

Then, in the 1880's and 1890's, as immigrant ships brought the hopeful from all lands, the growing industries of New Jersey absorbed them. The Hungarians, the Poles, the Swiss, the Russians, the French, the Czecho-Slovakians, the Lithuanians and the Scandinavians came to add their virtues to the melting pot. Jersey's three centuries of growth have taken vitality from the varied people who came to its shores.

Jersey's diversity offered some reminder of the homeland to these newcomers, for nature has split the state into three varied areas: The mountain country, the central hill and valley country, and the coastal plains of South Jersey.

In the mountain country, rich iron mines—plus fast-running streams and unlimited forests—attracted the ironmakers to Morris, Passaic, Warren, Sussex and Hunterdon. Farmers broke the hilly ground and struggled for a living, until they found that dairy cattle brought dividends greater than anything which could be grown in the fields. Estates of the wealthy clustered on the mountains, and when railroads came the North Jersey commuter was born. Today the cattle and iron and homemakers have been joined by the vacationists who know and love the lakes in the Highlands.

Nevertheless, the most vital portion of New Jersey is the central strip—that corridor linking New York and Philadelphia. This is the "city belt," and, with the exception of Atlantic City, every major city in the state is in this corridor. This is the heart of New Jersey industry, the homeland of the commuting population whose very life revolves about New York and Philadelphia. Over this corridor stretch the busiest highways and railroads in the world, linked at either end with docks and piers which give and take in world markets.

Finally there is Southern New Jersey, itself a study of sharp divergence. These are the components of South Jersey: A thin strip of land running from Cape May to Sandy Hook, where surf and sand combine to make a seaside playground for the nation; a vast area of pines and scrub oak trees, where mere man has met only frustration and economic collapse; a wide belt of verdant, prolific soil spread in an arc around the western edge of the pines.

Atlantic City, barely a hundred years old, is probably the nation's best-known vacation resort. Cape May and Long Branch had national fame by Civil War time, while Asbury Park has grown rapidly since its founding right after the Civil War. The Jersey shore is known to countless millions of people, most of whom have not the slightest interest in anything else in the Garden State.

If New Jersey deserves the name Garden State, incidentally, it's largely because of the rich strip of soil which starts in Monmouth County and circles down through the lower parts of Middlesex and Mercer counties, through the western part of Burlington and on into Camden, Gloucester, Salem and Cumberland counties. Most of the state's potatoes, tomatoes, vegetables and fruits are grown in this garden strip and the state's major food processing plants are here.

South Jersey has more, much more, than seaside resorts and farmlands. It has chickens, with Monmouth, Ocean, Atlantic and Cumberland counties (plus Hunterdon in North Jersey) accounting for nearly all the state's huge annual $133 million income from poultry. It has glassworks, in Salem and Cumberland counties (and can boast that the industry goes back to 1738). It has the thriving and picturesque oyster fleet in Cumberland County and the important commercial fisheries all along the coast. It has the rapidly expanding industrial region strung all along the Delaware River below Trenton.

Jersey's strategic geographical placement has always modified its history. There is the story of

New Jersey's leading role in the Revolution—admittedly because troops constantly marched and counter-marched across the state to attack or to defend the vital ports of New York and Philadelphia. General Washington and his armies spent more than one-quarter of the war on Jersey soil. Four major battles and nearly a hundred minor engagements took place between the Hudson and the Delaware.

Three times Washington took to the New Jersey hills for winter headquarters, twice in Morristown and once in Middlebrook. South Jersey food and North Jersey iron supplied the troops constantly. Bloody footprints in the snow and starvation in wretched quarters were as much a mark of Jockey Hollow as Valley Forge. Jersey's "Summer soldiers," "sunshine patriots" and outright Tories contrasted with Jersey's minutemen and seashore privateers.

But as the nation grew, it divided, and New Jersey was caught in the middle. The Quakers of South Jersey long had opposed slavery, with Mount Holly's John Woolman a vigorous advocate of emancipation in the eighteenth century. Warren County's Benjamin Lundy won recognition early in the nineteenth century as the leader of the Abolitionists. Slavery-haters strung out from Salem to Hoboken helped fleeing Negroes escape their pursuers.

However, the boot and shoemakers of Newark and the snuffmakers of Middlesex County opposed the war, fearing loss of their Southern markets. One quarter of the state lay below the imaginary Mason-Dixon line, including Cape May, where Southern aristocrats long had gathered. Half of Princeton University's student body came from the South.

But Copperhead sentiment couldn't eclipse the fact that the North's first volunteers came from New Jersey's Warren County, or that Cumberland County supplied a greater number of volunteers in proportion to its size than any other county in the north. New Jersey did its share, particularly after war contracts proved to be every bit as lucrative as the lost Southern trade.

Then industry edged into the Garden State. Railroads reached almost every part of New Jersey by 1870 and by 1900 the state had the greatest concentration of railroad track in the country. The Hudson County waterfront grew from mudflats to busy piers. Factories arose beside the tracks—in Jersey City, Hoboken, Bayonne, Harrison, Kearny, Newark, Elizabeth, New Brunswick, and on down to Trenton and Camden.

Iron mines in the Morris hills and zinc mines in Sussex prospered. Phillipsburg grew from hamlet to city. Paterson stopped building locomotives and made silk. Trenton found that pottery and iron combined to make a stable economy. Camden's star rose on soup, shipbuilding, steel pens and victrolas.

The movie industry started and grew in New Jersey, beginning in Thomas A. Edison's laboratory and spreading to the Palisades, where the earliest movie companies filmed thrillers at Fort Lee. Edison gave the world the electric light, the talking machine. Everywhere Jersey was abustle, always in the stream of industrial progress, often far ahead of the current.

Strikingly enough, despite this industrial growth, New Jersey didn't move from rural to urban status until the census of 1880, when 54 per cent of the population was adjudged urban. That same census also saw New Jersey's population top the 1,000,000 mark for the first time. Yet, in 1900, when the population soared to 1,883,669 (70 per cent urban) farms also reached a new high in number—34,650.

Since then, farm acreage has been cut nearly in half but farm output has soared spectacularly as Jersey farmers moved well out in front of the nation's agriculturists in increasing the rate of milk production per cow, egg production per hen, and yield per acre for many crops.

The state's most spectacular increase has been in egg production, which in the last 25 years alone has increased 316 per cent. Dairy farmers have moved ahead remarkably, too, increasing milk production almost 60 per cent since 1925. Seabrook Farms in Cumberland County has helped stimulate a big jump in vegetable production for quick freezing. Potatoes, tomatoes, string beans, asparagus, celery, onions, peas, cabbage, all continue to be important Jersey crops.

The garden patches partially gave way as soon as the railroads rolled over the mountains to Morristown, down the plains to Somerville and across the meadows to Paterson and Hackensack; people started to move out into the country. Still, it took the automobile to accelerate the move (and, to make it possible for New Jersey to absorb the 3,000,000 new residents who have arrived since 1900).

Nowhere has the increase been more startling than in once-bucolic Bergen County, where the population has rocketed from 78,441 in 1900 to more than 550,000 today. Completion of the George

Washington Bridge in 1931 had much to do with the increase, but the fact is that Bergen grew 75 per cent in population between 1900 and 1910, another 53 per cent from 1910 to 1920, and still another 73 per cent from 1920 to 1930.

Such residential increases as those in Bergen—and in Morris, Essex, Union, Passaic and Somerset—have added to North Jersey's reputation as a "dormitory for New York." Similar increases in population in Camden, Burlington and Gloucester counties also have made a "dormitory" for Philadelphia.

So, New Jersey has variety, even if it escapes most people (and in a way you can't blame people, who must also judge a state by headlines from Bergen and Atlantic and Hudson counties). But, putting the headlines aside, one way to grasp the Jersey variety is to contrast and compare the component parts, the twenty-one counties of the state.

Compare Atlantic County's recreation industry and small year-around population with the teeming population and heavy industry of Bergen. Put Burlington's farmlands and pinelands against Camden's growth in the shadow of Philadelphia, then contrast both of them with the quietude of old Cape May, where it is said that there are more descendants of Mayflower passengers than there are in Plymouth, Massachusetts.

Take tidewater Cumberland, with its oysters, glass, chickens and frozen foods, and contrast it with Essex, where factories, department stores, insurance houses and economic importance mingle with the pleasant homes in the Orange Mountains. They differ, but nothing like the difference between old Gloucester, the "Garden Patch of Philadelphia," and Hudson, the railroad and dockside center of the state. Hunterdon, 70 per cent rural, has ·a farm atmosphere radically different from Gloucester's—and Hunterdon's pleasant hills are somewhat more attractive than Hudson's waterfront (in most opinions, at least).

The "M" counties—Middlesex, Mercer, Monmouth and Morris—might well be called the "heritage" counties, because within them are found a major portion of the state's Revolutionary War importance. The "M's" include historically-important Princeton and Rutgers universities, and Middlesex and Mercer combine to make up the tiny 32-mile waistline across the state's center. Much of New Jersey's history has been shaped along this waistline, of course, because of its transportation vitality. The iron of Morris helped influence New Jersey manufacture, the marl beds of Monmouth influenced state-wide agriculture. The state capital at Trenton has made Mercer County a logical center, while Middlesex has always been a transportation key.

Salem's lush fields and quiet dignity compare favorably with both the estate country in the Somerset hills and the dairy farms on the rocky Sussex mountain slopes. Through these three counties can be glimpsed a picture of Jersey's differing topography—ranging from the flat swampy Salem lowlands where muskrats live, through hills leveling into valleys in Somerset, and on up to Jersey's highest spot in Sussex County.

Finally, place Union's heavy industry and convenient commuting towns against Warren's beautiful hill scenery, where only Phillipsburg has the right to claim itself industrial. Lest anyone think that Warren has all the scenery to the disadvantage of Union, however, let him drive through Union County's Watchung Reservation.

Somehow New Jersey escapes the words which praise it (and, fortunately, the words which damn it). That's because New Jersey is more than people, more than geography, more than history, more than industry, more than agriculture.

Jersey is a flotilla of sailboats on a North Jersey lake, a picnic in a state forest. It's the old streets of Cape May, the newness of the New Jersey Turnpike. It's the red and gold touched on North Jersey maple leaves in the fall, the magic of Atlantic City in July. It's the George Washington Bridge and the wooden covered bridge at Columbia.

Jersey is old, Jersey is new. It struggles to be all things to all men, and both fails and succeeds. It is factory, it is farm. Jersey is High Point, Jersey is Cape May.

Diversity—that's the spirit of Jersey.

The HILL COUNTRY

In New Jersey we call them mountains, yet we know that in Colorado or Utah—or even New Hampshire—they might be considered mere mounds. But visitors agree that these midget mountains, these rolling hills, have a rugged handsomeness all their own.

The Hill Country sets the topographic pattern for New Jersey, starting at the very northern tip on High Point and rolling southeastward through a series of declining hills to the plains below the Watchung Mountains.

This is the Hill Country, where streams dash downward to the sea and give to the land the richness to sustain abundant dairy farms and prime estates; where cool, blue lakes offer relief from the summer sun; where the quiet of the forests is the unobtrusive background for a falls tumbling a hundred feet through a clearing in the trees.

This is the Hill Country, where iron abounds in the Highlands, and zinc and lime add variety; where the Falls of Paterson, cascading from a rocky precipice, gave America's heavy industry its birth; where modern laboratories and research buildings fit harmoniously into the neatness of residential life.

This is the Hill Country, where Washington three times brought his weary Revolutionists to rest and to re-arm. This is a land of heritage, of industrial beginnings. A land of vacationists and homemakers. A land of beauty and opportunity.

This is the Hill Country; this is our scenic best.

South from Sunrise Mountain in Stokes State Forest, overlooking broad, fertile Kittatinny Valley.

SUSSEX

Somehow Sussex County's geographic position at the very top of New Jersey and its standing as the state's leading dairy county fit easily together, almost as if the cream of New Jersey has risen to the top.

Obviously, Sussex has no monopoly on natural beauty, but it can boast of a major share of mountain scenery, lakes, and state forests and parks. Sussex has the highest point in Jersey and a share in Lake Hopatcong, the state's biggest lake. Scenically, it cannot be denied that Sussex has a high cream content. Literally the county has a high cream content, too; Sussex has long been regarded as the state's prime milk-producing county.

Still, the rich farm potential and the mountain scenery were not the attractions that lured Dutchmen down from what is now Kingston, New York, in the 1640's. Had agriculture been on their minds these Hollanders probably would have ignored Sussex,—because rolling country that was unlike their homeland did not overly interest Dutch farmers.

But these newcomers were not farmers; they were restless adventurers seeking gold in the tree-covered mountains, and by 1645 they had followed the range down to a rocky mountain slope just north of the Delaware Water Gap. There they found copper, possibly as early as 1640, definitely by 1657. They took the copper back along the mountains and as they went they developed the first road in the United States, a 140-mile thoroughfare linking the Pahaquarry copper mine with Esopus (now Kingston).

No Indian trouble developed, even though these tree-covered mountains had long been the location of Kittatinny, the Lenni-Lenape "chief town."

Other Dutch and French Huguenots from Esopus also came down the old mine road, some remaining in the valley to plant crops along the Delaware, others climbing over the mountain to the flat marshy "Drowned Lands" where the sluggish Wallkill River overflowed its banks near the New York border.

High Point, elevation 1803 feet, is "Top of New Jersey."

English, Irish and Scotch emigrants came overland soon after 1700 to the Kittatinny slopes, which they called the "Blue" Mountains. Colonel Thomas De Kay exchanged sixty acres of land in lower Manhattan for twelve hundred acres along Hamburgh Mountain—considered a rather neat bargain in 1724. Germans came up from Philadelphia in the 1740's, led by John Peter Bernhardt and Caspar Shafer, and settled along the Tockhokkonetkong River (now called by the less jaw-cracking name of Paulins Kill).

So while many knew of the lands near the Blue Mountains, Philadelphia leaders heard to their astonishment in 1730 that people lived west of the mountains—and without getting English permission at that! Up the Delaware River went Nicholas Scull, famed English surveyor, and John Lukens, chain-bearer, to investigate.

Sure enough, there on the fertile lands of the Delaware they found many Hollanders. Samuel Dupui, their leader, welcomed Scull and Lukens (who marveled at the orchards—"greater than any in Philadelphia"). Dupui told Scull of the old mine road, by then used to take Delaware Valley wheat

and cider to Kingston and to bring in supplies. The Philadelphia-oriented Scull asked Samuel why he didn't use the Delaware River to get to market. Dupui replied simply that he didn't know where the river ran to.

Scarcely six hundred people lived in the whole county region in 1750, when settlers first started to grumble about going all the way to Morristown for court. There were no towns, not even any plantations, and in general the vast acreage had little economic importance. Morris County did not particularly regret losing the area when the Legislature created Sussex County on June 8, 1753.

Leaders of the new county met on November 20, 1753, to grant tavern licenses and to fix fees for liquor and provender. This reflected a major interest of the day, since for many decades the Sussex County tavern keeper's position meant a big boost in the climb to economic and political success.

In the following spring, county fathers levied taxes of £100 annually, two-thirds of which went to pay bounties for the killing of wolves and panthers. The remaining money went to build a log

Portion of Old Mine Road, earliest road in the United States.

Old Cochran House, built in 1840 in Newton, is one of North Jersey's most noted inns.

gaol, a lockup so flimsy that the sheriff complained he couldn't keep prisoners in. For their part, prisoners said they wouldn't stay in the jail if the sheriff couldn't keep the sheep out.

Sussex courts returned temporarily to Morristown in 1757, driven there by savage Indian uprisings along the Delaware valley. Indians who had long brooded over the loss of their territory in the valley struck back at white settlers in 1755. Alarmed state officials appropriated £10,000 in December, 1755, to build stone forts along the river.

The most noted of the Indian killings took place near Swartswood Lake, where in May, 1756, Anthony Swartwout, his wife and a daughter met death, and two young children became Indian captives. Other killings prompted Governor Belcher to offer rewards for male Indians over fifteen years of age, dead or alive. Tom Quick, an Indian killer of repute (or disrepute, depending on what kind of a humane yardstick is used for measurement), boasted of single-handedly killing scores of Indians.

Fortunately, wiser heads succeeded in ending the killings by persuading the Indians in 1758 to relinquish peacefully their territorial claims. The end

of the bloody Indian struggle focused attention on another battle, the war over the New York-New Jersey borderline which raged with more or less heat for fifty years after it started in 1719. Many beatings and shootings ensued before bi-state action fixed the border in 1722 at its present line.

Jonathan Hampton of Essex County, a man of some influence in Trenton, in 1761 shoved into prominence a place called New Town when the Legislature authorized the county to build a courthouse and jail a half-mile from Henry Hairlocker's house (on Hampton's property). Surveyors chained off the half-mile and found the location in the middle of a stream. A bit of chain-stretching moved the site halfway up the hill (and ever since, Newton folk have wished the surveyors had really stretched the chains and gone all the way to the hilltop, where the courthouse logically belongs.)

A substantial stone courthouse was built in 1765 on a plot of ground conveyed to the county by Hampton for five shillings. No one questioned Hampton's public spiritedness, but few missed the fact, either, that his adjacent lands quickly increased in value.

Days of scarcity and struggle marked Sussex

from 1760 to 1775, but in the latter year the free-holders found the rebellious courage to face up to the Crown with the announcement that Sussex County no longer would pay the salaries of any Royal judge. The Revolutionary War passed Sussex County by, except for supplies which flowed from field and forge—and except for Bonnell Moody, one of the best known of all British spies. Moody hid out in a cave located between Big and Little Muckshaw Ponds, near Springdale, from whence he sallied out to contact British sympathizers.

The price on Moody's head rose sharply in May, 1780, when he led six men into Newton to free the prisoners in the jail. "Poor Jemmy," the jailer, "trembled like a leaf" and handed over the keys. Moody threw open the doors, gave three lusty cheers for the King—and tradition says the cheers and the Indian war whoops of Moody's men frightened Newton people so badly that all of them fled the town. Moody fled, too, and most historians agree that the Americans never caught up with him.

Sussex County's economic position sagged during the Revolution, and assessment against it in 1781 of £8,038 to help pay for the war staggered the county. The economic struggles of these Jersey frontiersmen so absorbed them that they scarcely noticed an influx of big landholders from 1780 to 1810. Robert Ogden became Sparta's first permanent settler in 1778 and the Ogden family worked the rich mines in Sparta Mountain. Others came to start great estates—Lewis Morris, Thomas Lawrence and John Rutherford, to mention a few.

Census figures in both 1800 and 1810 showed Sussex County second only to Essex County in population. The building of turnpikes between 1804 and 1815 helped boost the county and, after stages began to run in 1808, newcomers filtered in. The influx of new residents lifted county population to 32,754 in 1820, making Sussex first in the state in population. True enough, Sussex then included all of Warren County—but second-ranked Essex then also included all of Union and the Paterson area of Passaic County.

Most of Sussex County's prosperity and population centered well below Newton, however, and that region began to stir discontentedly in 1815. The defeat of an 1819 act to permit the alternating

Harvesting grain in Sparta. Sussex is highly rural—and hence, highly scenic.

Cattle grazing on a farm near Augusta in New Jersey's leading dairy county.

of courts between Oxford and Newton hastened a split; constant pressure finally caused the Legislature to cut Warren County away from Sussex in 1824. Sussex County population dropped to 20,346 in 1830 and remained stationary throughout most of the nineteenth century.

Temperance leaders in the 1830's shook their heads in despair. An early chronicler tells of the consumption of "liquid poison," which increased "until, like the great deluge, it seemed to flood the land." Lovers of the spirits seemed especially numerous near Swartswood Lake, where three towns within a few miles of one another were known far and wide as "Gin Point," "Brandy Hook" and "Rum Corner."

William Rankin, who founded a famous private school at Deckertown (Sussex) in 1833, felt that education was the answer to drinking and lawlessness. Indeed, he advertised in 1834 that after only a year of his school in Deckertown the village "now contains a goodly portion of pious and moral citizens." Be that as it may, the fact remains that Rankin's school within twenty years turned out nearly five hundred graduates who went on to become schoolteachers elsewhere.

Rankin's school vied continuously for county educational leadership with a school that Edward Stiles opened in 1833 at nearby Mt. Retirement. In 1844 Rankin had seventy-six students, Stiles seventy-four—all private scholars. Sussex County looked unkindly on free education; as late as 1853 a town meeting in Newton rejected the idea of raising money for free schools.

Interesting enough, therefore, is the fact that Daniel Haines of Hamburg, who became governor of New Jersey in 1843-44 and 1848-51, led a fight to improve the state's educational system, particularly the free schools. His success in establishing New Jersey's first normal school (plus his leadership in the adoption of the new 1844 State Constitution) made his administrations outstanding.

The building of the Morris Canal boomed the iron mines at Andover and gave new life to forges, such as those at Stanhope, Waterloo and Franklin Furnace. Yet, of all the ore digging, that at Franklin was most vital, because there Dr. Samuel Fowler, distinguished physician, became the first to appreciate the value of the zinc ore in the Sussex hills.

Dr. Fowler, whose medical practice spread over five counties, moved from Hamburg to "The Plains" in 1810. He built mills, shops, and dwellings, and called the village Franklin. Soon he recognized the presence of zinc and interested other mineralogists in the ore he called "Franklinite."

Among other things, Dr. Fowler perfected a process in about 1830 for making a bluish-white zinc oxide powder to use as a paint base. He naturally took great pride in 1838 when the Federal Government used Franklin zinc in making the nation's first standard set of brass weights and measures. His death in 1844 opened the mines to others, and when two companies were organized in 1848 and 1849 to exploit the mines, a fifty-year legal battle over ore rights started.

Nevertheless, an experimental plant at Newark started to use Franklin zinc in 1852 to make zinc oxide. Shortly after the Civil War the manufacture of metallic zinc began in Newark, with the "Horse Head" and "Bertha" brands of Franklin slab zinc quickly becoming recognized as the acknowledged world zinc standards.

The nature of Sussex agriculture underwent a radical change after the Sussex Railroad rolled into Newton in 1854. First of all, Newton became the center of farm trade. Wagons which once hauled Sussex County farm produce to Chester in Orange County, New York, now headed for the railroad depot in Newton. Even the butter wagons which had gone overland twice weekly to Chester stopped running.

Western competition killed markets for Sussex County beef and pork and corn and flour, but the ability of the railroads to get milk to big city outlets changed the cattleman's emphasis from beef to dairy cows. The county's first milk trains started in 1863 and, as other railroads laid tracks over the county, milk depots sprang up everywhere. Railroads employed milk agents to roam the countryside, seeking new shippers. Dairying became the county's prime industry before the end of the Civil War.

Sussex County paused for the war, of course, although there were plenty of people who didn't particularly relish the pause. In fact, many of the county's young men joined the "Skedaddle Army" which marched off to Canada in May, 1862, to avoid

Works at Franklin zinc mine, long one of nation's top zinc producers.

Typical of the rural beauty of Sussex is this hillside haying scene.

the draft. In March, 1863, a Southern-minded assailant fired a bullet at Reverend G. W. Lloyd, pastor of Branchville Presbyterian Church and an outspoken Union advocate, but fortunately the bullet missed its mark.

The defections of the Copperheads did not hide the fact that Sussex County had a full-sized hero in Hugh Judson Kilpatrick of Deckertown, who as a West Point cadet asked permission to leave the academy to join the troops in the field in 1861. He entered service as a lieutenant, fought throughout the war, and wound up as a major general. Some years later, in 1878, he induced the Grand Army of the Republic to hold its annual encampment at Deckertown (Sussex)—with the result that 40,000 people turned out (about twice the total population of the county) and literally ground the surrounding fields into dust.

Dairymen, perhaps making up for the time lost during the war years, overproduced so much in the 1870's that the glutted market crashed in 1879. Outside dealers fixed the price of milk so low that Sussex farmers revolted in 1880 and established the Milk Producers' Association under the leadership of Senator Thomas Lawrence of Hamburg. The

Dairymen's League succeeded the association in 1907 and proved its power with a tempestuous fourteen-day strike in 1916—when farmers overturned milk wagons, battled with nonconformists, and finally won their fight with dealers.

Iron mining had a brief upsurge after Scranton interests built a huge blast furnace in 1872 at Franklin Furnace. Then Thomas Edison bought the iron mining rights at Ogden mines in 1891, but after sinking $2,500,000 into the pits he abandoned his efforts in 1898. Iron faded, but lime works in Hardyston Township moved into prominence after 1875.

Much local industry thrived in the 1880's and 1890's, such as Virgil Crisman's mill at Branchville, which in the late days of the nineteenth century produced a buckwheat flour which became so well known that it was a household word as far away as the western states. A shoe factory and a silk mill moved into Newton, and the town of Sussex had a woolen mill and a big plow factory (where the much-respected "Sussex" and "Wantage" plows were manufactured). Generally speaking, however, industry was a local proposition, on a make-it-for-the-neighbors scale.

Zinc continued to dominate the industrial picture. Finally, borings in 1891 and 1892 showed rich zinc deposits 800 to 1,200 feet down. When the shafts had been sunk to 1,000 feet, water flooded in. Persistently the mine owners pumped out water—800 gallons a minute, 24 hours a day, for a full year—before man beat the elements to sink the shaft the rest of the way.

The richness of the new zinc deposits made it imperative to settle long-standing legal difficulties over ore rights, and that settlement came in 1897 when the New Jersey Zinc Company acquired stock of three other companies with plants in New Jersey, Virginia, Pennsylvania and Wisconsin. The company built a zinc refining plant at Palmerton, Pennsylvania, and Franklin's economy blossomed.

While dairymen and zinc men headed toward new prosperity, Sussex County began to realize its vacationland possibilities at the turn of the century. Vacationists had come to Sussex as early as 1840—to Sparta, to Newton, to Culver's Lake, to Swartswood Lake. Fishermen knew the attractions of the county's streams and hunters loved its woods.

Still, it took the automobile to popularize the Sussex lakeland, with the biggest spurt taking place after World War I. By then the state had fully recognized the natural virtues of Sussex. It started to acquire acreage for the Stokes State Forest in 1907 (and now has bought 12,429 acres spread across the slopes of Kittatinny Mountain). Colonel and Mrs. Anthony R. Kuser of Bernardsville gave 11,000 acres for a state park in 1923, including High Point—1,803 feet above sea level, highest spot in New Jersey.

Sussex farming entered a new era in 1912 with the coming of young H. W. Gilbertson as New Jersey's first agricultural agent. Increasingly improved methods have made farming an $11,500,000 enterprise in Sussex today, with about 75 per cent of that figure derived from dairying. Sussex County leaders insist that it is a base canard to say that cows still outnumber people (although it's a fact that the bovines have had top rank in numbers for a long time, and if people do lead in 1953, the margin is slight).

After all, Sussex in the 1950 census had only 34,423 people living within its borders—65 per square mile—both figures being the lowest in the state. If the price of milk would stay up, the county's human beings wouldn't mind being outnumbered by cows forever.

Not that all is well in Sussex County. The word is going around again that the zinc is petering out in the Franklin mines. If the zinc company goes, the economic blow will be tremendous. Hoping for the best, but preparing for the worst, Franklin leaders are earnestly seeking to attract new industry to the town.

It is highly unlikely, however, that Sussex County's green hillsides will be darkened by much factory soot in the near future, if ever. The county is admittedly remote from industrial centers, as most of the world's beauty spots are. Much of the county is as wooded and as handsome as it was two hundred years ago. Its streams and lakes continue to sparkle, its forests still offer peace. After two hundred years, Sussex is still the beauty spot, off the beaten path, where dairy cattle roam the rocky hillsides, where vacationists find rest.

MORE ABOUT SUSSEX

Bunnell, Jacob L., Sussex County Sesquicentennial, September 2, 1903.

Decker, Amelia Stickney, *The Old Mine Road.* Sussex, New Jersey, Wantage Recorder Press, 1932.

Schaeffer, Casper, 1907, *Memoirs and Reminiscences.* Hackensack, New Jersey, Private printing, 1907.

Snell, James P., comp., *History of Sussex and Warren Counties, New Jersey.* Philadelphia, Pennsylvania, Everts and Peck. 1881.

Sussex County, New Jersey. The first Sussex centenary, Newark, New Jersey, Daily Advertiser, 1853.

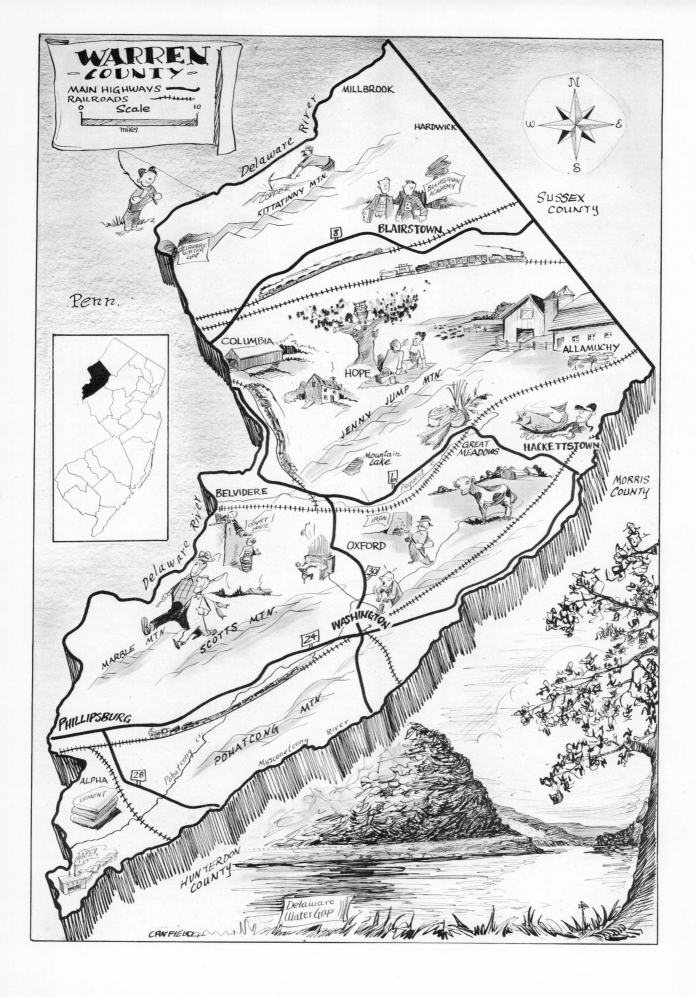

Brooks, such as this one at Mountain Lake, combine to give Warren County great water power.

WARREN

Only by a wide stretch of the imagination is it possible to visualize great industries spread all along the Delaware River from Phillipsburg to Belvidere, yet it might have been. In fact, viewed solely from the standpoint of the natural power of the streams pounding out of the Warren County hills to the Delaware River, it should have been.

Tick off the names of those streams—the Paulins Kill, the Pequest, the Pohatcong, the Musconetcong—whose waters have for countless centuries cascaded into the Delaware River. The mighty Delaware itself wore the tremendous gap through Kittatinny Mountain, and at Foul Rift the Delaware drops sixteen feet in less than a quarter-mile. That power, in the hands of an Alexander Hamilton, would have meant another Paterson on the banks of the Delaware.

But clouded land titles held the county back in the early nineteenth century, when great industrial expansion began everywhere else. No Hamilton came forward, and Warren County has remained through the years essentially rural.

Not that Warren got off to a slow start; as early as the 1650's, Dutchmen from Esopus (Kingston, New York) started to pick copper out of the Kittatinny Mountain, near the Delaware Water Gap. They built the Old Mine Road and laboriously hauled the copper northward to the Hudson, when with only moderate effort they might have floated it down the Delaware on rafts.

Of course there were no markets down-river when copper began heading for Esopus (Philadelphia didn't come into existence until 1682), and when the English took over all of New Jersey in 1664, the Dutch just stopped digging copper and

settled down to farming. Nevertheless, the Dutch exhibited not even mild curiosity in the Delaware River or where it ran; for seventy-five years their attention was focused upon the Old Mine Road to Esopus.

William Penn saw the power possibilities at Foul

Ruins of Oxford Furnace, early ironworks.

Rift, but he never developed the 5,000-acre tract he bought there in 1716. Ten years later, settlement of the county began in earnest when George Green and John Axford came overland from Long Island. Tradition says they climbed a tree, and from their vantage point agreed that Green should settle at the pond which is now Mountain Lake and Axford should settle at what is now Oxford.

Others followed—Abram Van Campen bought 1,666 acres on the mountain above Delaware Water Gap in 1732, Lodewick Titman bought land near the Gap in 1737, Harmon Shipman settled on Scott's Mountain in 1740, settlers built a log church at Mansfield (now Washington) in 1741, and that same year Aaron Depui established his famous store in John Axford's town.

Such colonization merely set the scene for the arrival of Jonathan Robeson in 1742 to build an iron furnace at Oxford. Robeson shipped his first ore on March 9, 1743, hauling it overland to a wharf just below Foul Rift and floating it in boats downstream to Philadelphia. Oxford immediately

became important; people from thirty miles around shopped at Aaron Depui's store. Robeson's iron works required great manpower to turn out two to three tons of ore a day—men to dig the iron, men to cut the timber needed to make charcoal, men to feed 400 bushels of charcoal into the furnace for every ton of iron produced.

Control of the booming iron enterprise slipped from Robeson's hands in 1754, when Dr. William Shippen and his brother Joseph acquired full control. The Shippens built an elaborate stone house in 1754 and Oxford became a social center, where wealthy Philadelphians frequented gay parties and exciting fox hunts—with "Gentleman Joe" Shippen ever in the fore.

Other small settlements emerged, such as Greenwich-on-the-Delaware, which Robert Patterson established in 1750 where the Pequest River met the Delaware. Helm's Mills had enough settlers in 1760 to make it worthwhile for Judge Samuel Hackett to call them together for a barrel of good spirits at the local tavern. As they imbibed, the Judge sug-

Portland-Columbia Bridge, only covered bridge left between New Jersey and Pennsylvania.

Immaculately kept truck farms in the Great Meadows.

gested that Hackett's Town might be a better name for the village than Helm's Mills—and the barrel-emptiers agreed.

Early farmers found it so difficult to till the rugged mountain slopes that severe food shortages occurred between 1753 and 1763, but Moravians from Bethlehem, Pennsylvania, saw the potential of the land and bought a thousand acres in 1768. They put up enduring stone buildings, including an indestructible mill, and as they built for the ages, they called their village Hope.

Possibly the first man to visualize the tremendous industrial potential of the Pequest River was Major Robert Hoops, who bought Patterson's holdings in 1769 and used the Pequest to turn mill wheels. Hoops officially called the settlement Mercer, but as early as 1777 he referred to it in letters as "Belvidere."

Hoops sent grain down the Delaware to Philadelphia in Durham boats, flat-bottomed craft which went downstream readily enough but had to be laboriously poled upstream. He built a slaughter-house just in time to be of tremendous service to General Washington's army during the bitter winter months in Morristown. At times every available wagon for miles around was requisitioned to carry Belvidere grain and meat to Morristown.

Oxford iron also helped the Continental cause greatly, although historians disagree on whether the Shippens favored the Crown or the Cause. At any rate, they left Philadelphia for Oxford during the British occupation in 1777. Dr. Shippen's niece, Peggy Shippen, met and married Benedict Arnold in Philadelphia—and may well have influenced Arnold's later treasonable actions.

Many Tories fled from other parts of the state to the Montana region of Scott's Mountain, but to its patriotic credit the county contributed Brigadier-General William Maxwell of Greenwich, commander of all New Jersey regular troops for most of the war. It also contributed Mrs. Margaret Vliet Warne, who lived in what is now Broadway. Peggy (as the countryside knew her) took over when the doctors of the county went off to service. She traveled on horseback with her nostrums packed in saddlebags, and continued her duties as an obstetrician and midwife well into the nineteenth century.

When Robert Hoops lost his fortune in the post-war depression, he left Belvidere in the 1790's to found the town of Olean, New York. Before he departed, Hoops sold a large tract south of the

Pequest to the celebrated Robert Morris. Morris gave the tract to his son-in-law and daughter, Charles and Mary Morris Croxall, in a deed which restricted title to the Croxalls and their heirs for all time. That hampering provision held up the development of Belvidere for nearly thirty years (and perhaps forever). It took an act of the Legislature to set aside the deed in 1818.

Also in the 1790's Phillipsburg began to suffer from competition with the young town of Easton directly across the river. Founded in about 1735, Phillipsburg grew slowly, but in 1790 it was bigger than Easton. Then the Penn family stepped in and inaugurated a series of land manipulations deliberately designed to stop development in Phillipsburg. As a result, land values declined so much by

1793 that Jacob Reese and Philip Seager bought the 92-acre town of Phillipsburg for $530.

Of so little significance was Phillipsburg that the charter for the Morris Turnpike in 1806 called for the pike to be built from Morristown to a point "opposite Easton." Actually, the principal reason for the pike seemed to be the mineral springs atop Schooley's Mountain, where the wealthy gathered to relieve their aches and pains. Wagons and carriages rolled right through Phillipsburg and over the covered wooden bridge to Easton. That bridge, incidentally, lasted for ninety years after its was built in 1805 from the proceeds of a lottery.

The early years of the nineteenth century brought varying fortunes. First, the old Oxford Furnace closed down in 1809 after timber supplies gave out.

State fish hatchery at Hackettstown, established in 1912.

Delaware Water Gap, natural wonder of New Jersey.

However, down the valley, Colonel William Mc-Cullough built the brick Washington House in Mansfield in 1811, and as the village prospered it took the name of Washington, after the tavern. John Rutherford's great estate spread out near Allamuchy, where Rutherford had come in 1778.

So prosperous had the area become, in fact, that residents pushed for freedom from Sussex County, to which they had been tied since that county's establishment in 1753. Finally, on November 20, 1824, the Legislature created a new county and named it for General Joseph Warren, Revolutionary War hero who fell at the Battle of Bunker Hill.

Among Warren's 18,000 residents at the time were many men and women of note, but none of greater proportions than Miss Catharine Learch, born in 1816 in Greenwich. Her mother died a few days after Catharine's birth and her father raised the baby "mit der spoon"—and did such a remarkable job that Miss Catharine grew up to weigh 764 pounds, with a waistline of nine feet, six inches. She married William Schooley of Greenwich and moved to Ohio, then later toured the country as possibly the fattest woman in all history.

Belvidere prospered after county fathers chose it as the county seat, in a decision reinforced by Garret D. Wall's gift of $1,000 and a plot of ground. Wall also gave land for the county park,

provided that it be "always kept as a public square." Land values jumped in 1826, with one corner lot bringing the "extravagent" price of $3,600.

No such good times pervaded Phillipsburg, even after the Morris Canal stretched across the state to Newark in 1832 with Phillipsburg as the western port. Scarcely a new house went up in the village, and industrial activity continued to center in Oxford, where William Henry rekindled the old furnace in 1831.

The new hot blast process was originated in England in 1828, and in 1834 at Oxford Henry used it for the first time in America. He refined the English blast so much that he raised temperatures to 500 degrees (compared with a maximum of 220 degrees in England). His blast revolutionized the iron industry everywhere; output shot up 40 per cent, costs dropped 40 per cent.

George W. and Seldon T. Scranton bought the Oxford Property in 1839, and a few years later joined William Henry in founding Scranton, in the mountains of Pennsylvania. Despite the departure of these leading iron masters, Oxford bloomed as an iron center and in the 1850's made great numbers of railroad car wheels.

Those railroad car wheels symbolized a new day for all Warren County, first because of the vigor the railroads eventually brought Phillipsburg, and secondly because of John I. Blair. Phillipsburg in 1848 had only forty-seven dwellings, but by 1852 it had attracted J. R. Templin's small iron and brass foundry and the furnaces of the Trenton Iron Company.

Later the same year, the Jersey Central Railroad rolled into Phillipsburg and within three years the Belvidere-Delaware and the Lehigh Valley railroads had entered town, making Phillipsburg the railroad gateway to the West (further augmented in 1865 when the Morris & Essex Railroad finally fought its way across North Jersey and through to Phillipsburg).

These were the days when the spread of railroads brought power on a national scale to a famed Warren County son, John I. Blair, whose life spanned almost the entire nineteenth century. He was born at Foul Rift in 1802 and died in Blairstown in 1899. In between, he became a highly successful merchant at Gravel Hill (which changed its name to Blairstown in 1839), founded Blair Academy in 1848, became a railroad builder and financier active throughout the United States, and amassed a fortune of $70,000,000. Despite his tremendous successes, he kept his home in Blairstown for almost eighty years and never lost his warm affection for the mountain slopes of Warren.

Although the railroads thrived and helped Warren County to grow, there were many who believed that the railroad could never replace the Delaware River as a means of transportation. Flat-bottomed Durham boats disappeared soon after the Morris Canal started, but the inception of steamboating stirred men along the Delaware. One noble effort ended tragically on March 6, 1860, in the attempt to run the steamer *Alfred Thomas* from Easton to Belvidere. Just as the ship slipped out into the river from Easton on her maiden trip she suddenly blew up, killing twelve persons, including two of her owners. That ended steamboating north of Phillipsburg.

Local tragedy faded into the greater tragedy of the Civil War, and a Warren County man, Benjamin Lundy, can be looked upon as the man who first systematically fanned the flames of discord over slavery. Lundy, born and raised in Quaker Settlement near Allamuchy, probably never saw a slave until he left his father's Warren farm in 1808 at the age of nineteen to visit Wheeling, West Virginia.

There he witnessed the brutal herding of bewildered Negroes into so-called "stock yards." His revulsion led to the founding of the American Abolition Society. Horace Greeley later called Benjamin Lundy "the first man to devote his life to the slaves," and it was Lundy who converted William Lloyd Garrison to the cause of abolitionism. As a Quaker, Lundy abhorred war, but his pen and his never-ceasing lectures did much to speed the open break.

Fittingly enough, then, Warren County supplied the nation's first volunteers after President Lincoln called for men on April 15, 1861, three days after Southern guns pounded Fort Sumter. Captain Edward Campbell of Belvidere rallied seven officers and fifty men about him and marched them off to Trenton on April 18, much to the astonishment of unprepared authorities. New Jersey, credited with supplying the first volunteer troops, earned that distinction because of Belvidere.

Industry moved ahead in Warren County after the war, particularly in Phillipsburg. Warren Foundry, established in 1856, grew rapidly. The Andover Iron Company succeeded the Trenton Iron Company and built two additional furnaces in 1868. Stove works, a boiler works, a rolling mill and a

Ingersoll Rand (Phillipsburg), Warren's major industry.

sheet iron company followed by the 1870's. Phillipsburg toiled and expanded.

Oxford continued to be as big an iron story as ever, particularly after the Oxford Iron Company took over in 1863 and built a new furnace, with a capacity of 12,000 tons per year. A new nail factory making 240,000 kegs of nails a year, a foundry, and a rolling mill kept men busy digging iron ore from the Oxford Hills.

John Riegel started an extensive paper mill along the Musconetcong River in 1862, and Hackettstown found prosperity in the manufacture of wagons and carriages, an industry dating from the factory Jacob Day built in 1815. By 1880 the town had ten carriage factories.

The village of Judge Hackett also catered to the carriage set who visited Schooley's Mountain, and it heard with satisfaction that the Newark Methodist Conference in 1867 had chosen Hackettstown as the site for Centenary Collegiate Institute (now Centenary Junior College). The Institute finally started classes for 183 students in 1874 in a new five-story brick building.

Culture also had something to do with the prominence Washington attained in the last half of the nineteenth century as the nation's organ-making center. The industry dated back to 1850 when John A. Smith started to make melodians. In Washington ten years later Robert Hornbacker made the first organ.

However, it took Daniel F. Beatty to make the organ industry big-time. Starting with a capital of one dollar, Beatty soon had a five-story factory in 1880 capable of turning out 500 organs a month, which he sold throughout the world. Fire leveled his factory in September, 1881, but within eight months Beatty had rebuilt it bigger than ever. The first month his men made 1,003 organs, but two years later Beatty failed. His rebuilding apparently had been too costly.

Others made organs, too—Star Parlor Organ Company, H. W. Allegar, and Cornish & Company, among others. Cornish, which at first specialized in large church organs, led the town in organ-making in 1900. By World War I the demand declined, possibly because Thomas A. Edison's phonograph made parlor singing old-fashioned. Organ-making became a thing of the past in Washington during the first World War, when the companies found themselves unable to collect on hundreds of organs placed in Europe on credit.

If Edison had anything to do with the lessened demand for organs, he partially made up for it in 1899 when he opened a huge Portland cement plant at New Village, close to Alpha, where the Vulcanite Portland Cement Company had opened a plant in 1894. The Warren cement plants made nearly 4,000,000 barrels annually before they began to decline in the 1920's. Edison's plant closed just before World War II.

Oxford's iron industry collapsed in the 1920's,

organs left Washington, carriages left Hackettstown—and despite its water power Belvidere never attracted much industry. Phillipsburg strengthened its industrial leadership after the Ingersoll-Rand Company decided to move its compressed air and hydraulic machinery plant across the river from Easton in 1904. Silk mills, too, played a part in Phillipsburg's growth.

All this time agriculture developed slowly. The 1870's saw thousands of acres of muckland in the "Great Meadows" reclaimed after an extended drainage program. At the turn of the century celery and lettuce growers began to utilize the rich black earth in earnest. Cattlemen began developing herds of milk cows in the 1880's and 1890's, particularly after dairying proved so profitable on the hilly farms in neighboring Sussex and Hunterdon counties. Today dairying stands supreme, with Warren's cows yielding an annual income of $8,000,000 from milk products (third in New Jersey behind Sussex and Hunterdon).

Actually, agriculture's role in Warren County has had no spectacular spurts, yet 62 per cent of

Phillipsburg, on the Delaware River, in less than a century grew to be a busy industrial city.

the county is still in farmland (with much more of the county in thick forests). Only Phillipsburg, with about 19,000 population and several excellent industries, can claim to be sizable. The rest of Warren's 55,000 population is widespread, Washington and Hackettstown being the only other towns with more than 4,000 residents.

Washington has the look of a town with a population much greater, since its busy, modern stores cater to a very wide shopping area. Hackettstown's well-preserved old Main Street, its college air, and its extensive state fish hatchery (established in 1912) make favorable impressions upon visitors.

Belvidere has a handsomeness all its own. Few towns in New Jersey—or anywhere else—can claim the atmosphere which surrounds the 125-year-old county park in Belvidere. The red brick courthouse, now expanded through the years to its present T-shape, dominates the square, but the old homes and the well-kept churches lend memorable dignity to this county seat.

Yet, the mystery of what prevented great industrial development in Belvidere persists, particularly after learning that the Pequest falls fifty feet in its last mile dash through Belvidere into the Delaware. In addition, the Delaware falls twenty-two feet within a mile and a half of Belvidere. But the power has never been fully used, and in the electric age is unlikely ever to be used.

Today the visitor to Warren County is secretly glad that the cascading water power did not attract the industry which might have made the river bank another Pittsburgh or Bethlehem. Think of no covered bridge at Columbia, no shaded square in Belvidere, no peaceful Harmony, no ruggedly charming Scotts Mountain. Think of no trout rising in the Pequest, the Paulins Kill, or the Musconetcong. Think of Delaware Water Gap as only a rocky nuisance rather than as one of the East's finest natural spectacles.

Take away the cattle grazing on sloping fields, the quaintness of Blairstown and Hope, the charm of Hackettstown, the bustling small-town character of Washington, and the old Oxford iron atmosphere. Surely all would have disappeared from the perimeter of a mighty industrial region.

Maybe many would prefer great factories clanging on the Delaware River banks. There are good arguments in favor of the theoretical industrial colossus, but none is convincing to the man who sees a trout strike in the rushing waters of the secluded Pequest.

MORE ABOUT WARREN

Brodhead, L. W., *Delaware Water Gap: Its Scenery, Its Legends and Early History.* Philadelphia, Pennsylvania, Sherman & Co., 870.

Cummins, George Wyckoff, *History of Warren County, New Jersey.* New York, Lewis Historical Publishing Co., 1911.

Mustin, M., *Warren County, N. J. 1931,* Warren County Board of Freeholders.

Shampanore, Frank, *History and Directory of Warren County.* Washington, New Jersey, Shampanore Bros., 1929.

Snell, James P., *History of Sussex and Warren Counties, New Jersey.* Philadelphia, Pa., Everts & Peck, 1881.

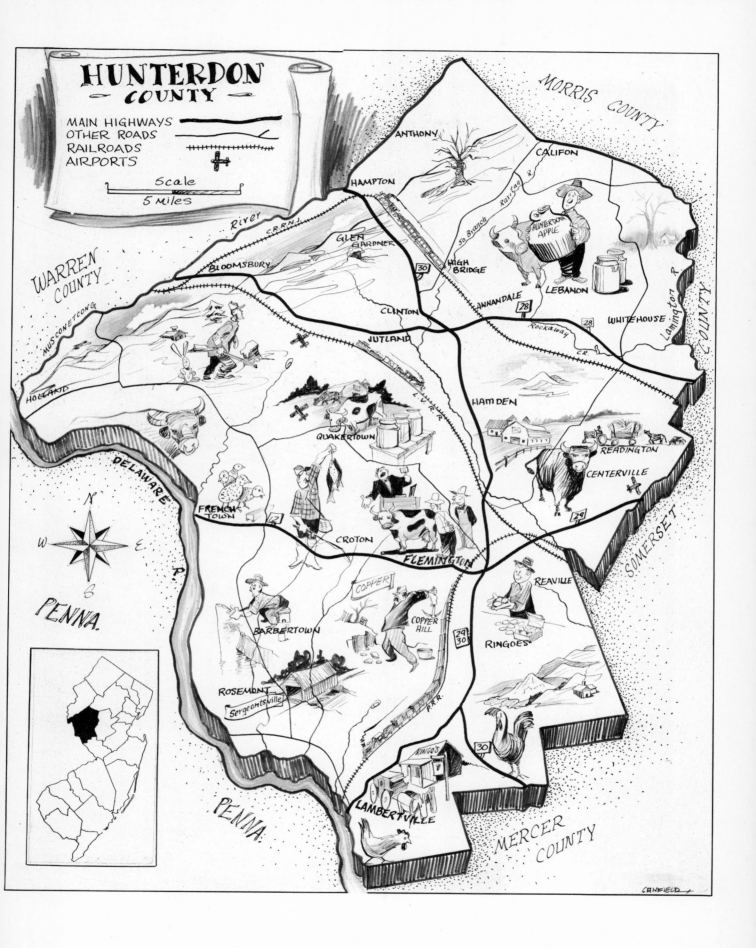

Modern version of the general store, in Annandale. Symbolic of rural nature of Hunterdon.

HUNTERDON

Every day throughout the first six weeks of 1935 the eyes of the world focused squarely on Hunterdon County—yet the world saw it not. The eyes skipped lightly over the lush farmlands and paused only briefly in Flemington to take in the exterior of the handsome old county courthouse. Within, on the second floor, a grim Bronx carpenter finally stopped the eyes.

Wintry blasts swept Flemington on January 2, 1935, when Bruno Richard Hauptmann sat down to face a Hunterdon County jury charged with determining whether he was guilty of the murder of Charles A. Lindbergh, Jr. A regiment of writers, radio announcers, photographers and communications men moved in to make certain the world got every detail.

As quickly and as noisily as it came, the regiment stampeded out of town right after the foreman of the jury rose on February 13 to declare Hauptmann guilty. The moving fingers, having writ, moved on—and left behind only memories and a mountain of empty beer bottles, crumpled sandwich wrappings, penciled note paper and stained coffee cartons.

To its eternal credit, Hunterdon quickly regained contentment in the pleasant rural status which some of the visiting press had deplored in dispatches to big city papers. But, as the editor of a local paper gently pointed out, Flemington had never aspired to be more than a country town. Chance, the very same chance which made Dayton, Tennessee, notorious for the Scopes "monkey" trial, and Callander, Ontario, famed for the Dionne quintuplets, shoved the most spectacular trial in modern history into Hunterdon's lap.

Take a look at the incredibly irregular border line set up when Hunterdon and Mercer counties were divided in 1838. The Lindbergh estate straddled the border line, but the house from which the baby was snatched lay on the Hunterdon side. So, Hunterdon received the designation for its forty days of agony, of drama, of pride, of frustration.

These were days in painful contrast to the placidity which had marked Hunterdon ever since the early 1700's when the first settlers drifted up from Burlington, over the rocky slopes of the Sourland Mountain and down into what is now Hunterdon County. They came singly, in pairs, in small groups, mostly without definite colonization aims.

1828 courthouse, Flemington. Scene of Hauptmann trial.

East Jersey and West Jersey joined hands over Hunterdon, an immense catch-all when it gained county status in 1713. It extended from Assunpink Creek north to the New York border and included most of what is now Mercer, Morris, Sussex and Warren counties. The last three separated from Hunterdon in a loosely defined chunk in 1738. A full century later (1838) Hunterdon and Mercer divided on an arbitrary line through the Sourlands, a line so deviating that it prompted latter-day wags to wonder if the surveyors hadn't been sampling Hunterdon's splendid apple brandy.

This land of plenty had room for all; long before the Revolution, English, Irish, Scotch, German, Dutch and French settlers came to Hunterdon, took one look and decided to remain. Thus, Hunterdon became the state's first genuine "melting pot," where nationality met nationality without prejudice and creed met creed without rancor.

The soil richly rewarded those who didn't mind callouses. Swiftly rushing streams watered the red,

shaly soil and provided power for gristmills and sawmills. Every natural feature predestined Hunterdon County's well-being to rise and fall in direct relation to the fortunes of its farmers.

Travelers headed over Indian paths criss-crossing Hunterdon and pushed the region into an important secondary role—assistance to wayfarers. John Ringo, who built a log hut in 1720 at the junction of two cross-county trails, soon found himself entertaining strangers. John's hut grew into the widely known "Ringo's Tavern," a pleasant place to stop before venturing on to the Delaware River ferry Emanuel Coryell established in 1732 at what is now Lambertville.

Up the Raritan River came the Dutch, following as ever the banks of a fertile stream. Germans, heading overland from Philadelphia to New York, spread throughout most of the county before concentrating in the section now known as Tewksbury Township. So many had arrived there by 1750 that the area became "German Valley" and their principal settlement "New Germantown" (changed to

High Bridge, long an important iron town.

This covered bridge near Sergeantsville is the only one wholly within New Jersey.

Oldwick when World War I engendered anti-German feeling).

An Irishman, Samuel Fleming, gave the county seat its name in 1756 by building his "castle" (a trim white structure, castlelike only in contrast with other houses in the area). Almost a decade before, John Philip Kase and understanding old Indian Chief Tuccamirgin had come to terms in the village, but villagers were more lastingly impressed by Fleming's domicile.

Another young Irishman, Robert Taylor, arrived in 1758 and taught school for a while before becoming bookkeeper at the Union Iron Works in the deep valley at what is now High Bridge. William Turner and Joseph Allen built the works in 1742, near the site of a much older Union Forge, and when young Taylor joined the firm Turner and Allen were surreptitiously operating an iron slitting mill in defiance of British orders. Taylor became works manager at the age of 27 and by Revolutionary War time had full control. (Incidentally, he was the first of five generations of Taylors to direct the operation, which since 1912 has been the Taylor-Wharton Iron & Steel Company.)

Taylor turned diligently to making ammunition

for Washington's armies, but except for the Union Iron Works and the food production of Hunterdon's farms, the war touched the county mainly at the ferry slips. Part of General Washington's badly-weakened army crossed over Coryell's Ferry after the gloomy November, 1776, retreat across New Jersey. The following year some of the British prisoners captured after General Burgoyne's defeat at Saratoga crossed the Delaware, at what is now Frenchtown, on the way to prison camp.

Washington's army broke camp at Valley Forge and surged back across the Delaware in June, 1778, to begin the cross-state pursuit of the British which was climaxed by the Battle of Monmouth. Washington stopped briefly in Coryell's Ferry at the home of Richard Holcombe. There Mrs. Holcombe, with female curiosity, asked Washington where he was headed. "Madam, can you keep a secret?" the General asked. "Why, yes!" responded Mrs. Holcombe. "Well," said Washington, "so can I!" Next day the army climbed the hills to the east and started after the British.

Flemington became the county seat in 1785, after farmers argued that Trenton (then still in Hunterdon) was too far away. The same year Thomas

Lowrey, Samuel Fleming's son-in-law, bought extensively up the Delaware River, at what is now Milford and Frenchtown. Lowrey sold 968 of his up-river acres to Paul Henry Mallet-Prevost, who fled the French Revolution in 1792, just one neck ahead of the guillotine. Mallet-Prevost stunned "Old Quicksilver" Lowrey (who loved his interest) by paying cash. The land became known as "French's Town," because no one ever bothered to learn that Prevost was really a Swiss, not a Frenchman.

Hunterdon County felt the pinch of the Revolution badly, so much that it was not able to build a courthouse until 1791. The tremendous war effort of the Union Iron Works all but closed the only early industry in the county, mainly because the furnaces had burned up all available timber on surrounding mountain slopes.

Creeks and streams dashing out of the mountains proved both a godsend and a troublesome matter; the former because of the impetus they gave to rising farm prosperity and the latter because they hampered travel. As early as 1795 county freeholders began levying taxes to bridge inland creeks. The spanning of the Delaware, however, was left in the hands of private stock companies, two of which built bridges across the river at Coryell's Ferry and Center Bridge (Stockton) between 1812 and 1814. Through the years, rampaging river waters smashed the Delaware bridges (particularly in

Lambertville's India rubber works, about 1880.

1841, 1862 and 1903) before steel framework fended off the fury of the river.

Coryell's Ferry ended with the coming of the bridge and even the name disappeared in 1812 when Senator John Lambert secured a post office and changed the village title to Lambert's Ville. Descendants of Emanuel Coryell heatedly rejected the new name ("more likely Lambert's villainy," they declared), but they pouted in vain.

The riverfront village had expanded enough by 1828 to challenge Flemington's right to the county seat after the original courthouse burned that year.

Chicken ranch above Frenchtown, a center of poultry experimentation and hatching.

Centerville on Old York Road was once an important stagecoach stop.

Flemington's fitness satisfied the Legislature, however, and later in 1828 the county built the courthouse in which the Hauptmann drama took place 107 years later. Flemington had a good case—boasting the Fulper Pottery Company (one of the nation's first potteries) as a leading industry and pridefully pointing out that at least one resident had laid a sidewalk and set out trees.

The entertainment of visitors continued to be a leading Hunterdon business: in Flemington at Fleming's Castle; at Centerville, half-way point on the Swift-Sure stage route between New York and Philadelphia, and at Larison's Corner, where the old inn lured sporting men bent on gambling or cockfighting.

In the northern part of the county the New Jersey Turnpike, built in 1806 to link Phillipsburg and New Brunswick, led to the building of many new inns and the revived popularity of old taverns. The sparkling white walls of the Whitehouse tavern attracted many overland passengers, but others preferred the inn on "Jugtown" Mountain or the Brick Tavern at Perryville. The latter became a gathering place for scores of cattle and sheep drovers

on their way to New Brunswick by way of the pike. Needless to say, the fastidious avoided Perryville and went on to Hunt's Mills (Clinton) to stay in the hotel near the old mill.

Most of the taverns naturally featured Hunterdon apple brandy, made from home-grown apples. The county's extensive nineteenth-century apple orchards dated back to early deeds requiring every land buyer to plant one apple tree for each acre of ground purchased. Cider millers found that Hunterdon County cider readily ripened into smooth apple brandy.

The taste for Hunterdon "apple" spread; soon wagonloads rolled to Trenton and Philadelphia for sale at twenty-five cents a gallon. Union Township became especially known for its brandy with ten distilleries spread along Spruce Run and Mulhockaway Creek.

The Belvidere-Delaware and the Jersey Central railroads gave the county an economic lift in the 1850's. Lambertville boomed as a locomotive and railroad car manufacturing center. Junction (now Hampton) sprung up in anticipation of the junction of the Jersey Central and the Delaware, Lacka-

35

wanna & Western Railroad in 1856, and for its fore-sight the brand-new village gained extensive rail-road shops.

Above all, the Jersey Central gave High Bridge both an economic shot in the arm and a new name, the latter for the extensive bridge the railroad built high over the valley. Taylor's Forge revived when the Jersey Central brought in anthracite to feed its long-hungry furnaces. Business at Taylor's in-creased threefold within two years and the upsurge of the forge led to extensive iron ore mining in and near the Musconetcong Mountains—at High Bridge, Cokesbury, Asbury, Jugtown and Glen Gardner. The West End Mine at Jugtown con-tinued until 1888, and produced a million tons of ore in its last decade of existence.

Many a man digging Hunterdon iron ore wished he was in California with James Marshall, Lambert-ville local-boy-turned-famous. Marshall, who had drifted westward from Lambertville in 1834, started the 1848 gold rush when he accidentally discovered gold nuggets while digging a raceway for a saw-mill at Fort Sutter, California. Gold did Marshall no good; he enjoyed few comforts before he died alone in a California county hospital.

Meanwhile, on farms close to Flemington, sev-eral companies dug copper in a spectacular craze which lasted from 1836 to 1865, when the last of the copper mines closed. Hugh Capner, who sold his farm to a copper company, was said to be the only honest man to make money from the copper rush ("honest" being a necessary qualification be-cause a stock-jobbing outfit used the mine near Copper Hill to perpetrate a huge swindle).

Nevertheless, the real Hunterdon County gold lay for the taking in the fields and pasturelands, and for 150 years the ripe lands gave and gave and gave. The farmer, on the other hand, took and took and took, with the result that farming ran into sad days throughout most of the last half of the nine-teenth century.

Railroad competition hurt, because Hunterdon beef, pork, wheat and wool couldn't compete with lower-priced western products. The taste for Hun-

Main Street in Lambertville still retains typical nineteenth-century look.

Cattle in a cornfield near Ringoes. Hunterdon ranks second to Sussex in dairy industry.

terdon apple brandy disappeared by Civil War time and apple orchards wasted on the hillsides. Above all, the fabulously rich soil finally rebelled at the poor husbandry. What happened is partially illustrated by county population. After rolling steadily upward to 40,758 in 1865, population began an unchecked slide which dropped the total to 32,885 in 1920. Hunterdon had its first population gain in 65 years in 1930 and did not go above 40,000 again until the late 1940's.

Peaches at first seemed a way out; farmers became enthusiastic after Joseph K. Potts of Franklin Township and Dr. George H. Larison of Sergeantsville started large orchards in the 1850's. Eventually 2,000,000 trees covered the county in 1890, the year the peach crop failed completely. Worse, the 1891, 1892 and 1893 crops were so tremendous that the bottom dropped out of the market. Finally, the deadly San Jose scale ate into the orchards in the late 1890's. Farmers, taking their axes to the peach orchards, chopped down more than 1,700,000 trees between 1895 and 1909. Today Hunterdon has fewer than 25,000 peach trees.

Hunterdon farm values reached a low point in 1900. Yet, even as agriculture stumbled through its most bitter days, the foundations of today's farmland prosperity were laid in the last part of the nineteenth century when farmers started to raise dairy cattle instead of beef cattle and began growing chickens commercially. Railroad shipments of milk to the cities started modestly in the 1870's and grew quickly after the Lehigh Valley Railroad built

through the county's heartland. Establishment of local creameries in the 1880's gave additional impetus to the Hunterdon dairy business.

Meanwhile, introduction of the portable incubator spurred the county's poultry business in the 1880's. Many objected to incubators, expressing concern over what being mothered by a hunk of tin would do to a baby chick. Others believed incubated chicks would forever smell and taste of kerosene. When a few of the less squeamish found the incubators profitable, even the most scrupulous readily revised their thinking—and today a hatchery like Kerr's in Frenchtown produces between five and six million chicks annually.

As dairy cattle spread over the hillsides and chickens peeped beneath incubators, Hunterdon's farm prosperity edged upward; farm values doubled within the first decade of the twentieth century. Not that the county sped out of the economic woods. Indeed, Hunterdon's fiscal picture never looked blacker than it did after the county borrowed $315,000 between 1910 and 1915 to resurface its archaic roads. Unfortunately, the resurfacing proved as fleeting as the bonds proved firm. Bitter farmers slogging over rutted roads in the early 1920's complained that the county had built "one-year roads on 30-year bonds."

By 1930 the county debt rose to $1,500,000 and the roads continued poor. The darkness was blackest, but just ahead was economic dawn.

Some of the "city folk" who had bought small Hunterdon farms in the 1920's began to get the hang of the land by 1930. That year, for the first time in six decades, the county census showed an increase over the previous ten-year mark. Then, county freeholders voted in 1930 to issue no more bonds. Finally, and possibly most important, the Flemington Auction Market started.

Hunterdon farmers, long used to accepting for their products whatever they could get, showed little enthusiasm for the auction at first. More than 1,200 chicken farmers were contacted; only forty sent eggs for sale at the first auction held in a Main Street basement in August, 1930. A leading auctioneer predicted that the venture would be a certain failure, and refused to sell the eighty cases of eggs on hand for the first sale.

Within a year, however, the cooperative venture proved itself. In 1931 the group began to auction live poultry and in 1936 added livestock auctions. Today auction sales are in the neighborhood of $8,500,000 annually, and the auction market is a continuing factor in improving conditions on farms, because farmers know prices and know breeding and marketing techniques.

Moreover, the cooperative auction market has led the way to other noted Hunterdon cooperative agricultural ventures. In 1939 the Hunterdon County Board of Agriculture established near Clinton the nation's first cooperative artificial cattle breeding unit in the United States. The New Jersey Poultry and Egg Co-operative Marketing Association, a statewide farmer cooperative, chose Flemington in 1946 as its central point for packaging state certified eggs.

Working together, Hunterdon County farmers made their own prosperity. Nearly 70 per cent of the county's acreage is farmed—and farmed so well that it represents $15,000,000 a year in income (mainly dairy products, $7,000,000, and poultry products, $6,600,000).

Much of the country's prosperous state can be traced to a tax windfall dating from 1937 to 1945, when more than . 170 large corporations from all over the nation set up offices of record in Flemington to take advantage of low local taxes. Standard Oil started the parade in 1937 by moving in from Linden. More than $275,000,000 in ratables fol-

Round Valley corner, reminiscent of the nineteenth century, with milk cans and picket fence.

lowed—and, while the corporations existed in the borough mainly in filing cabinets or as names on office doors, local tax rates dropped.

The state acted in 1945 to end collection of intangible corporation taxes by Flemington (or any other individual municipality), but the staggering blow saw Hunterdon emerge happily, its roads in good shape, its budget firm, and its bonded indebtedness reduced to zero. Today, of course, the tax rate has jumped back up, but the county has far fewer tax worries than many of its neighbors.

The Hunterdon Hills in 1952 are sheltering a relatively new type of settler, the wealthy and the artistic who have bought some of the handsome old stone houses and beautiful rolling acres. A select commuting class has also entered the county, and so many of them have become businessman-farmer combinations that the county agricultural agent keeps his office open Saturdays.

The practice of working together extends outward from the farmer cooperatives into such intercommunity ventures as the recently completed North Hunterdon Regional High School near Clinton, sponsored by eleven North Hunterdon school districts, and the $2,000,000 hospital north of Flemington, the product of countywide volunteer contributions.

However, the best example of cooperative action is Flemington's Choir School, where children of the town's five churches—Protestant and Catholic—have been learning music since 1895. Miss Elizabeth V. F. Vosseller, who founded the school in the Presbyterian Church, soon asked Miss Bessie R. Hopewell to become codirector and the two women guided the school through most of its years. Hundreds of Flemington youngsters have learned not only music but many of the amenities of life in the school of the Misses Vosseller and Hopewell.

Intense though the Hauptmann trial proved to be, Hunterdon County has far transcended it. World news usually overlooks Hunterdon today, possibly figuring that six solid weeks in 1935 was enough. Hunterdon—proud of its past, secure in its present and confident of its future—doesn't care.

MORE ABOUT HUNTERDON

Allen, Alexander B., *Where Town and Country Meet.* Flemington, New Jersey, Board of Trade, 1909.

Fargo, Clarence B., *History of Frenchtown.* Frenchtown, New Jersey, published by author. 1893.

Mott, George S., *The First Century of Hunterdon County, New Jersey.* Flemington, New Jersey, E. Vosseller, 1878.

Snell, James P., *History of Hunterdon and Somerset Counties,* New Jersey. Philadelphia, Pennsylvania, Everts and Peck, 1881.

Schmidt, Hubert G., *Rural Hunterdon,* New Brunswick, New Jersey, Rutgers University Press, 1947.

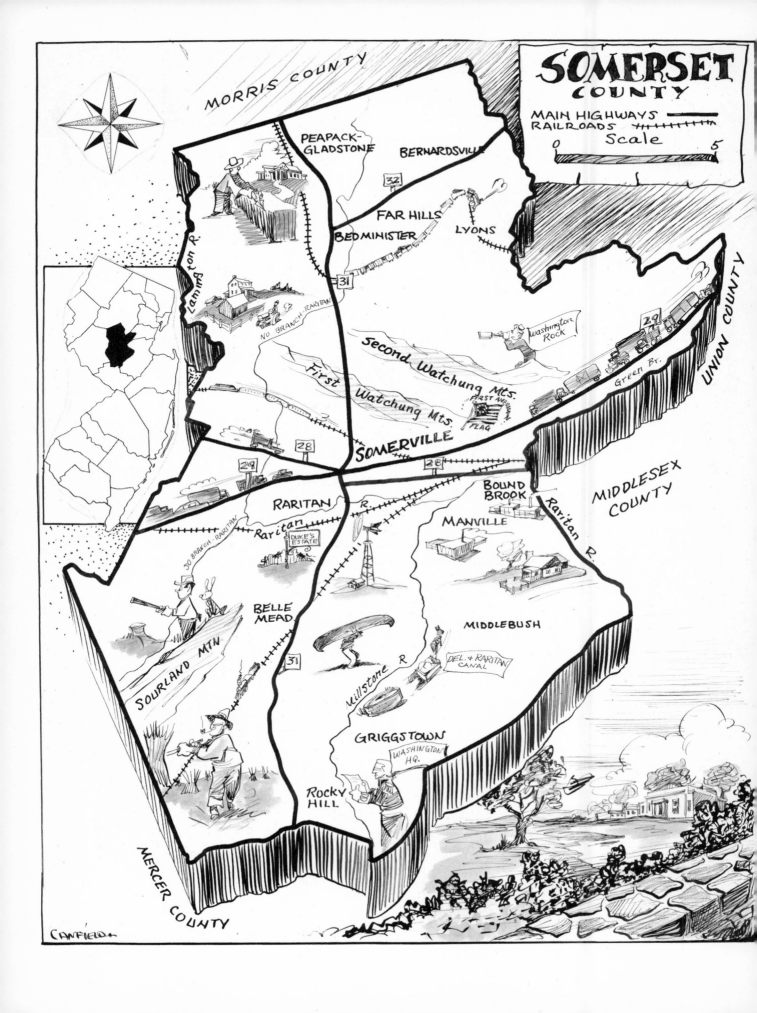

SOMERSET

Much of New Jersey's geographical diversity comes together in Somerset County, where North Jersey's rolling hills level off into South Jersey's flatlands; where gently flowing streams swell into the Raritan, "Queen of Rivers," and where widely varied soils tempt the farmer.

This pleasant land has always attracted the wealthy; for more than 200 years the "Somerset Hills" have meant landed gentry, riding to the hounds, and lavish living. The fertile valleys along the rivers have meant prosperity for less well-heeled farmers, too. Finally, transportation men through the years have made Somerset County the North Jersey hub where highways and railroads meet.

Thus, with the area apparently destined to be a North Jersey crossroads and a region of expansive living, it seems strange that the English families who stopped briefly along the Millstone River in 1642 did not tarry longer before moving on to Philadelphia. For that matter, though, few paid much attention either when a Dutch traveler visited the Raritan Valley in 1650 and called it "the handsomest and pleasantest country that man can behold."

Land sales in 1681 marked the beginning of settlement, with Thomas Codrington and John Royce taking up large tracts in the vicinity of what is now Bound Brook. Many followed, particularly French Huguenots and Dutch farmers from Long Island. Generally, the Dutch stayed in the lowlands while the English and Scotch favored the hill country.

The Provincial Assembly split Somerset County away from Middlesex on May 14, 1688, because "the uppermost part of the Raritan River is settled by persons, who, in their husbandry and manuring their lands, are forced upon quite different ways and methods from other farmers and inhabitants of Middlesex County. . . ."

Unique though their husbandry and manuring might have been, the residents of Somerset County were not numerous, because they remained under the jurisdiction of Middlesex County courts until 1713, when Somerset finally received permission to build its first courthouse, at Six Mill Run (now Franklin Park).

Population then centered near New Brunswick, where a group of Dutch farmers had settled down to farm and to raise large Dutch families. Villages came into being along the Raritan River and its tributaries and in the hills near Basking Ridge. The population was heterogeneous, both in nationality and rank—English and Scottish gentlemen and yeomen, Dutch burghers and peasants, German masters and redemptioners, French Huguenots of varied

Old Dutch parsonage in Somerville, built in 1751.

Historic Washington Rock, which overlooks a broad region of central New Jersey.

fortune. One historian has pointed out that the abundance of Dutch names in Somerset is no proof that the Lowlanders did all the settling—they merely had the biggest families.

No brood better illustrates that than the family of Christian Van Doren and his wife Altje, who moved from Monmouth County to Middlebush in 1723 and proceeded to boost Somerset's population by seventeen young Van Dorens—twelve boys and five girls. The young Van Dorens carried on, bearing 129 children among them, and when Mrs. Van Doren died at the age of ninety-five she left 352 descendants!

Another remarkable Somerset County family started soon after, when Reverend Theodorus Jacobus Frelinghuysen came to Three Mile Run near New Brunswick to establish the Dutch Reformed Church in Somerset County in 1719. His duties extended over 300 square miles, as far as the church "op der Millstone."

The congregations of the Raritan Valley invited Mr. Frelinghuysen's second son, John, to become their pastor after the death of Reverend Theodorus.

John returned in 1750 from Holland, where he had been to obtain from the classis of Amsterdam a license to preach. He brought with him a young bride, Dinah Van Bergh, and in 1751 the young Frelinghuysens built a home of bricks imported from Holland.

John was the only one of Theodorus Frelinghuysen's five sons who left descendants, with the Frelinghuysen name being continued by John's illustrious only son Frederick—teacher, lawyer, patriot and statesman. Frederick's three sons, in turn, became lawyers, with son Theodore becoming a United States senator, Vice Presidential nominee on the 1844 Whig ticket, and president of Rutgers University in 1850.

Young John Frelinghuysen died in 1754 after only four years in the ministry, but before his death he gathered about him in the Dutch parsonage four ministerial students in the first seminary of the Dutch Reformed Church in America —which may properly be regarded as the birthplace of Rutgers University (chartered as Queen's College in 1766 to train Dutch Reformed ministers).

The rich pasture of a dairy farm near Liberty Corner.

One of many pleasant spots on the Millstone River.

New Brunswick Theological Seminary also traces its roots back to the old Dutch parsonage. After John Frelinghuysen's death his widow married one of his students, Jacob Rutsen Hardenbergh, who became the first president of Queen's College. The Frelinghuysen influence at Queen's was even more intimate, since John's son Frederick became the first tutor.

As Somerset moved toward the Revolution the county grew slowly. Millstone assumed enough prominence in 1738 to be named county seat after the old courthouse burned at Six Mile Run. Basking Ridge attracted settlers to the 3,000-acre tract John Harrison bought in 1717, and in 1751 Reverend Dr. Samuel Kennedy started his famous academy in that village.

Grand estates became an established part of the Somerset scene before the war, with an outstanding early example being Lord Neil Campbell's lavish 1,600-acre estate at the junction of the north and south branches of the Raritan. None of the early estates, however, rivaled that of Lord Stirling (William Alexander), who in about 1760 returned to the 700-acre family holdings at Basking Ridge, intent on "settling a good farm in the wilderness."

Lord Stirling lived in the grand manner "and altogether affected a style and splendor probably unequalled in the colonies."

The Revolution touched Somerset first at Basking Ridge, where the recalcitrant General Charles Lee was captured in Mrs. White's Tavern on the morning of December 12, 1776. Thirty British dragoons surrounded the house and took the crestfallen Lee off to New Brunswick in his nightshirt. Lee returned to American lines in a prisoner exchange (and later earned a besmirched page in history for his dilatory tactics at the Battle of Monmouth in 1778).

Brighter pages remained in the war ledger for Somerset, starting after the Battle of Princeton in early January, 1777, when General Washington led his revived troops up the Millstone Valley and on to winter quarters in Morristown. The following May and June his troops took positions on the Watchung Mountains, overlooking the plains where General Howe tried in vain to coax the Continentals into battle.

Nearby, at Camp Middlebrook, tradition says the first Betsy Ross flag flew after adoption of the thirteen-star flag on June 14, 1777. Those who say the flag flew there point out that Washington stayed near Middlebrook before and after June 14—and where but at the Commander-in-Chief's quarters would the first American flag have flown?

The Americans returned for the winter of 1778-79, when Washington stayed at the Wallace House in Raritan (now Somerville). Relaxation marked that winter. Washington enjoyed a Christmas party at General Nathaniel Greene's headquarters in the Van Veghten house in Finderne in 1778, when he "evinced his esteem for Mrs. Greene by dancing three hours with her without sitting down."

Even greater gaiety marked the party given by General Henry Knox at Pluckemin on February 18, 1779, to celebrate the first anniversary of the French Alliance. Reviews and fireworks enthralled army men and their visitors and that night between 300 and 400 gentlemen danced until dawn with 70 of Somerset's handsomest maidens.

But there was no such joy in a tiny house in Griggstown where young Mary Honeyman and her family lived, left alone much of the time by husband John. Mary's neighbors despised John as a Tory and she feared for his life, keeping locked in her Irish heart the knowledge that John Honeyman was in truth an American spy. War's end brought Honeyman the fame he deserved, particularly after Somerest County learned that John's reports paved the way for the tide-turning Battle of Trenton in 1776.

The valley of the Millstone felt the swiftly moving feet of British Colonel John Graves Simcoe and his Queen's Rangers on October 27, 1779, when he led his Rangers out of New Brunswick to Somerville and back on the road to New Brunswick in a brilliant 55-mile dash in the course of a night and a morning. The Rangers coolly drew supplies from an American quartermaster, burned the courthouse in Millstone, and pillaged the countryside as they went, striking terror in the valley. Pursuers captured Simcoe at Middlebush, but many military authorities nevertheless called his raid the most daring single episode of the war.

General Washington came back to Somerset County once more, to write his Farewell Address while he stayed at the Berrien mansion at Rocky Hill from August to November, 1783. Nearby, in Princeton, the Continental Congress sat to draft peace terms with Great Britain.

The county decided to relocate its county seat after Simcoe burned the Millstone courthouse, and Raritan (Somerville) was selected in 1782. A general vote of freeholders meeting in Tunison's Tavern accepted a proposition from the Dutch Consistory that county and church unite in building a combination courthouse-church. The courthouse was completed in 1783 and a year later the consistory withdrew, being reimbursed £228 as its share of the courthouse-church cost. In 1798 a new courthouse and jail were built, "similar to that at Flemington."

Life soon centered in Somerville (as it became known in 1809), both because of county business and because the village straddled both the Old York Road (Elizabethtown to Philadelphia) and the New Jersey Turnpike (Easton to New Brunswick). Drivers of grain-laden wagons stopped overnight at Mrs. Fritts's tavern in Somerville, then left at dawn for New Brunswick. Many of the wagons trundled back into town bulging with supplies for Somerville merchants.

Attempts to harness the power of the Raritan River moved from the gristmill stage to a broader utilization in 1819, when a dam was built across the river just below the junction of the north and south branches. Water from the dam powered industry more or less effectively for decades, but the force of Raritan River freshets, and the even stronger force of continued law suits over control of the river, eventually ruined the industrial scheme.

Up in the Somerset hills Lord Stirling's estate fell into ruins, with chickens roosting on the gilded coats-of-arms and pigs rooting in the courtyard. Nearby, Basking Ridge knew both prosperity and intellectual reputation, however—the latter for an

Mansion where Washington wrote Farewell Address.

Veterans Administration Hospital, Lyons, is set in the midst of the Somerset hills.

academy opened in 1799 by Reverend Robert Finley, whose students included Samuel Lewis Southard and William L. Dayton, both of whom went on to distinguished careers in the United States Senate.

Somerville's position as the center of county trade declined after 1834, when the Delaware & Raritan Canal was built through the county in the Millstone and Raritan valleys. The county economy shifted to towns along the canal, particularly Bound Brook. That sleepy little town, with fewer than 500 inhabitants, quickly became an important point on the cross-state waterway (where upwards of 2,000,000 tons of freight passed annually from 1860 to 1880).

Some of the good old trading days seemed about to return to Somerville in 1842, when the Jersey Central Railroad came into town, thus making Somerville an important terminal point for West Jersey grain wagons. But the same year the railroad rolled onward to Phillipsburg, taking over most of the grain hauling. Eventually, of course, Somerville regained its importance as a local farm center because of the railroad connection.

Somerset County underwent important surgery in 1838 and 1850. On the first occasion the Legis-

lature added to Mercer County a slice of Somerset which included land along all the north side of Princeton's main street (across from the college buildings). The 1850 cut took away from Somerset and added to Middlesex the triangle in Franklin Township where Rutgers College was located. Thus, within a dozen years, Somerset lost both its "college towns."

Transportation advances marked the 1870's when the Lehigh Valley Railroad built its line across the center of Somerset and the Delaware & Bound Brook Railroad laid its track to link Bound Brook with the South and West. Both railroads, plus the Jersey Central, came into juxtaposition near Bound Brook, intensifying that town's vitality as a transportation axis.

Somerset County had no town of more than 3,000 population until 1880, when Somerville had just 3,100 residents, and the county's total population in 1885 was only slightly more than 27,000. Newly founded North Plainfield (1872) was little more than a country village. But one of Somerset County's residents might well have been counted as two—Colonel Ruth Goshen of Middlebush, Barnum's Circus giant whose seven-foot nine-inch stature made him the world's tallest man. His death in February, 1889, attracted thousands to gape at the largest single grave ever dug in New Jersey.

Improved railroad facilities in the 1880's and 1890's made Somerset more popular than ever with the wealthy, who now could live in the lush hills and commute to their work. Somerset County provided an ideal spot for those seeking large pieces of ground, since from the earliest days landholders were estate-minded, and wealthy industrialists, stock brokers and financiers moved into the quietude of the mountains, buying 200, 500, even 1,000 acres.

None of these buyers, however, matched the imagination (or the bankroll) of James Buchanan Duke, tobacco tycoon who scorned the natural hills when he came out to buy land in 1893. Starting with the 400-acre Veghte farm on the banks of the Raritan, he had assembled more than 2,200 acres by the turn of the century.

Then, as one writer put it, "he waved his magic wand, the check book" and wondrous things took place on the flat plains. Men and machines built

hills, transplanted full-grown forests, made lakes appear where open fields had been before. Hundreds of thousands of rhododendrons and other shrubs brought the atmosphere of woodland to the fabulous estate. Duke spent an estimated $15,000,000 to remake his flat open farmland into a hilly forest.

Duke's pride in his estate prompted him to open his lands to visitors, but one day in 1915 a party in 180 cars pulled into Duke Park and picnicked on the front lawn of his mansion. Duke threatened to close the park and made good his threat in 1917 when a visiting motorist promised to thrash him if Duke didn't get his phaeton and team of horses off a park road so uninvited automobilists could get through.

An obscure institution in North Carolina, Trinity College, faced a problem in 1924 when Duke signed papers at Duke Park for a $46,000,000 trust fund for charitable and educational institutions. Of the total, $6,000,000 was for Trinity—if it would change its name to Duke University. Trinity didn't hesitate. Duke died the following year, and left the

Johns-Manville plant, and part of the town that has grown up around it since 1912.

Basking Ridge Oak in Presbyterian Church yard is more than 400 years old.

bulk of his $100,000,000 estate in trust for his daughter Doris, who became the world's richest girl on her twenty-first birthday in 1933.

The early 1900's gave to the song-and-dance world two Somerset County girls. First, young Ruth Dennis, a native of Somerset, made her way from a nearby farm in 1900 to dance on the stage of the old Somerset Hall and leaped from there to world-wide fame as Ruth St. Denis. At about the same time Anna Case, daughter of a South Branch blacksmith, impressed church-goers with her voice in the Flemington village choir. Eventually Anna Case found her way to the Metropolitan Opera House and a great concert career.

Somerset's pride in its noted daughters could not hide its shame for its decaying old courthouse, so run-down that it brought only $125 when sold at public auction in 1906. Removal of the 107-year-old building made way for a new $300,000 white marble courthouse, dedicated in 1909 and still in use. It was here that Mrs. Edward W. Hall and two of her

brothers were acquitted after they faced trial for the murder in 1922 of Reverend Edward W. Hall, rector of a New Brunswick church, and Mrs. Eleanor Mills, a choir singer.

Fewer than 35,000 people lived in the county when the new courthouse was dedicated, and most of those earned their livings from surrounding farms. However, just before World War I, the excellent railroad facilities at Bound Brook at last attracted sizable industry to Somerest. In 1912 the Johns-Manville Company built the biggest asbestos plant in the world in the flats southwest of Bound Brook (where the town of Manville has since grown up). Three years later Calco Chemical Company started making dyes in Bound Brook for Somerville's Cott-a-Lap Company, a manufacturer of floor covering.

Somerset County had intimate knowledge of the end of World War I, because on July 2, 1921, President Warren G. Harding sat down at a desk in the home of U. S. Senator Joseph S. Frelinghuysen in Raritan and signed the Knox-Porter resolution proclaiming peace between the United States and the Central Powers. Harding had come to the Frelinghuysen estate for a Fourth-of-July week-end of golf and relaxation.

As Somerset moved through twentieth-century transition it took measures to preserve its past. Frelinghuysen descendants stepped forward in 1907 after the Central Railroad purchased the old home of Reverend John Frelinghuysen and planned to demolish it for a right-of-way. The Frelinghuysens bought the house and moved it 1,500 feet, and so well built was the old Dutch parsonage that not a crack was caused by the moving.

In Basking Ridge, members of the Presbyterian Church heard the alarming news in 1924 that their 400-year-old oak tree faced rapidly increasing decay. Experts filled in 72 cavities with three tons of concrete and stretched 1,150 feet of cable through the tree to hold up the ponderous limbs of Somerset County's most noted natural spectacle.

Industry surged forward in the 1920's and 1930's after highway building programs caused three major roads to meet near Somerville. Since World War II Somerset has become one of the fastest-growing industrial counties in the state, with new industry centering in the Somerville-Bound Brook-Manville area. Industrial employment in 1951 was up 250 per cent over 1940.

The Veterans Administration Hospital at Lyons, in the midst of the Somerset Hills estate country, is one of the oldest and best known veterans' hospitals in the United States.

North Plainfield, set off from Warren Township in 1872, grew rapidly in the last 25 years of the nineteenth century, doubling its population to almost 5,000 by 1900. Immediately adjacent to Plainfield (which juts westward out of Union County as North Plainfield juts eastward out of Somerset), North Plainfield early became noted for its residential fitness. The building of State Highway 29 through the borough also aided North Plainfield's growth; today it is the most-populous municipality in the County, just a shade ahead of Somerville. As a further mark of distinction, the famed Washington Rock is within North Plainfield's boundaries.

Population is bounding upward in Somerset County and has moved over the 100,000 mark—an increase of more than 35 per cent over 1940. Tangible evidence of the county's new administrative responsibilities as a result of its growth is the $1,600,000 Somerest County Administration Building dedicated in 1952.

Nevertheless, estates and farms still are the mark of Somerset, with its 1,100 farms yielding products valued at $7,500,000 annually. The Somerset hills continue to harbor the very wealthy while the towns and villages in the valleys reflect the prosperity to be found in the rich soil.

Today, 300 years after the first Dutch traveler saw the Raritan Valley, Somerset is still "handsome and pleasant to behold."

MORE ABOUT SOMERSET

Mellick, Andrew D., *The Story of an Old Farm, or Life in New Jersey in the Eighteenth Century.* Somerville, New Jersey, Unionist Gazette, 1889.

Messler, Abraham, *Centennial History of Somerset County, New Jersey.* Somerville, New Jersey, C. M. Jameson, 1878.

Schumacher, Ludwig, *The Somerset Hills.* New York, New Amsterdam Book Co., 1900.

Snell, James P. Comp., *History of Hunterdon and Somerset Counties, New Jersey,* Philadelphia, Penna., Everts and Peck, 1881.

Somerset Press, *Somerset County, 250 Years.* Somerville, New Jersey, Somerset Messenger Gazette, 1938.

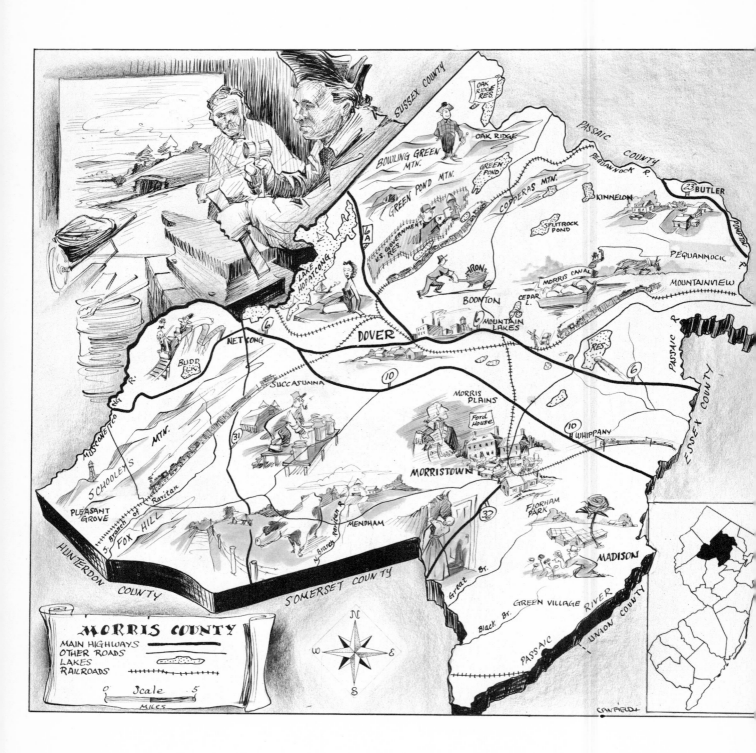

MORRIS

If someone were to write a musical suite for Morris County, the temptation would be strong to let variations on "Yankee Doodle" and the minuet carry the theme—in tribute to the county's Revolutionary War importance and in recognition of two centuries of opulent living in the Morris Hills. It would make pleasant listening but it would be inadequate.

Actually, to make the Morris Suite complete, music symbolizing patriotism and gentle living would have to be harmonized with the stridency of metal clashing against metal. The simple fact is that iron made Morris; all else grew around the iron backbone in the hills near Dover. Thus, in justice, the "Anvil Chorus" is as basic a Morris song as "Yankee Doodle."

Morris County's base rests solidly on "Sucky-sunny," the "black stone" which Lenni Lenape braves showed white men soon after 1700. Until then, the course of settlement had been routine: Dutch colonists came over from Bergen in about 1695 to take up 1,500 acres near Pompton Plains; German and Dutch wanderers headed overland from Philadelphia to New York and stopped at Schooley's Mountain in 1707; New Englanders came over the mountains from Essex County to settle at Whippanong in 1710 and spread westward to "West Hanover" (now Morristown).

Hanover quickly became dominant because of the old forge built on the Whippany River about 1710. Soon after, a forge began operations in "the hollow" (Morristown) and within twenty years others followed—at Dover, where John Jackson lit his forge fire in 1722, and in Rockaway in about 1730. Most of the ironworks centered along the Rockaway River, where proximity to the ore was combined with dashing water power and thick forests—a highly significant factor, since a single forge "fire" alone burned 1,000 acres of woodland annually.

Most of the early ironmen used ore from the mine opened in 1713 near Succasunna, where the "blackstone" cropped out on the surface and required little digging. Horses plodded from mine to furnace, carrying ore in leather bags. Then, when the ore was melted, the weary beasts plodded on to tidewater, hauling iron pigs shaped to their backs.

Jacob Ford, Sr., leader of all the early Morris ironmen, led the agitation to have Morris County cut away from Hunterdon, at a time when Morris had only two settlers per square mile. Hunterdon relinquished all of what is now Morris, Sussex and Warren counties in 1738, and fifteen years later (1753) Sussex and Warren counties cut away from

Mount Hope's 2700-foot shaft reaches deep for iron.

Hilltop Church in Mendham is a landmark in West Morris.

Morris. Actually, the Morris freedom was limited; until 1772 the county had no representatives in the State Legislature.

Morristown assumed both its name and designation as county seat in 1740. Elsewhere the early villages of Pompton, Whippany, German Valley, Chester, Dover, Rockaway and Mendham expanded, but by 1750 Morristown ruled supreme as a commercial center. Ironworkers trekked to Morristown once a week for supplies and much of the official business was done there.

Morris County ironmasters rebelled at the 1750 British decree that henceforth no rolling or slitting mills could be operated in the colonies. Quietly the Morris mills kept operating in defiance of the decree, and this a full twenty years before violation of British laws became widespread.

An excellent premise might be established to the effect that the Morris hills gave birth to full-scale rebellion, except that the most noted of the surreptitious slitting mills, the one at Boone Town, was run by men who became Tories after the war started. This rebellion of the 1750's was more a rebellion of the pocketbook than of principle.

John Jacob Faesch came on the Morris scene in 1772, when he bought several thousand acres at Mt. Hope after leaving the London Company at Ringwood. Faesch built a furnace, expanded his holdings near Mt. Hope to more than 10,000 acres,

and became the county's supreme ironmaster, more powerful even than the Fords, Jacob, Sr. and Jacob, Jr. His richness did not extend to the spirit, however, since he believed religion was a "very good thing—to keep the lower classes in proper subordination."

Morris County attracted the landed gentry even before the Revolution. In addition to Faesch and the Fords (who in 1774 built the mansion Washington occupied in the winter of 1779-80), great landholders included Peter Kemble, who became a Tory; Lucas von Beaverhoudt, who entertained impartially both British and American soldiers at "Beaverwyck" in Troy Hills, and Captain Michael Kearny of His Britannic Majesty's Navy, whose Whippany estate became known as the "Irish Lot."

When war flared, Morris County had the iron backbone to stiffen rebellion. General Washington led his bruised troops north to Morristown from Princeton early in January, 1777, and remained until the spring. He familiarized himself with the ironworks (a Washington letter written in 1777 tells of between 80 and 100 ironworks "great and small" in Morris County).

Munitions poured from the forges and furnaces, particularly those at Hibernia and Mt. Hope. Shovels, axes, cannon, cannon balls, grapeshot and other supplies went to the Continental Army throughout the war. In return, ironworks employees

Hilltop view of Dover, an iron town ever since John Jackson lit first forge fire there in 1722.

Ford Mansion, at Morristown, where Washington spent winter of 1779-1780.

were exempted from service. Colonel Jacob Ford built a powder mill near Morristown in 1776, probably the only Revolutionary War powder mill in New Jersey.

All New Jersey mourned the death of both Fords in January, 1777. Jacob, Jr., died January 11 of pneumonia, and eight days later Jacob, Sr., died of fever. Thus Morris County lost its most important early leaders at a time when the American cause sorely needed both of them.

Washington spent his first winter in Morristown in Jacob Arnold's Tavern while his men camped in the Loantaka Valley. Surrounding hills made the village easy to defend and even then it must have been a handsome town, since the Green had been set aside as early as 1771. The ease of defense, the pleasantness of the village, and the strength of the iron region lured Washington and his army back for the winter of 1779-80.

That winter truly tested the endurance of the American cause. The war had dragged on for almost three and a half years when Washington and his troops arrived in town on December 1, 1779. Washington established his headquarters in the Ford Mansion, his men went to live in Jockey Hollow. Everything added up to despair—poor food, meager pay, wretched quarters for the men. On top of everything else, Benedict Arnold faced

a court-martial board in the Dickerson Tavern, Morristown, in December, 1779. Accused of favoring Tories in Philadelphia, Arnold received only a reprimand from Washington, but it stung him deeply enough to make him desert to the British a few weeks later.

Despite the generally low spirit, Washington and his staff had some high moments in Morristown. Count Pulaski helped maintain morale by his exhibitions of brilliant horsemanship. Lafayette, returning from a journey to France in May, 1780, reported that a powerful French force was on the way with help. Young Colonel Alexander Hamilton courted his Betty Schuyler, who lived just around the corner from Ford Mansion.

Hopes for an early peace soared high when the army moved out of Jockey Hollow in June, 1780. Thus the bitterness of two Pennsylvania brigades, still in service and back in Morristown the following winter, can be understood. Many of the men had been fighting for more than three years; most had not been paid for a year. Their grumbling culminated in mutiny on New Year's Day, 1781, when they killed one of their officers, Captain Adam Bettin, and marched off toward Philadelphia. Their commander, General "Mad" Anthony Wayne, followed the mutineers to Princeton and at a series of meetings promised better things for the men. Satisfied, the troops returned to Morristown.

Out of the mutiny came one of the best-known Revolutionary stories, that of Tempe Wick and her horse. The young colonial miss fought off mutinous Pennsylvania brigade troops who tried to seize her beloved horse. She galloped home and, according to legend, led her horse into her bedroom to conceal him from the troops.

Chartering of turnpikes in the first decade of the nineteenth century slowly increased the county's population. A toll pike from Elizabethtown to Morristown via Chatham and Bottle Hill (Madison) encouraged travel (but also prompted the more thrifty to travel via the parallel "Shunpike" a mile to the south). The Morristown-Phillipsburg Turnpike, chartered in 1806, made the Schooley's Mountain "health" business spurt wonderously. Although the Alpha Hotel had been built on the moun-

tain in 1795, it took the turnpike to help make Schooley's Mountain a nationally-known health resort.

"The most gay and fashionable company" harkened up Schooley's slopes, to the Heath House and later to the Dorincourt Hotel. They came for their health (or said they did), and, their illnesses vanished after drinking from the miraculous springs, the waters of which contained many minerals and health-giving elements (not the least of which was sodium bicarbonate).

Meanwhile, ironmakers burned timber furiously along the Rockaway River. Most forges and furnaces continued to depend on the old Succasunna mine (renamed Dickerson Mine after the family of Governor Mahlon Dickerson bought the property in the 1780's). From 1826 to 1830, a hundred forge fires in an area from Hamburg to High Bridge used Dickerson Mine ore. Some other pits—

First iron mine in Morris County, near Mine Hill, dates back to about 1700.

A mural in Wharton Borough Hall shows operation of Morris Canal inclined plane.

notably Mt. Hope—supplied ore, but the easiest digging was at Dickerson Mine.

High costs of transportation and diminishing forest land seemed certain to doom the Morris County iron industry, until George P. Macculoch went fishing on Lake Hopatcong one summer day in 1822. Gazing over the lake, Macculoch noted the mountains sloping away to the east and his mind played with the thought of a canal, utilizing the waters of Lake Hopatcong and flowing to tidewater down the Rockaway and Passaic River valleys. He looked westward, conceived the possibility of sending the canal down the Musconetcong River valley to Phillipsburg, the approach to Pennsylvania anthracite.

Macculoch definitely had Morris County iron in mind when he sought financing for his plan. His scheme seemed fantastic; financial backing came slowly, but in August, 1831, the canal linked Easton and Newark—every inch of it dug by hand. Never before had such an engineering feat been accomplished; boats literally climbed mountains by an ingenious system of planes and locks. Anthracite flowed into Morris County. Iron again became a king.

Dover, Boonton and Rockaway all found new life. Henry McFarlan and Joseph Blackwell, New York merchants, expanded the old ironworks. In 1827 they laid out streets and offered lots for sale (with the canal-to-be their chief selling point). Smoke soon bellowed forth in thick columns from the village's two rolling mills, its foundries, its nail and spike factory, its forging shop and numerous smaller iron-connected enterprises.

Boonton had the most impressive boom of all,

however. Grass grew in Boonton's streets before the canal cut through, then the New Jersey Iron Company built a new mill in the village in 1830. The company brought in skilled rolling mill mechanics from England and started to produce in quantity. Paradoxically, as soon as the mill began to benefit from the canal its rollers began to turn out axles, wheels and rails for railroads, thus helping doom the canal before it was fairly started.

One of the most famous iron manufactories of all was the Speedwell Iron Works in Morristown. Its early achievements included the manufacture in 1819 of the driving shaft for the *SS Savannah*, first vessel to cross the Atlantic using steam. Samuel F. B. Morse and Alfred Vail brought the old mill its greatest fame, however, by their development of the electromagnetic telegraph—with the financial encouragement of Judge Stephen Vail, Alfred's father and owner of the ironworks. Three miles of wire looped around the old mill carried the first telegraph message on January 6, 1838, when Vail ticked out: "A patient waiter is no loser."

Iron entered a new era after 1850. Until then, products of Morris mines had largely been processed within the county. After 1850, most of the ore went out of the county for processing, with the change traceable to the coming of the Morris & Essex Railroad to Dover in 1848, ten years after it reached Morristown.

Quick transportation encouraged extensive mining and exportation of ore. In 1855 Morris County mines produced 100,000 tons of ore; twelve years later that total jumped to 275,000 tons, and by 1880 Morris was the third county in the nation in amount of iron ore mined, with 568,420 tons.

Iron mines pockmarked the entire backbone of western and northern Morris County. As many as fifty mines operated at once in the region from Long Valley to Hibernia. Then the iron industry discovered in 1882 that iron ore could almost literally be picked off the surface in the Mesabi region near Lake Superior. The crown moved from Morris to Mesabi.

The Jersey iron dynasty faced ruin, although full effects of the Mesabi interloper took forty years to upset Morris ironmen. Nevertheless, the ancient Dickerson mine closed in the 1890's after giving up more than a million tons of ore. Hurdtown's famous mine closed in 1898, after going down 2,600 feet for elusive iron. Hibernia, once the heart of the industry, heard the sound of the pick for the last time in 1913, seven years after thirteen miners drowned in flooded shafts.

The iron mines naturally attracted allied industries. Dover had an extensive plant in the 1870's for making mine equipment, in addition to its rolling mills. Boonton's iron processers gained additional

fame for nail production, while Wharton attracted the tremendous foundry of the Replogle Steel Company (whose closing in 1919, incidentally, brought economic collapse to Wharton).

Mines enticed the Giant Powder Company of California to Kenvil in 1871 to make dynamite. First devoted exclusively to dynamite, Giant turned to smokeless powder and during World War I (as Hercules Powder Company) added TNT.

Hercules strengthened Morris County's longestablished role as an arsenal of freedom, and the title became fixed in September, 1880, when the War Department purchased 1,866 acres east of Green Pond Mountain to build mighty Picatinny Arsenal (which now spreads over 5,125 acres of ground with installations valued at $100,000,000).

Meanwhile, the Morris & Essex Railroad changed the county's character by convincing men of wealth that they could work in New York and live in the healthful Morris Hills, in Morristown, Madison, Convent, Chatham and surrounding areas. Morristown's handsome streets became adorned with great homes, and splendid estates on the surrounding

Tempe Wick House in Jockey Hollow Park, Morristown.

A stretch of Lake Hopatcong, state's largest lake.

slopes harbored the wealthy and the famous. Writers and artists lived near Morristown in the last decades of the nineteenth century—including Frank B. Stockton, Bret Harte, Rudyard Kipling, A. B. Frost, Thomas Nast and many others.

At the twentieth century's dawn, Morristown could boast (probably with some truth) that within a radius of one mile of the Green more millionaires lived than in any other equal area in the world. The fabulous estates were numerous enough to fill the pages of a World War I vintage picture book, "Beautiful Homes of Morris County." Possibly the most opulent Morris dweller of all was Otto H. Kahn, whose "Cedar Court" on Normandie Heights was so lavish that a 1905 fire which destroyed only the east wing caused damage estimated at $750,000!

Interestingly enough, when the Morris County courthouse was built in 1827, a weathervane in the shape of a golden plow topped the structure. While rural dwellers could quip that the plow "showed politicians which way the wind was blowing," the Morris farmer did not come into his own until after the Civil War. Today the county's 1,000 farms have an annual business of more than $7,000,000, $1,500,000 of which comes from the horticultural business centered in Madison, the "Rose City,"

where rose growing has been big business since the 1880's.

Iron still has great significance for Morris County, since more than 500,000 tons of ore are extracted annually from Mt. Hope, Scrub Oak and Richards mines (most active iron mines in New Jersey). Ever present is the possibility of greater glory, since an estimated 600,000,000 tons of ore still give substance to the hills. If ever Mesabi slips, Morris could see a return of the king with the iron crown.

However, the iron hills today play host to a growing recreation business. Indeed, the iron region is now better known as the "Lakeland," mainly because of Lake Hopatcong. Largest of New Jersey's lakes, Hopatcong has been a popular resort for more than sixty years. Numerous smaller lakes dot all of north Morris, most of them close to former thriving iron ore villages.

Much of Morris continues to be rural, particularly north and west of Dover and west of Morristown. Another vast stretch of ground—the prehistoric "Great Swamp" between Chatham and Basking Ridge—has resisted efforts to turn it to usefulness. However, Morris is becoming an area of small homeowners, with many housing developments spreading over former great estates. Other large

A fisherman angles at Hacklebarny State Park.

land holdings now are being used as building sites for modern industrial plants. Not that great estates are completely a thing of the past in Morris, but many of the "old" names have moved elsewhere since World War I.

Some of the old homes and estates live on in other forms. A former private estate near Whippany is the home of the internationally-known Seeing Eye, where dogs are trained to lead the blind. Mead Hall in Madison, once the Gibbons mansion, is the administration building for Drew University, while a few blocks away Bayley-Ellard High School is housed in another old mansion. Nearby, in Convent, St. Elizabeth's College is set in an area which is still predominantly estate country.

Morris County obviously (and correctly) takes tremendous pride in its colonial heritage. Morristown National Park, established in 1933, has attracted more than 4,000,000 visitors. The Morristown Green, while of some nuisance in the automobile age, makes Morristown unique among all New Jersey towns.

Thus has Morris moved away from the iron monarchy, yet has seen nearly every movement directed or affected by iron. Iron is no longer king; yet, setting on a throne of 600,000,000 tons of iron ore, King Ferro may return any day—and to glory greater than ever before known.

MORE ABOUT MORRIS

A History of Morris County. New York City, Lewis Historical Publishing Co., 1914.

Munsell, W. W. and Co., *Munsell's History of Morris County*. New York City, W. W. Munsell and Co., 1882.

Platt, Charles D., *Dover Dates, 1722-1922*. Charles D. Platt, 1922.

Sherman, Andrew M. *Historic Morristown, New Jersey: The Story of Its First Century*. Morristown, New Jersey, Howard Publishing Co., 1905.

PASSAIC

Elbridge Gerry's philosophy that land areas should be manipulated in a manner most beneficial to politicians found full favor in February, 1837, when the legislators sat down in Trenton to establish Passaic County. If ever there was a gerrymandered county it is wasp-waisted Passaic.

South Jersey votes held back Passaic County until Atlantic County could be created as a counterbalancing vote. Moreover, by linking the little-settled country north of Pompton Lakes with the heavily industrial regions along the Passaic River, South Jersey politicians killed the continual clamoring for two logical new North Jersey districts—proposed as "Pompton" and "Paterson" counties.

The projected "Pompton" and "Paterson" counties clearly recognized the vast differences between the rugged hill country and the upcoming factory area in the crook of the Passaic River. But only the one hourglass-shaped county slipped by the Legislature—and few pondered the fact that North Passaic's forestlands had little in common with Paterson's factories. Intervening years have failed to make the two areas on either side of the narrow two-mile connecting corridor completely one. The corridor divides as much as it connects.

Long before 1837 the Passaic River brought Dutch settlers inland, the earliest of record being Hartman Michielsen, who bought an island in the river in 1678 from Captehan Peeters, an Indian. Two years later two Dutch missionaries visited the "Great Falls" and wrote awe-filled accounts of its grandeur. Then, in 1682, fourteen Dutch families acquired the Acquackanonk Tract (comprising most of modern Clifton, Passaic and Paterson).

Arent Schuyler and Anthony Brockholts bought 5,500 acres near Pompton in 1697, and all of the land in modern Passaic County had been purchased before 1711, including the acres on the rolling highlands to the north. Settlers stopped at the "little falls" in 1711, and Simeon Van Winkle built his "white house" on a river ford two miles below the "great falls" before 1719. By 1730 German and Dutch families lived in the rough hill country, among them John Jacob Kanouse of Holland (whose name is today perpetuated in Kanouse Mountain).

Cornelius Board, tramping up and down the Ramapo Valley seeking copper, found iron instead, and built a forge in the valley before 1740. That year the Ogdens of Newark bought land from Board and, styling themselves the "Ringwood Company," commenced the smelting of iron in 1741.

Word of the rich iron deposits spread to England, where the American Company (sometimes called the "London Company") commissioned an

Silk mills along the Passaic River, Paterson, about 1875.

Eye-catching view of north Passaic County's rolling hills.

energetic German, Peter Hasenclever, to represent them in American iron ventures. Hasenclever acquired 50,000 acres, including Ringwood. He imported 535 Germans to run his mines and iron works and built a thriving iron community at Ringwood in 1764 and 1765. Roads spread through the forestland to connect the Ringwood mines with Pompton, Charlottesburg and New Foundland furnaces.

Hasenclever lived like a feudal lord in the mountains, while in the surrounding forest deeply religious German colonists eagerly welcomed Reverend Ferdinand Farmer, the indefatigable Catholic priest who conducted services at Macopin (Echo Lake) in the 1750's. Father Farmer's services in those North Jersey hills were among the earliest Catholic masses in New Jersey.

John Jacob Faesch succeeded Hesenclever in 1769 and Faesch in turn yielded control to Robert Erskine in 1771. Erskine's diligent efforts at Ringwood mines provided munitions for the Revolutionary cause, and the young Scotchman rendered yeoman service as a mapmaker for the Continental Army.

General Washington often slept in what is now Passaic County. The main American Army encamped at Pompton, Wayne and Totowa in the summer and fall of 1780. Washington and his officers lived in the Theunis Dey Mansion at Preakness from July 1 to 29 and from October 9 to 27, both 1780, and the General hurried back again in January, 1781, after the abortive Jersey Brigade mutiny at Pompton on January 20.

Nevertheless, Washington's most important visit of all possibly was on July 10, 1778, when the General stopped for lunch at the foot of the majestic "Totowa Falls." One of his officers, young Alexander Hamilton, particularly exulted in the pounding volume of the falls as they plunged 70 feet into their rocky gorge.

Thirteen years later Hamilton, Secretary of the Treasury in Washington's Cabinet, sent to Congress his vital "Report on Manufactures." He insisted that the new nation could never be truly free until it

Industry is keynote of Passaic River today.

Looking up Bloomfield Avenue, now Broadway, Passaic, at the turn of the century.

manufactured its own products. Possibly he envisioned an industrial city at the foot of the falls he had first seen as an Army colonel. Certainly he rejoiced on November 22, 1791, when New Jersey's Governor William Paterson signed the charter for the Society for Establishing Useful Manufactures.

The Society (even then abbreviated as S. U. M.) invited proposals from New York, New Jersey and Pennsylvania—and Hamilton offered no objection to an engineer's declaration that the falls offered "the best situation in the world." An S. U. M. committee accepted the appraisal on May 17, 1792, and named their projected city in honor of Governor Paterson.

The Society hired Major Pierre Charles L'Enfant to design the city. L'Enfant sketched elaborate plans, with streets 200 feet wide, but the S. U. M. budget failed to match L'Enfant's imagination and the Major took off with his plans (which later proved very valuable when he laid out Washington, D. C., in 1801).

Peter Colt, treasurer of the State of Connecticut, succeeded L'Enfant in February, 1793. He started digging a raceway to lead the powerful river to the society's cotton mill (which became known as the "Bull Mill" because Colt operated it with oxen while awaiting water power). America had few skilled craftsmen; Colt imported them from England, Scotland and Ireland.

Gloom descended on the budding city when S. U. M. ran out of money in 1796, but individual operators came to the city to lease S. U. M. property. John Clark, for example, started Paterson's first machine shop in about 1800. John Parke built a small cotton mill of his own, then in 1810 built a large brick stone mill.

Parke disdained sending his products to New York via sloops tied up at Acquackanonk Landing; instead, he packed his cotton in "gorgeously painted" covered wagons and went overland to Philadelphia. It cost more, but Parke found it paid to advertise. Business boomed for Parke and the city's six or seven other cotton millers in the War of 1812, but the industry collapsed when peace came. A new tariff in 1816 pumped life back into the mills; Paterson's ever-recurring boom and bust cycles were under way.

A dozen cotton mills used S. U. M. power in

1825 and twice that many used Passaic Falls power in 1829. Moneyed men invested in the mills and built fine homes on the hillsides surrounding Paterson. The big industrial leaders scorned free schools, although they set up Sunday schools where youngsters working in the mills could study on their day off without hindering production. In 1832 Paterson had twenty "pay" schools, one free school.

Paterson and Acquackanonk came to a mutually satisfying break in 1831. Paterson decided it wanted to keep its tax revenues; Acquackanonk leaders found satisfaction in the thriving trade carried on by Passaic River steamers which touched their docks—and saw no reason why Paterson votes should run their little community.

A cholera epidemic struck the Passaic River lands in 1832, killing 140 in Paterson alone, but it failed to stop completion that year of the Morris Canal and the Paterson and Hudson River Railroad (Paterson to Jersey City). Paterson absorbed coal brought in by the Morris Canal and sent increasing amounts of finished goods to tidewater on the railroad.

The new transportation eventually helped up-county farmers, too, by opening great new markets. The Morris Canal boosted Little Falls industry and

gave it enough prominence to entice Robert Beattie's carpet mill out from New York in 1842. Only Acquackanonk (Passaic) suffered, because the canal and railroad doomed its dockside trade.

Meanwhile, in Paterson, the Colt family took over complete control of the S. U. M. by purchasing 1,991 of the Society's 2,620 shares before 1814. Roswell L. Colt, largest shareholder and "the greatest of the Colts," became governor of the Society in 1814 and served until his death in 1856.

Other Colts had genius, too. John Colt started to make cotton duck in Paterson in 1827, being the first man ever to substitute cotton for flax in sail duck. Samuel Colt first made his Colt "revolver" in the Paterson "Gun Mill" in 1836. Sam's gun seemed a failure, so he sold his last automatic to an Indian trader in 1842—and when the government finally recognized the gun's merits in 1847 and gave him a large order, Sam had no model from which to work. He redesigned the revolver and resumed manufacture in Connecticut.

Another Colt, Christopher, established Paterson's first silk mill in 1839, but the true "father" of Paterson silk industry was John Ryle. Colt sold his silk plant to George W. Murray, who brought Ryle

Modern-day view of thriving Paterson.

from England to superintend operations. Ryle set up a battery of silk looms in 1842, bought out Murray in 1846. The "Silk City" was born.

Cotton supremacy gravitated from Paterson to New England, but the mechanical "know-how" and the pool of experienced hands remained behind. Thus, when Tom Rogers and others began to make locomotives in the 1830's, Paterson had an edge on all the nation. The simple fact is that Paterson's workmen could make anything. It was no anomaly that Paterson became the "Iron City" at the same time it became the "Silk City."

Paterson and Passaic County were synonymous before the Civil War. No one challenged the city's right to become county seat in 1837. Seventy per cent of Passaic's 16,734 population lived in or adjacent to Paterson in 1840—a ratio which continued unchecked for almost another fifty years.

Amidst the clanging of factories and the whirring of looms, Paterson became a city in 1851. Its 11,341 people had great pride. In fact, too much pride and too much sense to permit aldermen to continue wearing the leather badges on their hats which proclaimed: "ALDERMAN, FIRST WARD" (or any other ward). That was too much for democratic Paterson, whose citizens ridiculed this show of snobbishness. The badges disappeared.

Down the river, people living in sight of Dundee Island clung to their quaint name of Acquackanonk and stubbornly demanded high prices for their land. Finally, after thirty years of fruitless attempts to harness the river as Paterson had done seventy years before, the Dundee Manufacturing Company gave in to exorbitant demands and bought two key farms in 1858. The company built a 450-foot dam across the river and let it be known that open arms awaited manufacturers.

A small brick and anvil factory responded initially, and the New York Steam-Engine Company works, a wire mill and a print works followed. By 1873, when Acquackanonk incorporated as the city of Passaic, about fifteen mills fringed the Dundee water power canal. Nevertheless, fewer than a thousand people lived in the city.

All Passaic County expanded in the last three decades of the nineteenth century. Wayne Township boasted in 1880 of the Laflin & Rand Powder Company (capacity, 600 kegs daily). Mountain View had four brick factories producing more than 120,000 bricks daily. The Beattie Company greatly enlarged its carpet plant at Little Falls, and four other mills and an iron moulding plant built nearby.

Ringwood Manor, traditional ironmaster's home.

North of the "wasp waist," iron and water paced the advance. Martin Ryerson and family took over the old Ringwood works in 1807 and operated them until 1853, when Peter Cooper bought the 22,000-acre property. Cooper, New York glue magnate, inventor and promoter, pushed the old mines to their greatest prominence—aided by Abram Hewitt, who merged his personal and business fortunes with Cooper in 1855 by marrying Peter's daughter Amelia.

The Cooper-Hewitt combine made the mines pay. The 1880 census showed that a total of 896,000 long tons had been taken from 20 Ringwood mines. Some estimates say 2,500,000 long tons have been taken from the mines since colonial days—a great percentage of it during management by Cooper and Hewitt interests. The mines, worked sporadically since 1931, now are once again being studied as a source of ore.

Late in the 1870's, Newark leaders cast envious eyes on the crystal-clear waters in the Pequannock and Wanaque watersheds, convinced of the practicability of tapping upper Passaic to provide drinking water. However, while city fathers debated the proposal, a group known as the East Jersey Water Company quietly bought up most of the land in the Pequannock watershed.

Accordingly, when Newark finally decided in 1889 to build reservoirs, it found the East Jersey interests held a monopoly on the land. The city had to negotiate with the water company to build reservoirs at Oak Ridge, Echo Lake, Clinton and Macopin at a total cost of $6,000,000. East Jersey lived up to its agreement and by May, 1892, the reservoirs were built and a 48-inch steel pipe carried Passaic County water 21 miles to Newark faucets.

Construction of another reservoir at Canistear before 1900 and improvements to the other reservoirs through the years have raised the Pequannock storage area to more than eleven billion gallons. All of it came under complete Newark control in 1900 when court decisions forced the East Jersey Water Company to convey its water rights to the city.

Even greater plans engrossed Newark water men in 1907 when the city revived study of the Wanaque watershed as the location of a fifty-million-gallon-per-day reservoir. This time Passaic County interests stood in the way, alarmed that the Pequannock watershed had slipped completely away from the county.

Eventually eight municipalities joined to build Wanaque Reservoir: Paterson, Passaic and Clifton in Passaic County; Newark, Montclair, Bloomfield and Glen Ridge in Essex; and Kearny in Hudson. Much legal maneuvering delayed the project, most of it occasioned by the stubborn refusal of large

property owners to give up land which they wanted to preserve as grazing pasture for their prize cattle.

Nevertheless, on November 23, 1920, ground was broken for the tremendous reservoir capable of supplying a hundred million gallons of water daily. A dam 1,500 feet long and 100 feet high was completed in 1928 and water started to back up through the valley. Work on the $26,000,000 project was completed in 1930.

Paterson, "fastest-growing city in the East" in 1880, had a tremendous influx of emigrants in the 1880's. Emigrant trains stopped nightly in town, and many of the newcomers also made their way to mushrooming Passaic, where the population jumped from about 1,000 in 1873 to 6,632 in 1880 and 27,777 in 1900. Passaic's famed woolen mills, started in the 1890's, led the advance.

Locomotive production began to decline in Paterson during the 1890's, but silk production and silk processing took up the slack. Paterson also became one of New Jersey's prime shopping centers, with

Macopin farm points up rural nature of north Passaic.

Part of the business section of Clifton.

scores of small shops and supply houses lining the city's old streets.

Celebration of the S. U. M.'s hundredth anniversary in 1891 served as the occasion to "remember in passing"—to remember that the process for making paper in a continuous roll was developed in Paterson, that a Paterson man invented the steam radiator, that Paterson made nearly all the railroads' rotary snow plows and a big percentage of the nation's fire engines.

Some remembered John Philip Holland, the supposedly eccentric Paterson schoolmaster who on July 23, 1878, tried out in the Passaic River the first submarine. Naturally, his 1881 launching of the "Fenian Ram" (paid for by Irish Fenian Sympathizers) raised him in the city's estimation—but not until submarines wrecked havoc on shipping in World War I did Paterson (and the world) understand the true significance of John Philip Holland's invention.

Active in the S. U. M. celebration was Garret A. Hobart, prominent businessman and politician who had been a lawyer in Paterson since 1866. Hobart's political star ascended rapidly in the early 1890's, climaxed in 1896 when he was elected Vice President to serve with President William McKinley. Hobart's death in 1899 cut short a promising career in national politics.

Everything else took a back seat in 1902 and 1903 when the elements tried vainly to eradicate Paterson. First a fire in February, 1902, swept through 54 acres and destroyed 456 buildings. Three weeks later violent floodwaters surged through the streets, and soon afterwards a tornado twisted through the city. Finally, in October, 1903, floodwaters again inundated the city. Miraculously, however, in every instance the silk mills escaped damage.

Although they had survived flood and fire, the mills suffered from a violent strike in 1913. When Paterson's 25,000 silk workers struck, led by the International Workers of the World (I.W.W.), all of the city's 350 silk mills came to a standstill. Mill owners described the "red" strike leadership (undoubtedly with some justification), but the trouble had roots reaching back to 1794, when Paterson had its first strike. Intermittent trouble through the nineteenth century pointed up the tremendous economic and social gulf between worker and mill owner. Industrial strife was inevitable, but the fact is that both labor and management suffered bitterly from the five-months-long strike in 1913.

Silk management began an exodus from the city in 1925, but in 1926 another Paterson industrial era began when the then little-known Wright Aeronautical Corporation moved into a silk mill to start making airplane engines. Paterson went into its fourth distinct cycle: from cotton to locomotives to silk, and now airplane engines. The eggs still remained largely in one basket.

As Paterson and Passaic grew, they spilled over into the farmlands of Clifton, whose greatest early prominence had been from 1886 to 1891 when a race track flourished in the village. Since it proclaimed its independent status in 1917, however, Clifton has had an amazing growth. Even in the doleful 1929-1934 days, 1,500 new homes were built in Clifton; 5,000 more were added from 1934 to 1940. The years since World War II have accelerated the increase. Today Clifton's 65,000 population is second to Paterson in the county. Textile, steel and chemical plants prosper within its borders.

Paterson remains the county's greatest city. Hundreds of smaller industries hum in the many factories where in the recurring cycles of the past only a single product was made. City fathers believe that diversification is good; too long has Paterson risen and fallen on a single industry—the latest blow being when Wright moved out after World War II. Silk is still a major industry, and textiles in general comprise the greatest bulk of production. Downriver, in Passaic, the vital woolen mills share industrial honors with the production of mechanical rubber goods and—interestingly enough—the city of Passaic is the greatest producer of handkerchiefs in the nation.

North of the waist, Passaic County possesses some of New Jersey's finest vacation lands. Exceptional scenery rewards the visitor who climbs a mountain range to view Wanaque Reservoir or the Bearfort and Kanouse valleys. Some of the lakes close to Paterson have become all-year living centers; others bustle with sound and excitement only in the summer months.

Wanaque Reservoir supplies eight municipalities in Passaic, Essex and Hudson counties.

The automobile has helped tie north and south together, although a high percentage of Passaic County's 340,000 residents still live south of Pompton. Actually, however, what was political expediency in 1837 is now a blessing. Diversity never hurt any county.

MORE ABOUT PASSAIC

Clayton, W. Woodford, comp., *History of Bergen and Passaic Counties, New Jersey*. Philadelphia, Pennsylvania, Everts and Peck, 1882.

Scott, William W., 1855, *History of Passaic and Its Environs*. New York, Lewis Historical Publishing Co., 1922.

Trumbull, L. R., *A History of Industrial Paterson*. Paterson, New Jersey, C. M. Herrick, 1882.

The CITY BELT

At one end there is New York, at the other there is Philadelphia. Between, on either side of a thin railroad corridor linking them, live more than two-thirds of all the people in New Jersey.

This is the City Belt . . .

Where trains thunder over the busiest stretches of railroad tracks in the world, where heavy trucks and untold hundreds of thousands of cars grind away at cement and macadam; where factories and shipyards and research laboratories and chemical plants combine to make New Jersey the sixth most important industrial state in the land.

This is the City Belt . . .

Where the upper half revolves around New York, where the lower half sees Philadelphia as its axis; where transportation has been the key ever since the first foot paths linked the Dutch village of New York and the Quaker village of Philadelphia.

This is the City Belt, where "dormitories" for New York and Philadelphia have become a way of life; where teeming waterfronts reflect the vigor of the state, where most of New Jersey's colleges and universities have been born and brought to maturity. This is the City Belt, which is all that most of Jersey's millions of visitors ever see. This is a land of industry, of slums, of housing developments, of progress, of noise, of culture. This is the land which Benjamin Franklin likened to a barrel, "tapped at both ends."

This is New Jersey's City Belt . . .

Nature of New Jersey's teeming city belt is vividly portrayed in this aerial view of Newark.

ESSEX

Robert Treat, just off the boat from Connecticut, spoke angrily in the warmth of a May afternoon in 1666. He expressed himself flatly as being all for going back to Connecticut and leaving these lush meadows on the shores of the beautiful Passaic to the Indians. According to Treat's argument, Governor Carteret had indicated that the land already had been bought from the Indians. Now, however, the Indians ordered the Connecticut colonists back to their boats—"no wampum, no land."

Treat stayed, despite his initial anger; the New Englanders settled down, and official purchase of the land was consumated in July, 1667, the eventual transaction ranking high among all-time real estate bargains. The Indians exchanged most of what is now Essex and Union counties for what seems today more like a collection of assorted items to satisfy the personal desires of the braves than a calculated asking price.

Apparently the Indians went off in high glee with their receipts, which included, in addition to 850 fathoms of wampum, this miscellany: "50 double hands of powder, one hundred bars of lead, 20 axes, 20 coats . . . four barrels of beer, two pair of breeches, two ankers of liquor (about 32 gallons) or something equivalent, and three trooper's coats." Ten years later, by the additional payment of "two guns, three coats and 13 kans of rum" the settlers secured a deed to land all the way to the top of Orange Mountain.

By then "Our Town on the Pesayak" had changed its name from Milford to Newark (New Work, incidentally, rather than New Ark). Its growth had been quickened from the start by the arrival of Reverend Abram Pierson and his flock from Bran-

ford, Connecticut, who demanded and got an agreement that only members of "some or other of the Congregational churches" could vote, hold office or attain chief military trust.

Newark was a compact town by 1682, when the East Jersey Legislature established Essex County. Laid out around Broad and Market streets, the village had a church, "an ordinary (inn) for the entertainment of travelers," a ferryman, a town drummer, a cornmill, and a sawmill (which Thomas Davis was permitted to build after agreeing that "he shall let any of the inhabitants have boards as cheap as others and before strangers"). Still, Newark life was primitive enough; the killing of wolves and bears within the village was encouraged and rewarded by bounty.

The few who had pushed beyond the village limits by 1700 found that the Dutch had already come over from Bergen County to settle along Second River (Belleville) and in West Essex, particularly in the sprawling meadowland where the

The landing of the Milfordites at Newark, May, 1666.

Passaic River looped in a broad arc to form "Horse Neck."

Slowly Newarkers spread outward to the hills and to the meadows of West Essex. Sons of original colonists led the movement up the mountains, where settlement centered around individual farms —proof of which lies in early village names: Speertown (Upper Montclair), Wardsesson (Bloomfield), Morehousetown (Livingston), Doddtown (East Orange), Camptown (Irvington) and Williamstown and Freemantown (both West Orange).

So many had gathered on the Orange Mountain slopes that "The Mountain Society" established itself in 1719 to build a church. Farmers prospered, particularly because their apple orchards produced top-grade cider and vinegar (and if a goodly bit of the cider ripened into wonderful "Jersey Lightning," so much the merrier).

Thus, when the East Jersey Proprietors in 1745 challenged the land claim of farmers living in "Big Piece" and "Little Piece" meadows, all of West Essex stiffened. As a lesson to others, the law clamped one of these farmers, Nehemiah Baldwin, into Newark jail in 1745, but 300 rioters from the "back settlement" smashed into the jail and freed him. A similar riot in 1746 convinced the Proprietors that they were in the wrong territory.

Newarkers smiled genteely at the impetuous farmers. The town had grown and acquired some dignity· by 1746, despite the bitterness generated when Colonel Josiah Ogden broke away from Old First Church in 1733 because Old First objected when, rather than let his wheat be ruined by rain, he harvested it on a Sunday. Ogden and several followers helped found Trinity Church soon after.

The controversy split the village, and to soothe wounded spirits Old First finally brought 20-year-old Reverend Aaron Burr to Newark in 1737. He

Market Street in Newark in the 1890's.

Broad Street, near Market, Newark, about 1845.

landowner in West Essex (in the region now marking his memory as "Hetfield Swamp"), openly supported the British. Newark had considerable Tory spirit among its 1,000 inhabitants; discord split neighbors and friends—even families.

So, when General Washington led his bewildered troops into Newark from Hackensack on November 22, 1776, the reception failed to cheer the soldiers. Thomas Paine began to write "The Crisis" while sitting in a Newark park, saddened by the knowledge that the "Summer soldier and sunshine patriot" had already begun to desert the American cause.

Lord Cornwallis leisurely entered North Newark on November 28, at almost precisely the same time that Washington left the southern limits. Cornwallis, presuming victory, paused in Newark while Washington slipped across the state to regroup his riddled legions.

succeeded admirably, and his leadership was responsible for the choice of Newark in 1748 as the location of the College of New Jersey, transferred from Elizabeth after the death of Jonathan Dickinson. Mr. Burr became the second president and led the college through pioneer days until it moved permanently to Princeton in 1756 and eventually became Princeton College. His son, Aaron Burr, Jr. (later Vice President of the United States), was born in Newark.

Essex County had prosperity enough in 1776 to provoke serious internal dissension over the Revolution. Wealthy farmers like Caleb Hetfield, large

Essex County's well-ordered farms endured the merciless attention of foraging parties and punitive sorties. On the night of January 25, 1780, a group of British soldiers and Tory allies swooped into Newark and burned the academy. Returning to New York, they stopped by the house of anti-Tory

Broad Street, Newark, from north of Old Trinity Church.

Justice Joseph Hedden and forced him to accompany them across the frozen meadows. Justice Hedden died within a few months, from illness brought on by that night's ride.

Foundations for industrial Essex developed quickly after the Revolution—in about 1785 James Condit set up Orange's first hat factory and at the same time Moses N. Combs started producing shoes commercially in Newark. Tanning had been important in Newark almost from the start, because water from streams gushing off the hill and down to the swamp south of Broad Street proved ideal for the process. Many tanners located in "The Swamp," but it took Combs to change Newark shoemaking from a strictly local enterprise to a far-flung commercial proposition. Others emulated Combs, of course, and within twenty years the town became celebrated for the fine shoes which were sent by the wagonload to New York, Philadelphia and Savannah.

Newark was not exactly a metropolis. Indeed, Essex County's total population of 20,000 in 1800 lagged behind Sussex County. West Essex was highly rural; cattle and sheep on their way to Newark market stirred the dust in the narrow mountain passes and met swine being driven westward to summer rooting along the Passaic River at West Caldwell.

Dutch traditions lingered in Bloomfield and Speertown, where storekeepers spoke both Dutch and English. Wagons rolled over county roads constantly in the fall, bringing farm products eastward from Morris and Sussex counties and taking winter supplies westward to the farms.

Essex County's need for better roads began to be met in the "turnpike era" of the early 1800's. Charters granted in 1806 opened the way for turnpikes to Elizabeth, Belleville, New Brunswick, Springfield and Pompton (via Bloomfield). The latter, destined to become Bloomfield Avenue, was the personal promotion of Israel "King" Crane, high-powered Bloomfield entrepreneur whose wide-traveling fleet of wagons brought him power and wealth.

Newark Township split into Newark, Orange and Bloomfield wards in 1806 to facilitate tax collections. The following year scandal touched Essex as citizens voted on whether a new courthouse should be built in Newark or Elizabethtown (what is now Union County was all then part of Essex). Newark won because its individual citizens voted far more often and much more illegally than Elizabethtown's, but the Legislature ruled the result

A street view in Orange, in the 1880's.

fraudulent. Newark got the new courthouse anyway in 1811.

Newark's industrial pattern became set in the 1830's. Improved transportation provided the impetus—first with the completion of the Morris Canal in 1832, then through the building of the New Jersey Railroad and the Morris & Essex Railroad in the middle 1830's. In addition, enough sailing vessels moved in and out of the bay to make Newark a port of entry in 1834. Imports that year totaled $2,500,000, while exports reached $8,000,000.

Newark finally became a city in 1836, amid the thundering of cannon and the vigorous stirring of its 19,000 citizens, whom an observer called "a remarkably industrious people, pounding away at their trades from 5 A.M. to 10 or 12 at night."

Railroads spelled change for the "back settlements," too. The Morris & Essex gave new life to Millburn's many paper mills and added markets for Orange's 32 booming hat factories in the late 1830's. More important, the M. & E. enticed the first of a new breed known as commuters to the Essex hills. Essex County grew along the thin line of the Morris & Essex, snaking its way through the mountains to Morristown.

The Panic of 1837 prostrated the infant city of Newark and struck the Orange hatters hard, but expanding markets of the 1840's gave new life to the resurgent industries. Newark's post-Revolutionary character as a "genteel neighborhood where there is much tea drinking" gave way before progress. The original New England descendants were augmented by steady streams of Irish and Germans entering the city, the latter to work in the breweries (although, interestingly enough, it was a Scotchman, Peter Ballantine, who established the city's first large-scale brewery in 1840 after he bought the

Airview of Bloomfield Avenue showing broad stretches of West Essex near Montclair.

small brewery that General John Cummings had started in 1803).

Progress in the city, however, meant dissatisfaction in the hinterlands. Farmers felt that city people who discussed such things as gas lights in the streets and watchmen "by day and by night" were peculiar enough without expecting farmers to pay taxes for such extravagances. As a consequence of such differences, Essex County slowly began to break up into separate municipalities.

Orange split from Newark in 1806, Bloomfield Township became independent in 1812, Clinton Township broke away in 1835. Then, like a cell dividing as life develops, the townships in turn split up. Belleville cut away from Bloomfield in 1839, Irvington from Clinton in 1852, and Millburn from Springfield in 1857 (when all of Union County was separated from Essex). Later, in 1868, Montclair seceded from Bloomfield when the latter refused to bond a railroad venture.

Division proceeded briskly in Orange Township after Orange incorporated as a town in 1860, thus gaining the right to spend money for such "frills" as a police department, street improvement, school development, and other municipal departments. Orange's outlying regions wanted no part of the subsequent taxes. South Orange became a separate village in 1861, East Orange and West Orange both incorporated in 1863, satisfied that they had both frustrated modernization and saved money.

The economic concern of Newark manufacturers mounted when the Civil War shattered the tremendous markets the city had built up with the South in boots and shoes, carriages, clothing, saddles and harness. Leather men in the "Swamp" sulked in bitterness over the loss of their markets below the Mason-Dixon line. But the city and county rallied to the cause (possibly because the "Swamp" found Union war contracts every bit as lucrative as Southern peacetime contracts). President Lincoln received a tremendous welcome when he visited Newark in February, 1861; a crowd of 25,000 jammed the streets to greet him, despite a lively snowstorm.

The first fully outfitted soldiers to reach the Capital were 3,000 armed New Jersey troops, led into Washington by Brigadier General Theodore Runyon of Newark (later mayor and state chancellor). Back home, the Hewes and Phillips Iron Works gave each of its men who entered the service a blanket and revolver, paid full salaries to volunteers, and kept their jobs open. Dr. Marcus L.

Ward led a successful movement to have a 1,400-bed army hospital opened in the city.

The 1870 census showed 143,839 people in Essex County, with 105,000 of those living in the bustling city of Newark. It was at this time that the city began to assume its "melting pot" character—increasing numbers of Italian and Polish immigrants streamed in to join the Irish, the Germans and the descendants of "first families." More than 45,000 people labored in Newark (including an estimated 15,000 people sewing garments in their homes), with shoes, carriages and buggies, and jewelry pacing the industrial life. In its pride Newark staged a memorable 1872 industrial exhibit in the skating rink to show off the city's "Made in Newark" might.

Many felt that the one man who would have most enjoyed the exhibit would have been Seth Boyden, who had died in 1870. Boyden came to Newark from New England as a young man and in 1818 produced the first patent leather in the United States. He announced the successful manufacture of malleable iron in 1826 and in the 1830's built locomotives and steam machinery. Newark's "Uncommercial Inventor" profited but little by his discoveries, however, and in 1855 he moved to Hilton (near Maplewood) where he lived as a poor farmer. There he perfected the amazing Hilton strawberry, which brought a dollar a quart, but not to Boyden, since he gave away his plants.

Thomas A. Edison's house in Llewellyn Park, West Orange.

Port Newark with the New York skyline in the rear.

Inventors found a fertile atmosphere in Essex County. Thomas Alva Edison moved from Menlo Park to open a research laboratory in West Orange in 1887, and built a phonograph works there between 1887 and 1890. John Wesley Hyatt's invention of celluloid in 1870 gave Newark an important industry overnight, and D. Edward Weston's pioneering in electrical instruments in the 1870's led to another important Newark firm.

Newark's industrial growth was accompanied by the growth of its banking and insurance companies. Banking dated from 1804, when the Newark Banking & Insurance Company was founded in a private house on a shaky capital of only $40,000. Major insurance companies had equally small beginnings; Mutual Benefit started in 1845 without even the $300 to pay for its charter. Thirty years later John F. Dryden's pioneering in industrial insurance met with little financial support, yet he founded the Prudential Insurance Company in 1875 and watched it grow rapidly.

Industry had a more limited growth in the suburbs. Orange's hatters celebrated a hundred years of their enterprise in 1892 by turning out 400,000 dozen hats in 21 firms, but a 1909 strike over the use of union labels doomed the suburban industry. Some hatters moved to Millburn after the Civil War; eight firms prospered there in the 1880's, only to suffer eventually the same fate as the Orange plants.

The advent of the trolleys in the 1890's made possible the broader development of the suburbs as residential areas. Several noted early real estate developments prospered (and attracted the prosperous)—Llewellyn S. Haskell's "Llewellyn Park" grew after its establishment in 1875, and Stewart Hartshorn's "Short Hills" was successful after he announced it in 1877. The wealthy bought homes in Benjamin Small's summer colony at St. Cloud, and such noted people as General George B. McClellan bought in Dr. Marcy's development on "The Ridge" in West Orange.

Before they attracted home buyers to the suburbs, the trolleys opened the Orange mountaintops to Sunday excursionists at Eagle Rock and Cable Lake. Thousands of Newarkers rode trolleys up to Vailsburg for picnics in the 1890's. Other thousands joined in German songfests at Becker's Grove in Irvington (where even "My Old Kentucky Home" was sung in German).

Significantly, at this time the Essex County Park Commission was formed (in 1895) to preserve for the public some natural beauty spots—Eagle Rock, South Mountain, Branch Brook, for example. That the commission was formed was an exceptionally progressive step, since at the time the only other place in the nation which had anything of the sort was cultured Boston.

The automobile—rather than inflexible railroads and trolleys—finally metamorphosed Essex County farmland into homeland. At the turn of the century only Orange and East Orange had more than 10,000 inhabitants, with industrial Orange's 15,000 population the largest outside of Newark. More than two-thirds of Essex County's 359,000 people still lived in Newark in 1900; it was just too hard to get even as far out as Vailsburg on the trolleys.

Automobiles brought demands for improved roads—and more suburban dispute. In wide-spread Caldwell Township, for example, arguments over the disposition of road funds between 1898 and 1908 dissolved the once huge township into the smaller municipalities of North Caldwell, West Caldwell, Caldwell Borough, Verona, Cedar Grove and Essex Fells. In the division the house where President Grover Cleveland had been born in 1837, and where he had lived for four years, stayed within Caldwell Borough limits.

Through its first 240 years Newark had struggled along without a real port, but in 1907 the Board of Trade announced optimistically that a port was coming. The Board's predication began to assume reality in 1915 when a 20-foot channel was dredged in the Meadows, and with government help the port became an actuality during World War I. Nearby, in the 1920's Newark Airport grew in the Meadows, too, making the marshland more useful than it had been since cattle of the early settlers roamed through the marsh hay.

Newark's skyline jutted upward in the late 1920's and early 1930's, climaxed finally by construction of the 34-story Raymond Commerce Building in 1930 and the 35-story National Newark and Essex Building in 1931. The city embraced new ideas—radio, for example, by welcoming Radio Station WJZ, second in the nation. Radio's impact on the county and nation became indelible with the first broadcast of a World Series game in 1921 from Newark's Station WJZ. A year later station WOR began broadcasting from L. Bamberger & Company.

Everything spurted in Newark in the 1920's. Factories boomed, banks and insurance companies expanded, great department stores became the mecca of suburban housewives. That made the depression even more cruel, since more than 600 factories closed their doors and business lagged. Such days are at the moment behind, of course, and today Newark continues to rank among the top cities in the nation in diversity of manufactured products (and more than 50 of its industries earn more than $1,000,000 apiece annually).

Essex County's economic life centers in Newark, but the city's population has become almost stable in the last twenty years. People prefer to live elsewhere, and rapid transportation makes that preference possible to achieve. The once-impregnable mountains and valleys to the west are covered with homes and shopping centers. Many of the towns also have welcomed research laboratories and modern factories, so that suburban economic life is on a far broader economic base than mere commuter income.

Airplanes, railroads, superhighways and trucks link Essex County and the world. The greenness of Treat's Meadows is cinder-stained; the twentieth-century industrial smells have replaced the odors of apple blossoms which wafted from the mountains in May, 1666. Closely packed slum dwellings are in sad contrast to the six acres of land allotted to each of the early Newark settlers. Essex County today is the nation's eleventh most populous county, with nearly 1,000,000 population.

It is of little moment to wonder what Mr. Treat would think of the modern Essex County; he probably wouldn't like it. Yet, with his New England sagacity, he would unquestionably agree that he had bought a bit of a bargain.

MORE ABOUT ESSEX

Shaw, William H., *History of Essex and Hudson Counties, New Jersey*. Philadelphia, Pennsylvania, Everts and Peck, 1884.

Folsom, John Fulford, ed., *The Municipalities of Essex County, New Jersey, 1666-1924*. New York, Lewis Historical Publishing Co., Inc., 1925.

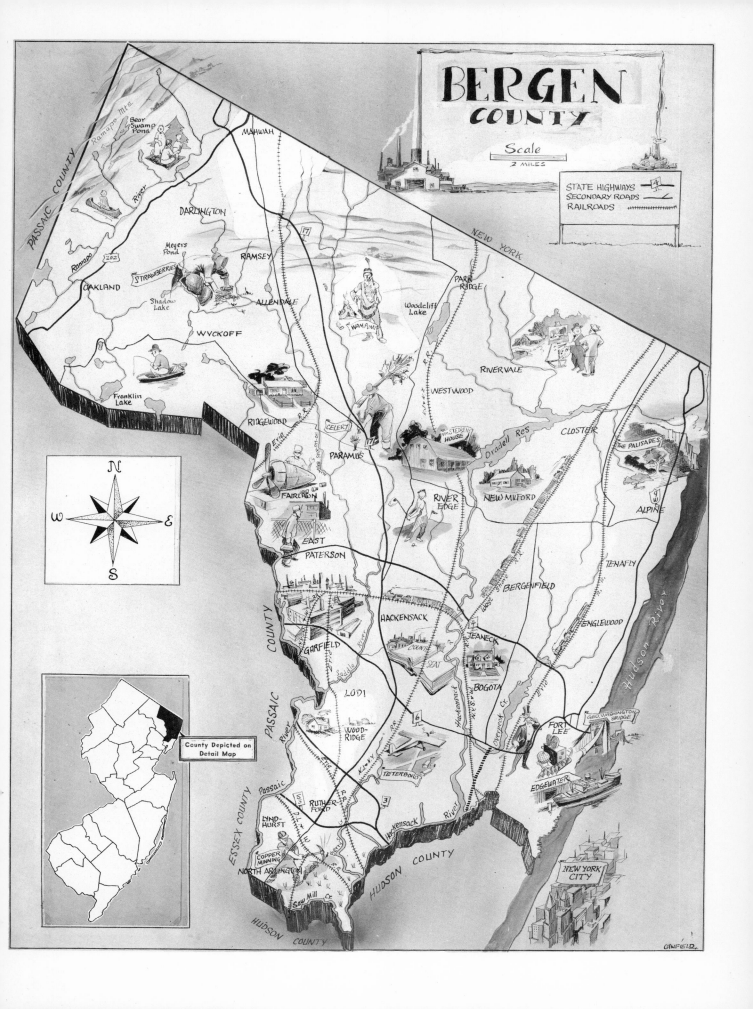

Roads twisting in geometric patterns lead traffic to and from George Washington Bridge.

BERGEN

So much of the story of the development of Bergen County as a residential area can be seen in the houses by the roadsides that there is a temptation to sum it up like this: from genuine Dutch Colonial to modified ranch house in three centuries. Add the George Washington Bridge and the Indian names which dot the county; vital keys to knowing Bergen are close at hand.

Dutch Colonial homes and the George Washington Bridge are very much part of the same heritage. The Dutch who came in the seventeenth century, and built houses with brick walls two feet thick and strong gambril roofs, sought and found a place to live. Through the decades other homeseekers have found the answer to their needs in Bergen. The bridge merely quickened the search and made it easy for many, many thousands to live in Bergen and work in New York.

Indeed, George Washington Bridge, started in 1927 and finished in 1931, may well be said to rest on a foundation begun in 1618. That was the year adventurers and fortune seekers of the Dutch East India Company established a trading post in Bergen. Even at this time the Bergen dwellers found their strength across the river where the Dutch had set up Fort Amsterdam on the island of Manhattan.

One of Bergen County's all-time great citizens welcomed the Dutch. He arrived ahead of the fur trappers by the simple expedient of being born on the banks of Overpeck (Awapaugh) Creek in the year 1577. As Oratam, the great sagamore and sachem of the Hackensack Indians, his decision to live in peace with the usurpers of his land eased the way for settlement of Bergen.

Oratam had help from the Dutch in his peaceful intentions. Mrs. Sarah Kierstede, wife of a Dutch doctor on the Island of Manhattan, took the trouble to learn the Indian language and as an interpreter she helped conclude treaties. Oratam, in gratitude, granted her title in 1638 to 2,120 choice acres on the banks of the Hackensack.

Chief Oratam, sachem of the Hackensack Indians.

Captain David Pietersen de Vries, adventurer and mariner of note, settled on the banks of the Hackensack River in 1640 and quickly earned the trust of the Indians. His interest in the fertile lands west of the Palisades was predicated upon the conviction that the panthers and wolves in the Bergen woods were more dangerous than the Indians.

Unfortunately, not all the Dutch sought peace. A brutal massacre of Indians in Bergen County touched off bloodletting in 1643 which not even the wisdom of Oratam and the sympathy of de Vries could stem. Warfare continued almost until 1664, the year the English took Fort Amsterdam (New York) from the Dutch.

Colonization proceeded quickly in Bergen under the English, mainly because they dealt in friendly and just fashion with the tribes of Oratam. The great Indian was nearing the end of his days—he was too old to go to Newark to sign a treaty in 1666—but when he died in 1669 at the age of ninety-two he had seen peace come to the land he loved.

Paradoxically, neither the Dutch nor the English founded Bergen's first permanent colony. That honor fell to David des Marest, a French Huguenot who objected to helping support the Dutch Church in New York. He sailed with his family up the Hackensack in 1677 to what is now New Milford and settled down to farming and religious peace.

Six years later (1683) Bergen's boundaries were fixed between the Hudson and Hackensack rivers from the New York province line to Newark Bay. Settlers pushed westward to the Ramapo Mountain by 1700 (enough lived in Yaughpaugh, now Oakland, in 1700 to require the services of a circuit-riding dominie). Then, in 1709, Essex County ceded New Barbadoes Township to Bergen and the thriving village of Hackensack became the county seat.

Port of call for ocean-going ships and center of a rich agricultural section, Hackensack boomed. New settlers built spendid brick and red sandstone homes, shops lined the shaded streets and stage-coaches regularly brought new faces and the mail. Life in the religious-minded colonial village cen-

Historic Steuben House, New Bridge, now home of Bergen County Historic Society.

Truck farms along New Jersey route 17, near Westwood.

tered in the stately Dutch Reformed Church on the green, built in 1696. The Old Demarest heart-stone bearing that date is still in the east wall of the church.

So well established was Hackensack that in 1767 the State Legislature debated the merits of the village along with New Brunswick for the location of Queens College (Rutgers). The vote ended in a deadlock, with the Bergen County delegate to the Legislature, Dr. David Wilson, scrupulously not voting. New Brunswick won on the tie-breaking vote of the Governor, and Dr. Wilson returned to Hackensack to established in 1768 the widely renowned Washington Institute to work "for the preservation of the morals of youth" (and to educate them, too).

Bergen's Dutch and English lived harmoniously, respecting one another as well as other nationalities who came to the shores of the Hackensack, Ramapo, Saddle and Passaic rivers in the eighteenth century. Their knowledge of persecution in their native lands forged a common bond against the British in 1776. They were fully aware from the first crackling of guns at Lexington that the Brit-

ish would find Bergen the gateway to New Jersey.

They had not long to wait. Lord Cornwallis led 5,000 British regulars and Hessians across the Hudson in early November, 1776; he overwhelmed the garrison at Fort Constitution (Fort Lee) and sent the Continentals reeling across Bergen to the little bridge over the Hackensack at New Bridge. Cornwallis failed to follow up his advantage, in what historians regard as a colossal blunder. One writer declares that "the crossing of the Delaware was made safe by the crossing of the Hackensack a month earlier." Washington regrouped his ragged and despairing troops in Hackensack and led them across New Jersey to prepare for the inspiring smash at Trenton on Christmas night, 1776.

No great battles engulfed Bergen but the county felt the Revolution constantly. Foraging parties stripped its fields and orchards. Washington was often in the county and in 1780 British and Hessian troops drove the county government from Hackensack to Yaughpaugh. A disastrous raid in 1778 cost the lives of several Americans when a British party caught an American regiment sleeping in the old Blauvelt red-stone house and barns at River Vale and, following orders of Major General "No Flint" Grey, bayoneted many Continentals to death in the infamous "Baylor Massacre."

One important defection from the American cause was that of John Zabriskie, who built a pretentious home at New Bridge in 1739 and grew prosperous from his big gristmill and his extensive dock on the river. He remained loyal to King George and, in retaliation, his home was taken from him by patriots and presented in gratitude to General von Steuben (who never occupied it) for his services in the American cause.

War wounds healed quickly. Peace brought freedom to till the Bergen fields again and the county's farmers moved to the fore. There was some industry, but it consisted mainly of such strictly local enterprises as gristmills, smithys and sawmills powered by the county's many streams. An exception was the sporadic copper mining in North Arlington, started in 1719 by the accidental discovery of a vein of ore on Arent Schuyler's farm.

Up Park Ridge way, John Campbell and his sons made plenty of wampum—literally. John took over

an abandoned mill in 1775 to make the Indian money from sea shells. He found wampum could be sold for good hard American dollars. Even John Jacob Astor came to the Campbells for the Indian wherewithal to conduct his fur-trading ventures. Indian traders from all over the country looked to Park Ridge for wampum until 1889, when the Indians decided that American dollars had come to stay. Wampum was no mere Park Ridge shell game, however, while it lasted.

Agriculture, nevertheless, was Bergen's big nineteenth-century enterprise. Even the slicing away of sizable chunks to add to Passaic County in 1837, and the creation of Hudson County from Bergen in 1840, failed to cut appreciably into farm income.

And small wonder, since (if you would believe the chroniclers of the day) the lush soil yielded pears a pound in weight, celery more than three feet long, and pumpkins weighing a hundred pounds (give or take a few inches or pounds). Hackensack melons and "Chestnut Ridge" peaches brought further fame to Bergen growers.

Most important of all was the strawberry trade,

An art class is attracted to the rural Saddle River area.

Where agriculture meets Bergen's residential growth.

which started about 1800 and reached a peak just before the Civil War. The period was fabulous, an era when buyers, sellers and pickers congregated in the inns at the strawberry centers in Ramsey and Allendale. Four to eight of the Erie Railroad's specially painted white boxcars left Allendale and Ramsey each morning in the season. Mostly, however, the strawberries went by the wagonload over rutted roads to New York, Paterson and Newark. The last week of June, 1858, for example, saw 1,100 wagonloads carrying 1,500,000 baskets of the ripe red fruit trundle through the toll gates of the Bergen turnpike on the way to market. The strawberry rash faded quickly after the Civil War, disappeared by 1880.

Farm prosperity brought demands for improved roads, but the railroads—led by the Erie and the Paterson and Hudson River—supplied the needed fast movement in the 1830's and 1840's. By the middle 1850's John Van Brunt and associates had pushed the Northern Railroad up the valley west of the Palisades. The New Jersey & New York, the West Shore and the New York, Susquehanna & Western followed later.

The railroads gave sudden birth to a new type of businessman, one who ever since has risen and fallen in good times and bad in Bergen—the real estate man, quick to envision paradise in fields "within five minutes' walk of the station" (which he hoped would be built).

Bergen's first official real estate development came in 1854 when Dr. Carl Klein led a group of New York Germans to a hillside north of Boiling Springs (Rutherford). They bought 140 acres, split it up into 270 plots, and appropriately enough called it Carlstadt (Carl's Town). Nearby, at Boiling

Springs, Floyd W. Thompkins began buying and selling home plots in 1858.

The Civil War temporarily shelved the building boom, partially because of the troubled times and partially because Bergen split in bitter wrangling over the war.

Much of the bitterness was occasioned by the tight political hold Garry Ackerson's Democratic political machine had on the county. Strong anti-war sentiment, combined with the Ackerson machine, in 1860 resulted in Abraham Lincoln's losing Bergen to Breckinridge, 2,112 to 1,455. In 1861, Copperheads threatened bodily harm to a newspaper editor who supported the Union cause. Finally, however, both political parties realized that the war was bigger than themselves, and in their political truce let the Union rather than Bergen benefit from their fighting.

Political excitement was about all that the agricultural county enjoyed, if the words of one editor be true. He rued the "monotony of bucolic existence" in Bergen and cried that "lawyers cannot incite the people to contention during the six days nor the preacher keep them awake on the seventh."

Then "outside folks" flocked in to stay. J. Wyman Jones, a lawyer, saw possibilities in the golden orchard country, the rolling land where Englewood now stands. His city friends came, settled on the land near the Northern Railroad, and commuted to New York. Local stores failed to meet early demands, it is said, and commuters from Englewood in the 1860's carried market baskets to and from the train each day.

Another newcomer, William Walter Phelps, made Teaneck his home in 1865, settling in the old Garrit Brinkerhoff home on Teaneck Ridge. Within thirteen years he and his Palisades Land Company owned 4,000 acres as far east as the Palisades and north to Alpine. Phelps became one of Bergen's noted citizens before his death in 1894. He personally defrayed the cost of thirty miles of road, paid half the cost of his town's railroad station, and ordered the planting of more than a half-million trees—plus being elected to Congress and serving as Minister to Austria and Germany.

Out along the Passaic River, Gilbert D. Bogart and Henry Marsellus bought property and laid out a town, called "East Passaic" until James A. Garfield was elected President in November, 1880. The next day Bogart strode into the office of the editor of the Passaic newspaper and announced: "From today on we're Garfield. No more

East Passaic." There was no more East Passaic.

Other towns and villages lost old Dutch and Indian names under the influence of the new arrivals. So much so, in fact, that in 1872 the Bergen County Historical Society, according to contemporary newspaper stories, sought to prevent "the old historic names of the county from being blotted out by namby-pamby sentimental 'Ridges,' 'Woods' and 'Parks.'"

(But Bergen grew away from its early names, although enough of the Indian names have survived to remind the visitor that Oratam also slept here— such as Kinderkamack Road, Hohokus, Pascack, Mahwah, Wyckoff, and, of course, Hackensack.)

Summer people flocked to such popular spots as Norwood Hotel and Edgewater's Buena Vista Hotel to enjoy Bergen's well-advertised healthful air. They were of course desirable. Somewhat less welcome (but apparently tolerated) were "hordes of New York ruffians of the lowest degree" who came to the illegal cockfights and the illegal horse race betting rooms in the area surrounding Fort Lee.

More than 300,000 visitors came to Fort Lee by ferry in 1879 and a goodly number of them came for more than the Jersey air, enforcement officials admitted, possibly setting the tone for more recent activities in Bergen.

But there were sweet, dreamy hours to be enjoyed at Fort Lee's Park Hotel and there were pleasant times at Clahan's Hotel in Edgewater. Francis R. Tillou's estate, "Tilliedudlum," attracted New York's Very Important (including Boss Tweed). Above all, the Octagon Building at Edgewater was a mecca for the fun seekers. Up county, the Park Ridge Town Improvement Association ran a big amusement center—and used the proceeds to defray the costs of streets and sidewalks and to pay the salary of the boy who lighted the oil lamps in the streets.

An acute attack of what one writer called "boroughitis" seized Bergen County in the 1890's, mainly because the Legislature voted a new borough act which made each township a separate school district, wherein taxpayers were obliged to pay,

Fairchild Aerial Surveys, Inc.

Thousands of residential streets have made Bergen a fast-growing county.

Ford Motor Company's assembly plant at Edgewater.

pro rata, existing debts of old school districts, as well as future school debts. There was one very important clause: the act did not apply to boroughs, towns, villages and cities.

Small wonder, then, that between January 23 and December 18, 1894, Bergen gave birth to twenty-six new boroughs, or that the county today has seventy separate municipalities in its 233 square miles.

The changes often took place in charged atmospheres. Bitter words were exchanged. A few noses were bloodied. Balloting was close, school taxes or no school taxes. Of all the misunderstanding, however, none was more cruel than that visited upon one Russell Jones, whose borderline house burned down while firemen of Bogota and Teaneck argued over who had a right to extinguish the fire.

Real estate men went on apace. They ran special trains and gave hot chowder and lukewarm music to induce 1890 settlers to Bergen. Their cause was boosted in 1900 when plans were drawn and approved in Washington for a double-decked $60,000,000 bridge over the Hudson from New York City to West New York. The bridge was not built, but population in Bergen zoomed from

78,441 in 1900 to 139,002 in 1910. In 1905 a New York newspaper summed it up: "Alas, the days of the Bergen farmer are numbered. Land worth $1,000 to $5,000 per acre is too valuable for growing cabbage." Newcomers bought the cabbage fields for home sites.

Magnetic names among those Bergen newcomers were attracted to Fort Lee, motion picture capital of the world from 1907 to World War I. Pearl

Rugged bluff of Palisades, familiar to millions of people.

White emoted much of her anguished series, "The Perils of Pauline," in the rugged Palisades. Edwin S. Porter made "Rescued From an Eagle's Nest" in 1908 with young David W. Griffith in the role of a mountaineer. Mack Sennett and his pie throwers arrived at Fort Lee in 1908, and 1909 the winsome Mary Pickford made her debut there in "The Violin Maker of Cremona."

Fort Lee enjoyed its position as the film capital. Samuel Goldwyn, William Fox and Carl Laemmle pioneered in movies in the town, and stars like Rudolph Valentino, Lon Chaney, Charlie Chaplin, Fatty Arbuckle, Theda Bara, Lillian Gish and Marie Dressler faced Fort Lee cameras. It was a sad day for the livery stables, the hotels, the restaurants and the town extras when movieland moved to Hollywood. Richard Barthelmess and Ina Claire made Fort Lee's last important picture in 1923.

Bergen County took World War I pride in Camp Merritt near Cresskill, from where more than a half-million young men left for France. It suffered wartime anguish on a bitter night in January, 1917, when the sprawling plant of the Canadian Car & Foundry Company at Kingsland erupted in violent explosion. German agents, they said, used that means to stop the $83,000,000 order of shells destined for Russia.

Explosion, camp, movies, real estate booms, strawberries, Revolution, colonization—those are the elements in Bergen's past. Yet, probably no Bergen happening was more important than that on October 24, 1931, when Governor Franklin Delano Roosevelt of New York and Governor Morgan F. Larson of New Jersey jointly snipped a ribbon to open the $80,000,000 George Washington Bridge.

Bergen had dreamed of a bridge since 1834, when the New York and New Jersey Legislatures first set up a commission to study the spanning of the Hudson. Now, just three years short of a century later, the bridge was ready.

Ready, too, were the real estate men; Bergen's phenomenal growth since 1931 can be attributed both to the bridge and the successful selling of Bergen as a place in which to live. Today home developments spread far and wide, edged up tight to the old stone Dutch houses and the disappearing farms.

Industry is important in Bergen, of course (and many of the development-swelled towns would give anything for a couple of nice clean little factories to help ease taxes). Mainly industry is concentrated along the Passaic (Fair Lawn, Garfield, Lodi), near the important Teterboro Airport (Wood-Ridge, South Hackensack and Moonachie) and along the Hudson, particularly at Edgewater (called the spot "where homes and industry blend"). Textiles, airplane motors, automobiles, paper, chemicals and widely varied metal products and delicate instruments flow from Bergen industry. Research laboratories and offices of erstwhile New York firms are locating in Bergen. All are a rich source of employment and county prosperity.

Still, Bergen must be looked upon essentially as "home"—the place to live in residential comfort, on income gained in New York.

MORE ABOUT BERGEN

Clayton, W. Woodford, comp., assisted by Nelson, William, *History of Bergen and Passaic Counties.* Philadelphia, Pennsylvania Everts and Peck, 1882.

New Jersey Writers' Project, *Bergen County Panorama.* Sponsored by Bergen County Board of Freeholders, 1941.

Koehler, Francis C., *Three Hundred Years; The Story of the Hackensack Valley,* Chester, New Jersey, 1940.

Van Valen, J. M., *History of Bergen County, New Jersey.* New York, New Jersey Publishing and Engraving Co., 1900.

Westervelt, Frances A., *History of Bergen County from 1630 to 1923.* New York; Chicago, Lewis Historical Publishing Co., Inc., 1923.

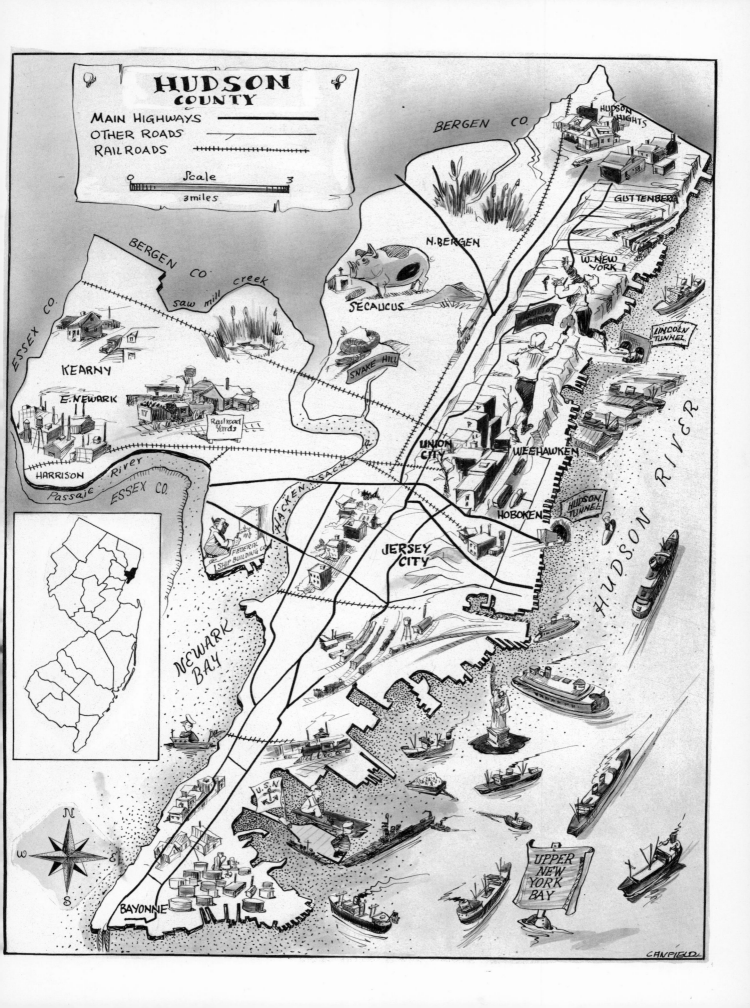

Hoboken piers, scene of busy waterfront activity for more than a century.

HUDSON

Maybe Dutch Burgomaster Michael Pauw really believed that peacocks strutted over the land he bought on the shores of Henry Hudson's River in 1630. Certainly the chronicles brought back to Holland by Hudson after his 1609 voyage would lead a burgomaster to be convinced that peacocks (at the very least) dwelled on the west bank of the river.

Much more probable is the belief that Pauw chose to honor himself (since Pauw means "peacock" in Dutch) when he purchased sight unseen an area comprising much of what is now Hudson County and named it Pavonia, "The Land of the Peacock." He never saw the land, never knew if peacocks really preened their feathers by the Hudson River, but early Dutch settlers agreed that Pavonia was a handsome piece of real estate, good enough for peacocks (or Pauws).

Pavonia was destined to become a key transportation center, and once the railroads rolled through Bergen Hill to the Hudson, the river-bank brilliancy faded, a victim of machines—both coal-fired and ballot-stuffed. Although these machines were not invented in Hudson County, unquestionably they attained perfection on the banks of Henry Hudson's river.

Hudson, an Englishman working for the Dutch East India Company, discovered the river and surrounding land somewhat accidentally as he poked about looking for a short cut to the Indies. No short cut existed, but glowing word pictures of the land convinced the Dutch that Hudson's voyage had merit anyway, so the Dutch West Indies Company set out to exploit the New World.

Dutch trappers came as early as 1618, and a few settlers put down shallow roots before 1650—such as Jan Evertsen Bout at Communipaw (Jersey City), Aert T. von Putten at Hobocan Hackingh (Hoboken), and Jacob Jacobsen Roy at Konstapel's Hoeck (Bayonne).

The early settlers prospered to a degree and von Putten even started America's first brewery at Hobocan in 1642. Then Dutch leaders savagely massacred Indians at Pavonia to spark intermittent warfare through the late 1650's. Governor Peter Stuyvesant forbade new settlements until 1660, and then approved the village of Bergen (New Jersey's first municipal government) on the slopes behind Communipaw, but only on the express provision that it be protected by a stockade.

Hudson County was then part of Bergen (the division was made in 1840), and the solidly Dutch region watched with only token interest as their overlords and the English bounced the province around. The English took it from the Dutch in 1664, the Dutch took it back in 1673, and finally

Cows walked through heart of Jersey City in 1800.

a treaty granted all New Jersey to the English in 1674.

The atmosphere of the county was unchanged by treaties, however; Dutch traditions and the Dutch way with the land persisted. The ready market across the river made the Dutch cabbage growers successful and they cared little whether the market was called New Amsterdam or New York. Down on Bergen Neck (Bayonne), Dutch farmers raised cabbages so big they were called "Governor's Head" (referring to size, not quality) and hauled in oysters so large they were called "Governor's Foot."

A few ventured westward, although barriers such as Bergen Hill and the meadows beyond made it much easier to stay by the river. Captain William Sanford and Major Nathaniel Kingsland, retired British Colonial officers, bought all the Harrison-Kearny area in 1668. Fifteen years later a few farmers ventured over the boglands to the high ground at Secaucus (from the Indian, Siskakes—"where the snake hides").

Almost a century slipped by before the county moved toward the transportation role which was to have such tremendous significance for the west bank of the Hudson. Philadelphia-bound stage-wagons began to roll in 1764 from Paulus (or Powles) Hook, down over Staten Island and then over to Woodbridge via the Blazing Star Ferry. The new route broke the monopoly formerly enjoyed by Elizabethtown and Perth Amboy and gave the passenger the advantage of a speedy two-day trip (weather permitting) to Philadelphia.

As many as twenty stages moved in and out of the Hook daily, but westbound passengers found themselves on the short end of a neat tavern-ferry parlay. Morning ferries, despite improvements inaugurated in 1764, arrived just too late to catch the westbound stage. The answer, naturally, was to stay in the tavern overnight and start off refreshed the next morning. The suspicious traveler could hardly help thinking that the ferry would have caught the stage had the same entrepreneur not owned both ferry and tavern.

The transportation network made Paulus Hook, Hoboken and Bergen Neck vital; even before the signing of the Declaration of Independence a series of fortifications arose on the Jersey side of the Hudson. New York's capitulation to the British made the forts untenable and the Hook fell into enemy hands on September 23, 1776, as the battered American Army reeled back across the Hudson from New York.

Except for a few dramatic hours in 1779, most

Part of Jersey Central's one-square-mile railroad yard at Jersey City.

Journal Square, heart of Jersey City.

of the coastline remained in Royal control throughout the Revolution. The exception came in the predawn hours of August 19, 1779, when Major Light Horse Harry Lee led 300 troops over the marshes from Hackensack for a bold smash at Paulus Hook. Lee's men routed the surprised British but the position could not be held with the rest of the area in enemy hands, so Lee retreated quickly. His troops took along 159 prisoners, at a cost of only two killed and three wounded.

The nearness of the British and the apparent hopelessness of the American cause prompted many riverfront "summer patriots" to embrace the English. William Bayard, son of one of the earliest settlers of the Hoboken area and one of the most active prewar promoters of the Colonial movement, made a fantastically wrong guess when he switched allegiance and accepted a colonel's commission in the British army.

That cost Bayard his estate and brought the county its most famous son, Colonel John Stevens, who bought the Bayard holdings for $90,000 at public auction in 1794. Just before the sale Baron von Steuben, German militarist revered for his wartime services to the Americans, tried to buy the

estate. Governor William Livingston replied that a private sale could not be arranged because of the Legislative approval of an auction. Anyway, Livingston added in his letter to the baron, ". . . never was there a place where mosquitos are more numerous."

Mosquitos didn't bother the versatile John Stevens. On the slopes of Castle Point he raised New Jersey's most illustrious engineering family, and in the study of Steven's Villa his fertile mind ranged through engineering projects far in advance of his day. The Stevens engineering saga has highlighted all the history of Hoboken and all the story of transportation. Many of his dreams came true through his energetic sons, others materialized in the work of Stevens Institute, founded on his estate in 1871.

The beauty of his holdings prompted Stevens to gauge correctly that New Yorkers would like to come over to live and to visit. Accordingly, in March of 1804 he mapped "The New City of Hoboken" and auctioned lots in New York. Soon after the Hoboken auction, speculative New Yorkers cast envious eyes on Paulus Hook. Encouraged by the advice of their distinguished attorney, Alexander Hamilton, a syndicate led by Anthony Dey bought the present site of Jersey City in 1804.

Only thirteen people lived in the sand hills of the Hook when the Associates of the Jersey Company bought the land, but Hamilton envisioned a great metropolis, pointing out that in all history great cities usually arose on the west rather than the east bank of a navigable river. Five months later, on July 11, 1804, Hamilton fell mortally wounded in a duel with Aaron Burr up the river on the famous Weehawken dueling ground (where, incidentally, more than fifteen duels were fought before the pistol play was outlawed in 1835).

Hamilton's loss stunned the Paulus Hook real estate developers, and in the days ahead, as their venture seemed perilously close to failure, the Associates wished for Hamilton's counsel. In spite of all the inducements they offered—they built a red brick tavern, set out 600 poplars along the streets, and put 1,340 lots on sale for only $100 apiece—in the first thirty years of existence the town had grown to only 1,500 persons. Changing the settle-

ment's name to Jersey City in 1820 caused no spurt in sales.

Dey and friends could look across the river for the principal reason for their slow progress. New York's tight hold on riparian rights gave that state control right up to the low-water line on the New Jersey side. However, the fact remained that the Associates also maintained too tight a grip on their land, refusing even the possibility of ferry rights to purchasers and subjecting property holders to civic as well as economic control by the company.

Everything changed for the better in 1834. First, a treaty set the boundary line between New Jersey and New York in the middle of the Hudson River; Jersey City finally had access to its own water line. Later in 1834 the first railroad from Newark chugged over the Meadows to forge a bond between Jersey City and the west.

So, the establishment of Hudson as a separate county by legislative act in February, 1840, found a solid basis for growth. Jersey City could pridefully claim the American Pottery Company, where

Entrances to Lincoln Tunnel at Weehawken.

Site of nation's first baseball contest.

the nation's foremost potters learned their trade; and Isaac Edge's fireworks plant, famed as a training center for American pyrotechnists. Dummer's Jersey City flint glass was widely known. Down neck, in Bayonne, industry dated back to the establishment of Hazard Powder House in 1812, while up in Hoboken the Land & Improvement Company was established in 1838 to encourage growing waterfront business without destroying the city's inland residential charm.

Out on the other side of the marshes Harrison came into being in 1840 by the same legislative act which set up Hudson County. A small trunk factory, opened in 1846, became the forerunner of Harrison's teeming factory region, but the movement of industrialists across the Passaic from Newark assumed no importance until the 1880's.

Actually, West Hudson won nineteenth-century acclaim for its residential charm, typified by General Philip Kearny's lovely "Belgrove," the estate he bought in the 1850's. He built "Kearny's Castle" in 1855, but his wanderings as a soldier kept him often away. Only ten weeks before his death at Chantilly in 1862 he wrote: "How beautiful Belgrove must look! If I were there, I would never leave. . . ." The Civil War soldier's funeral was held at Belgrove and when the region broke away from Harrison in 1867 it memorialized Kearny by taking his name.

Until the Civil War, as a matter of fact, much of Hudson County remained a playland. Hoboken's beer gardens, river walks and pleasant groves brought thousands over on the ferries from New York every weekend. Castle Point dominated the scene and Sybil's Cave, hewn into the Point's rocky base, became a lovers' rendezvous.

The magnificence of Elysian Fields, surrounded by stately trees, helped make Hoboken the playground of the East. There, on a cricket field laid out by John Cox Stevens (son of Colonel John), the Knickerbocker Giants faced New York on June 19, 1846, in the world's first organized baseball game. Nearby, the Hoboken Turtle Club met regularly to enjoy the mingling in their stomachs of turtle soup and good Hoboken beer.

Many of the visitors decided to remain in Hoboken, the most prominent being John Jacob Astor, who built a villa there in 1829. Many tarried, with vacationists including Washington Irving, Edgar Allan Poe, Martin Van Buren and William Cullen Bryant. Most came to play, however, although the sporting set switched to Jersey City from 1837 to 1845 to watch the races at the old hilltop Beacon Race Course.

New York aristocrats spurned all such plebeian pursuits, however, and in dignity went to Bayonne, "The Newport of New York." The oldest and wealthiest of New York's families acquired huge estates overlooking beautiful (and sweet-smelling) Newark Bay. Some boarded expensively and expansively at the Mansion House or La Tourette Hotel.

Hudson County came of age in the Civil War, and in donning the mantle of transportation vitality and industrial vigor it laid aside its adolescent playgrounds. Hudson assumed adult responsibilities in shepherding more than 60,000 fugitive slaves through Hoboken and Jersey City and on to freedom by way of the Underground Railroad.

The regular railroad systems moved quickly into riverfront dominance, too. Rail passengers streamed through Hudson (proof of which is found in an 1855 report showing that 7,000,000 passengers used Jersey City ferries annually—at a time when the city's population was only 22,000).

Railroad growth changed forever the shape of the Hudson River banks. Jersey Central Railroad, getting into Jersey City late (and then only by building an unprecedentedly-long bridge over

Newark Bay in 1863), dumped untold thousands of tons of New York garbage into South Cove to build its terminal. That and subsequent dumpings (which became less ordoriferous after Greenville residents violently protested garbage dumping by the Pennsylvania Railroad in 1875) eventually built the entire county riverfront out as much as 4,000 feet from its original line. Limited waterfront footage left Hudson County no alternative—it had to build out, not sideways.

Hudson County grew phenomenally. Starting with a population of 9,483 in 1840, it listed 163,000 by 1875 and 386,048 in 1900. Industrialists came across the river, attracted by the excellent transportation facilities and the zooming labor market. Jersey City, for example, was still young when it gained three of its basic industries: William Colgate brought his soap kettles over from New York in 1847; Joseph Dixon moved his expanding crucible plant from Salem, Massachusetts, at about the same time, and P. Lorillard Tobacco Company moved its snuff factory to the city in 1870.

Standard Oil Company, Bayonne, 1882.

Transportation stepped up to world-wide proportions with the coming of major steamship companies to Hudson. The Cunard Company built a dock at Jersey City in 1847 and the sailing of Cunard's *Hibernia* on January 1, 1848, merited a 100-gun salute. Upstream, four major steamboat companies (mainly German and Dutch controlled) adopted Hoboken as an American port.

Out in the western regions along the Passaic, Harrison and Kearny moved **ahead industrially.**

Jersey City dock area has been built out into the Hudson since the 1860's.

Bayonne Bridge over Kill van Kull, longest steel arch span in the world.

Starting with the establishment of Thomas A. Edison's first incandescent lamp factory in Harrison in 1881, the region also attracted William Hyatt's roller bearing factory in 1903, and soon the Meadows made way for Crucible Steel, Otis Elevator, Worthington Pump and dozens of other industries. William Howard Taft, stumping for re-election in 1912, exclaimed: "Why, this is a hive of industry!" —and that Republican exclamation became Democratic Harrison's slogan.

Huge population increases forced municipality realignments, but Hudson County partially reversed one statewide trend in the middle years of the nineteenth century when it consolidated towns and townships rather than creating numerous new municipalities (as in Bergen County). Jersey City absorbed Van Vorst Township in 1859, Hudson City and 210-year-old Bergen town in 1870, and the Township of Greenville in 1873. Bayonne consolidated Constable Hook, Bergen Point, Centerville and Saltersville into one city in 1869.

One by one Bayonne's aristocratic New Yorkers left town after the Prentice Oil Company established the first of Bayonne's many oil refineries in 1875. Others followed soon after—Standard Oil, Tidewater and Gulf—and the shad fishermen, hotel proprietors and bathing beach operators sadly moved elsewhere. Tidewater Oil Company, founded in 1878, brought the refinery business into a new era when it built the first pipeline to tap interior oil fields, but it took eight years of fighting the competition, the railroads and nature before the line stretched complete from Pennsylvania to Bayonne in 1887.

Nineteenth-century immigration altered Hudson County's character and speech just as transportation changed its face. The Germans and Irish started to come in the 1840's, with most of the Germans gravitating to Hoboken and North Hudson and most of the Irish heading for railroad work in Jersey City. Later the Scotch came to work in the mills in Harrison and Kearny, and the Swiss arrived to work in Union City's small industries. All of the Old World immigrants were joined at the turn of the century by increasing numbers of Italians.

German traditions dominated Hoboken and North Hudson until World War I, when a wave of intense partisan feeling suppressed the Scheutzen societies, the beer halls and the German parks. Hoboken's importance as the World War I port of embarkation for American troops boomed its industries but also destroyed many of its traditions.

Immigration altered Hudson County in another way by adding the voting strength needed to make the political machine all-powerful. The new arrivals eagerly listened to waterfront politicians, particularly the Irish who found themselves bewildered, alone, and in perilous straits when the railroads, which brought many of them over, hired them and fired them at will.

Hudson County politics have prompted millions of written and spoken words since the 1870's, without satisfying either Hudson County residents or out-of-county critics. Nevertheless, two facts emerge: first, the waterfront situation, with its waves of immigration and its periodic booms and busts, made the political machine a possibility—maybe even a necessity. Second, it took two-party interplay to bring the Hudson County machine to maturity.

The Republicans, for example, first forced the gerrymandered district on Hudson in the 1870's when they devised the infamous Jersey City "Horseshoe" to include nearly all Democrats (and thus leave the city and county free for Republican control). Frank Hague, significantly, was born in that "Horseshoe."

Actually, Democrats might never have gained Hudson County had the Republicans indorsed their own Mark Fagan and his "New Idea." Fagan served as Jersey City mayor from 1901 to 1907, and on his re-election for a third time as mayor in 1905, he took all twelve Hudson County Republican Assembly candidates into office on his ticket. The GOP bosses decided to dump Fagan in 1907 and succeeded so well that the Republican machine has never been righted in Hudson.

The Democrats took over the "New Idea," with few changes; put Frank Hague in the driver's seat, and by various devices and alterations steamrollered Hudson County and much of New Jersey for four decades. John Kenny and associates shouldered their way aboard the machine in 1949, but Republicans gained slight solace, if any, from that.

This is no place to judge Hudson County politics, but politics rules supreme in Hudson as in no other New Jersey county (partially because machines elsewhere have always been much, much more discreet, even if just as smoothly-oiled). Since the Land of the Peacock was transformed from the garden spot of the East to the transportation center of the East, politics has been a way-of-life.

Today, Hudson County's population of 647,000 is jammed into 45 square miles of land area, which means that 14,387 persons live in an average square mile (as against 7,000 per square mile in Essex, next largest, and 65 per square mile in Sussex, lowest in population density).

Nine trunk line railroads terminate in Hudson County and tremendous railroad yards sprawl over the Meadows. Industries smoke and steam along the Hudson and Passaic rivers, trucks clatter and bang over the maze of old waterfront streets in Hoboken and Jersey City. Millions of automobile passengers say "hello" and "good-by" to New Jersey by way of the Holland and Lincoln tunnels and the Kill van Kull Bridge.

The shrillness of transportation and industry and the stridency of politicians speak for Hudson County now. The voice of the peacock is heard no more.

MORE ABOUT HUDSON

Miller, Edmund W., Bergen and Jersey City: an historical souvenir of the 250th anniversary of the founding of Bergen. Jersey City, New Jersey, The Free Public Library, 1910.

Shaw, William H., History of Essex and Hudson Counties, New Jersey. Philadelphia, Pennsylvania, Everts and Peck, 1884.

Stinson, Robert R., Hudson County Today: Its History, People, Trades, Commerce, Institutions and Industries. Union City, New Jersey, Hudson Dispatch, 1914.

Van Winkle, Daniel, 1839, History of the Municipalities of Hudson County, New Jersey. New York and Chicago, Lewis Historical Publishing Co., Inc., 3 vols., 1630 to 1923.

Winfield, Charles H., History of the County of Hudson, New Jersey from Its Earliest Settlement to the Present Time. New York, Hennard and Hay Printing Company, 1874.

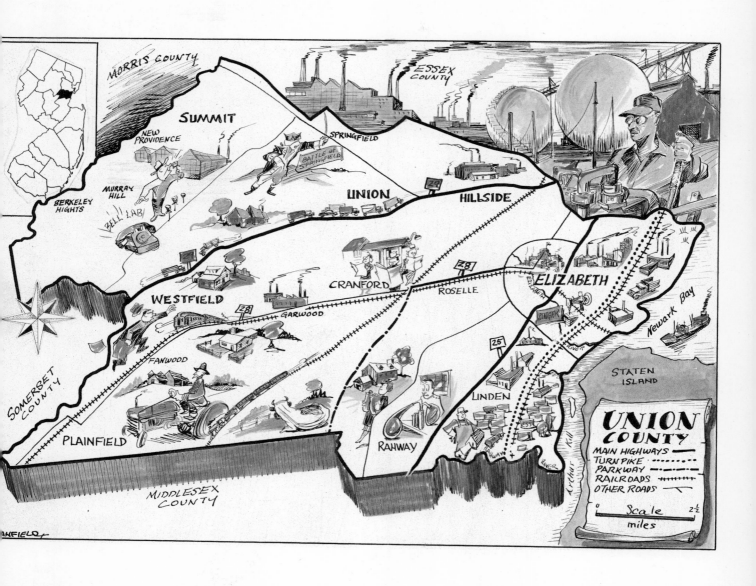

The New Jersey Turnpike, expressway north and south, touches busy Elizabeth.

UNION

All the national talk about secession in the 1850's found understanding along the Elizabeth River, where residents long had discussed seceding from Essex County. Slavery and states' rights had nothing to do with the secession sentiment in Elizabeth; local citizens simply chafed under Essex domination. They broke away on March 18, 1857 (with legislative approval of course) and called their seceded county "Union."

Actually the Essex-Union schism was predominantly an Elizabeth-Newark division, since life in the two county regions pivoted on the sister cities which had grown up in rivalry for more than 175 years. The House of Essex was not big enough to hold them both, particularly with slightly younger sister Newark taking most of the cake and leaving the crumbs for Elizabeth.

The divided house eventually benefited both Union and Essex, but in 1857 Union County lived mainly on memories. Boundaries of the new county roughly coincided with the early boundaries of Elizabethtown, the first English-speaking settlement in New Jersey. Oddly enough, this first-settled land became the last of New Jersey's twenty-one counties to be established.

Why the Dutch never settled the regions by the Achter Kol (Arthur Kill) is a mystery, since they knew good land when they saw it. New Englanders unsuccessfully negotiated with the Dutch in 1660 for permission to settle near what is now Elizabeth; soon afterward Dutch guns drove off a party of twenty Long Islanders seeking to buy a plantation near the Raritan River.

English guns had the final say in late August of 1664, however, when New Amsterdam (New York) capitulated to Colonel Richard Nicolls. Within a month three Long Islanders, John Bayly, Daniel Denton and Luke Watson, obtained Nicolls's permission to dicker with the Indians for a tract along the Achter Kol.

The Indians readily accepted the usual English offer of coats, gunpowder and miscellany, and in exchange deeded a plot of ground including all of present-day Union County and pieces of Essex, Middlesex, Somerset and Morris counties. Settlement started in November, 1664, after Denton sold his share to John Baker and John Ogden, with Ogden and his five grown sons being a powerful addition to the original property holders.

Meanwhile, the Duke of York sat down in England on June 23, 1664, and gave a couple of court favorites, Lord John Berkeley and George Carteret, the land of Nova Caesaria (New Jersey). Governor Nicolls obviously had no knowledge of this

Street scene in Elizabeth in the 1880's.

gift when he permitted John Bayly and friends to bargain with the Indians.

Philip Carteret, cousin of George, sailed from England to become Governor of Nova Caesaria, and his arrival on the Achter Kol on August 1, 1665, caused no particular joy among the few families already living there. Carteret's ship *Philip* anchored and the new 26-year-old Governor came ashore along with 30 immigrants, including 18 servants.

Carteret tried to make the best of a difficult situation. He greeted the old settlers, and in a show of husbandry shouldered a hoe as he marched up from the wharf. At the same time he named the settlement "Elizabeth Town" in honor of cousin George Carteret's wife.

Robert Treat and his Connecticut associates founded Newark in the Spring of 1666, but Elizabethtown moved into foremost prominence when Governor Carteret designated the town the capital of Jersey and summoned the state's first General Assembly there in 1668. Laws enacted by the As-

sembly covered everything from tippling in "tapp-houses" after nine o'clock at night to putting witches to death. But, as one authority said, "Puritan austerity was so tempered by Dutch indifference that mercy itself could not have dictated a milder system."

Village fathers met on Divident Hill on May 20, 1668, to settle boundary differences between Newark and Elizabethtown, and in the fall of that year little whaling vessels set out from the Elizabeth River. Soon Elizabethtown tanners began to cure leather, and quickly the village became the center of the colonial leather industry. Many leather enterprises in other colonies and other towns in New Jersey were started by "Betsytowners," including the first one in Newark. As early as 1678 Elizabethtown exported leather.

Farming occupied all male settlers, even those engaged in whaling or leather-making (and, in fact, the great number of cattle in the settlement led to the early leather curing). As demand for farm land increased, settlers pushed outward

Fairchild Aerial Surveys, Inc.
Jersey Central Railroad tracks link Plainfield and other towns in western Union County.

Celebrated home of Elias Boudinot in Elizabeth.

through the valley beneath heavily-forested Watchung Mountain.

Farmers from Connecticut moved down to what is now Union in 1667 and established Connecticut Farms; in the 1680's Scotch families from Perth Amboy came overland and stopped in the fields on the plain south of the Watchungs—and their villages became known as Scotch Plains and Plainfield. Quakers from Woodbridge came to the Rawack (Rahway) River at about the same time. Then, in 1699, Elizabethtown settlers divided the pasturelands to the west—the West Fields, of course.

A family named Briant stopped in 1717 to farm the fields where springs gushed forth into the headwaters of the Rahway River. The village name? It had to be Springfield! Isaac Sayre built his house in about 1710 on top of the plateau they later called Summit, and just to the west the preponderance of wild turkeys led new arrivals to call the area Turkey (now New Providence). If ever a region was settled easily and named naturally, it was Union County.

Yet trouble brewed and erupted through the area, because of the understandable feelings of early settlers that their purchase of the land directly from the Indians took precedence over arbitrary distribution of the region to English Proprietors. The Proprietors tried to collect quit-rents but the settlers stood firm—and ready to fight, even against royal authority.

Even as land troubles intensified, Elizabethtown moved into a position as the leading settlement in the state. The location of the original state capital in the town attracted men of substance and cul-

ture. Village life rotated around the Presbyterian and Episcopal churches, particularly after Reverend Jonathan Dickinson (Presbyterian) and Reverend Edward Vaughan (Episcopalian) came to the village in 1709.

Mr. Dickinson and Mr. Vaughan had remarkably parallel careers, both coming to Elizabethtown at about the same time and both dying in October, 1747. Mr. Dickinson gained particular attention as a preacher, teacher, farmer and practising physician of note. He was an obvious choice to become the first president of the College of New Jersey (now Princeton University) after its founding in Elizabethtown in 1746. After his death in 1747 the college moved to Newark (which made Elizabethtown residents feel no more loving toward Newarkers).

Rent battles with the Proprietors prepared the county for opposition to the King. In February, 1775, an Elizabethtown resolution cut off trade with Staten Island because the Island inhabitants "have manifested an unfriendly disposition towards the liberties of America." Tory sentiment pervaded the area, nevertheless, and became espe-

Where Parson Caldwell "gave 'em Watts" in Springfield.

Bell Telephone Laboratories, Murray Hill.

Fairchild Aerial Surveys, Inc.

cially strong after the defeat of American troops in the Battle of Long Island in the summer of 1776 and the subsequent retreat of Washington's army across New Jersey that fall.

Despite the sympathies of many for the Crown, the region which is now Union County had Revolutionary leaders aplenty. These included William Livingston, elected governor of New Jersey on August 27, 1776 (and re-elected continuously until he died in office in 1790); Abraham Clark of Elizabethtown and Rahway, one of the signers of the Declaration of Independence; Jonathon Dayton, an officer on Washington's staff and subsequently a leader in Congress; Aaron Ogden, distinguished field officer; and Elias Boudinot, outstanding member of the Continental Congress, who as president of Congress in 1783 signed the peace treaty with Great Britain.

Trouble with the Tories forced many Elizabethtown patriots to take to the hills. Tories struck often from Staten Island in the winter of 1779-80, making one particularly damaging foray on January 25, 1780, when Cornelius Hatfield, Jr. led royal sympathizers into Elizabethtown and burned the courthouse and Presbyterian Church. Proof of

the divided houses in the settlement, however, is the fact that Elizabethtown resident Cornelius Hatfield, Sr., father of the raider, immediately opened the doors of his "large red storehouse" as a temporary church.

The British made two desperate efforts to roll through the county to get at Washington's troops quartered in Morristown in June, 1780, but each time furiously fighting and badly outnumbered militia turned back the King's Men.

On June 7, 1780, General Knyphausen swung ashore at Elizabeth Point with 6,000 brilliantly uniformed troops and headed for the Short Hills. Colonel Dayton established twelve men at the eastern end of Elizabethtown, with instructions to delay the march. The dozen fell back doggedly while "Old Sow," the 18-pounder atop Beacon Hill above Springfield, called out the militia and summoned Washington's brigades from Morristown.

Knyphausen halted his mauled troops at Connecticut Farms, then fell back to Elizabethtown in the midst of a pounding rain storm. As his troops left the Farms they set the torch to the village. One of the British soldiers shot through an open window to kill Mrs. James Caldwell, wife of Reverend Caldwell, "The Fighting Parson" (or, "The High Priest of the Revolution," as the British called him).

Sixteen days later 5,000 British troops again headed towards the Short Hills, only to meet a militia savagely aroused by the burning of Connecticut Farms and the wanton murder of Mrs. Caldwell. Reverend Caldwell inspired the fighting Americans at Springfield, finally passing out Watts's hymnals for use as wadding in the defenders' guns. His ringing shout, "Now give them Watts, boys!" has rolled down through the years.

English troops fell back from Watts and Springfield after this last battle of consequence on Jersey soil, and the nation moved toward peace. War's end meant disaster for many old Tory families, forced to leave their homeland for exile in Nova Scotia or New Brunswick, Canada. General Washington paid a brief visit to Elizabethtown's Boxwood Hall, the residence of Elias Boudinot, on April 30, 1789, while the General was on his way to New York to become President.

Essex County—including all of Union—had about 17,000 residents after the war, with Newark and Elizabeth almost of a size, each having a population of about 1,000. The towns vied for leadership, although the people of Elizabeth slowly became charged with envy on account of the increasing prosperity of Newark. Even Elizabethtown's long-standing leather industry gravitated to Newark.

The smoldering battle broke out into the open in February, 1807, when Essex County voted for the location of a new courthouse. Citizens of both Elizabethtown and Newark voted often, if not wisely, with so many votes being cast that it was evident a glaring fraud had been perpetrated. Nevertheless Newark won the battle and got the new courthouse—but in her stubbornness, Elizabeth kept her old courthouse anyway!

A more personal battle involved John and Robert Livingston, Aaron Ogden and Thomas Gibbons, who fought for control of the waterfront, where ferries had been running to New York for a cen-

L. B. Coddington Company, Murray Hill, largest planter of eucharist lilies in the country.

tury. Ogden granted permission to the Livingstons to run the steamboat *Raritan* between Elizabeth Point and New York in 1808, then built his own steamboat in 1811. He ran afoul of a steamboat monopoly granted to the Livingstons by the New York Legislature. Protracted legal maneuvering finally ended in 1824 when the U.S. Supreme Court voided monopolistic steamboat practices and opened the waters to all comers.

That set the stage for the coming of the railroads in the 1830's (the New Jersey Railroad in 1834 and the Elizabethtown and Somerville in 1836). The routes of the twisting lines across the county's fields encouraged the development of the pasture-land surrounding Elizabethtown.

Union County had only about 25,000 residents when it became a separate county, compared with about 95,000 in Essex County. But in spite of this inferiority in numbers, Union residents were so happy to be free that the Republicans and Democrats agreed to split county offices equally, a spirit of harmony which has not prevailed since.

Industry of a widely varied sort came to the region in the first half of the nineteenth century. Plainfield, for example, found prosperity from the many hat factories and clothes-making establishments started in the first years of the nineteenth century. Rahway had twelve carriage factories in the 1830's and became famed as a center of fine carriages although the Civil War ruined its Southern trade.

Elizabethport was spoken of in 1844 as a "new and thriving place" because of its railroad connections. Elizabethtown boasted a population somewhat in excess of 5,000 in 1857 and had a few small machine manufacturers. Many Union County towns had paper mills in the 1840's, most of them concentrated in Springfield.

On the south slope of Watchung Mountain, David Felt came in 1845 to buy the old mill Peter Willcoxie had built on Blue Brook a century before. Felt, a New York printer and stationer, conceived the notion of a self-contained manufacturing village. He built homes, a school, a church and a country store. Things went along well until the Civil War, when markets collapsed and Feltville became a deserted village (Feltville still exists as "The Deserted Village" in Watchung Reservation).

Easily the most significant industrial happening in all Union County history took place in 1873, when the Singer Manufacturing Company consolidated its several separate sewing machine manufac-

turing plants into one plant in Elizabethport. Singer put $3,000,000 into a 32-acre plant employing 3,000 workers. Few industries in the nation exceeded the plant in size. Singer's success focused attention on the wide open Union County meadow land available for big industry.

Industrial development also hastened growth of residential towns along the railroads. The beautifully shaded streets of Westfield, Plainfield and Scotch Plains attracted settlers, many of them men of wealth. The Jersey Central Railroad itself started to develop Fanwood in 1867, and in 1878 a luxurious summer hotel was built at Netherwood at a cost of $175,000.

In the mountains, the Lackawanna Railroad snaked over from Essex County to Summit in 1837 and by the 1880's made the town easily accessible to moneyed commuters and equally well-off summer visitors. A branch railroad rolled out through New Providence and Berkeley Heights to link that region with the cities.

Strangely enough, in view of the excellent railroad connections, the land south of Elizabeth developed slowly. As late as 1890 Linden was an area of truck farms, while Rahway's carriage factories still topped industries in that town. Suddenly, however, within two decades the entire section burst forth into industrial prominence and Union County's die was cast.

Galloping Hill Park, a Union County recreation area.

Debutinization and stabilization plant in bustling Bayway Refinery at Linden.

Among the first to found an important industry in the area was J. Noah H. Slee, who developed his Three-in-One Oil in a Rahway shack and sold his first three dozen bottles there in 1894. George Merck purchased 150 acres of land on the Rahway-Linden boundary line in 1900 and by 1903 had completed construction of a three-story brick building, forerunner of today's tremendous Merck chemical and drug manufactory. Soon after, the Wheatena Company started to make cereals in Rahway.

At the same time Standard Oil Company, seeking to escape the congested conditions hemming in its refineries in Bayonne and Jersey City, built a pumping station in Linden and on January 2, 1909, the first battery of Linden stills was fired. Since then the Bayway Refinery has grown into one of the world's largest refineries.

Industry has spread throughout Union County from those beginnings—to Garwood, Clark, Plainfield, Hillside, Kenilworth, and to many new locations in Elizabeth, Linden and Rahway——until today Union is the third most important industrial county in the state, despite the fact that it is the second smallest in land area.

The last two decades have seen an influx of modern research laboratories and equally-modern production plants. Excellent examples are the Ciba Pharmaceutical Company plant in Summit, Bell Telephone Laboratories at Murray Hill, and the General Motors assembly plant at Linden. There are more, many more, as the postwar trend toward industrial decentralization continues.

In fact, a recent report of the Regional Plan Association, covering the five-year period ending in 1951, showed that Union County led all metropolitan area counties in number of new plants from 1946 to 1951. The report showed that Union gained 277 new plants in the period, with a construction value of $25,563,000.

This tremendous industrial growth since 1900 has jumped Union County's population from 99,353 in 1900 to 398,138 in 1950. Real estate booms have struck various parts of the county, with Hillside and Union being notable illustrations of what has happened to particular locales in the past thirty years.

Hillside and Union parted ways as a joint township in 1913, with each of their rural towns taking about half the total population of 3,500. Ten years later Union had about 4,000 population, Hillside about 5,000. Then the real estate men started to cut up the farmlands into small home plots. Today finds Union with a population of about 40,000 and Hillside with about 22,000.

Surprisingly enough, despite Union's recognized industrial prominence and its noted residential towns, the county has an agricultural income of well over $4,000,000 annually. Moreover, Union leads all New Jersey counties in value of nursery and greenhouse products, with the county's annual income of $2,500,000 from that source topping second-place Morris County by about $800,000.

The rapid growth has wiped out many of the old landmarks of Union County, with oldtime Elizabeth particularly buried under modern advances. Although little islands of antiquity linger, this oldest part of the House of Essex has been almost completely revamped.

Still somewhat short of being officially a century old, Union County retains its memories—and certainly still has a future. Statistics alone do not tell a story, but Union County has advanced from one of the state's lesser-populated areas to the fourth highest in population. Above all, Union has its pride—something its residents felt they had lost to Newark before 1857.

Thus the house divided did not fall. The sisters who went their separate ways both grew and prospered, and they're much friendlier than they were in 1857.

MORE ABOUT UNION

Honeyman, Abraham Van Doren, 1849, *History of Union County, New Jersey, 1664-1923*. Chicago, Lewis Historical Publishing Co. New York, 1923.

Ricord, Frederik William, *History of Union County, New Jersey*. Newark, New Jersey, East Jersey History Co., 1897.

Clayton, W. Woodford, *History of Union and Middlesex Counties, New Jersey*. Philadelphia, Penna., Everts and Peck, 1882.

Hatfield, Edwin Francis, *History of Elizabeth, New Jersey*. New York, Carlton and Lanahan, 1868.

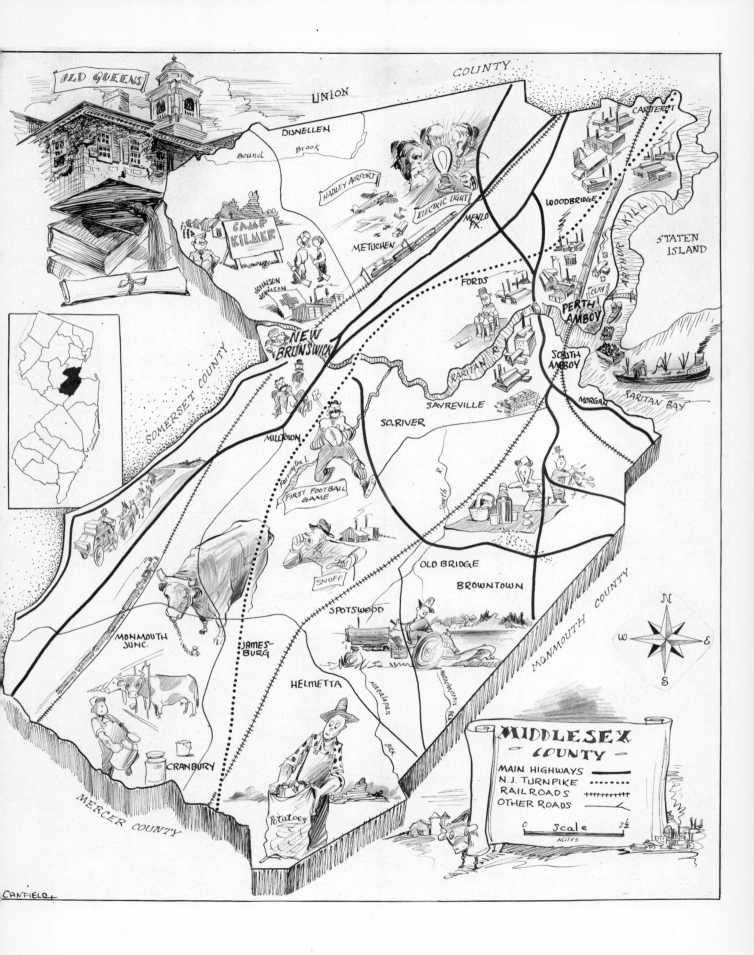

Fairchild Aerial Surveys, Inc.

Modern New Brunswick is a far cry from Inian's ferry.

MIDDLESEX

John Inian's vision possibly did not extend much beyond the east and west banks of the Raritan River when he established a ferry at what is now New Brunswick in 1686. Nevertheless, the fact remains that his ferry was the first exploitation of Middlesex County's ever-vital role as the connecting bridge between East and West Jersey, between New York and Philadelphia, between New England and the South.

Twentieth-century trains thundering over the county on the busiest stretch of railroad tracks in the world, and principal highways stretching over Middlesex owe their origin to the same simple reason which prompted Inian's Ferry. The reason is easily-demonstrated: trace a straight line between New York and Philadelphia, and astride the line is Middlesex County, the necessary link.

Travelers on horseback had been fording the Raritan for nearly thirty years before John Inian arrived in 1681. The calm waters of Raritan Bay lured colonists off the stormy Atlantic, the placid Raritan River enticed them inland. English settlers from the Piscataqua River in Maine established Piscataway in the 1660's, at about the same time Woodbridge sprang into being.

County courts alternated between Piscataway and Woodbridge for seven years before Middlesex County was established officially in 1682 (with its loosely defined county borders including most of Somerset County). Sprawling Woodbridge had 600 residents by that time, but the East Jersey Proprietors had their eyes on "sweet, wholesome and delightful" Ambo Point. They visualized it as the "London of the Western Hemisphere" (because of its "commodious situation upon a safe harbor").

Three buildings graced Ambo Point by August, 1683, but real growth began two years later when the Earl of Perth permitted 200 oppressed Scots to immigrate to the Point. Gratefully the Scots dubbed the village "New Perth"; reluctantly older Ambo Point residents gave ground in the compromise name of "Perth Amboy."

Middlesex County's "bridge" character began to emerge in 1686, when Perth Amboy became the provincial capital of East Jersey. That necessitated communication with Burlington, capital of West

Home of the East Jersey proprietors in Perth Amboy.

115

Jersey, and led to the gradual widening of Indian paths into roads across the narrow waist of New Jersey. Two roads traversed the length of Middlesex, the "Upper" road going to Princeton and Trenton via Inian's Ferry, the "Lower" road extending from South Amboy to Burlington via Cranbury.

Meanwhile the Raritan River led Dutch settlers westward to Hunterdon County. Some of those Dutch stopped off in New Brunswick early in the eighteenth century, and renamed the main street "Albany" Street to honor the New York town from whence they came. The struggling little river town became "New Brunswick" officially in 1730, ending years of casual designation (ranging from "Pridmore's Swamp" to "Inian's Ferry" to "The River").

Perth Amboy grew steadily, but its future suffered a setback in 1747 when Governor Belcher arrived in town, apparently to live there as had most Royal Governors before him. Governor Belcher delivered himself movingly: ". . . and you may

depend on everything on my part to render it a flourishing town. . . ." Then he went to live in Elizabethtown.

However, as the colonies moved toward an open split with England in 1776, Governor William Franklin established his residence at Perth Amboy. On the night of June 15, 1776, Colonel Nathaniel Heard of the Continental Army knocked on Franklin's door to present him with a parole. Franklin had his choice: either sign the parole and sit out the impending war in a town which Franklin could choose, or submit to arrest. The Governor scorned the parole; Heard placed him under arrest.

Middlesex County played a more-or-less unwilling host to Lord Howe's British army from December 2, 1776, to June 22, 1777. Patriotic feeling dominated the Raritan and produced such heroes as Colonel John Neilson, but 200 to 300 adults flocked into New Brunswick each day in December of 1776 to accept Howe's offer of amnesty in return for a renunciation of revoluntionary sentiments.

Howe found his position untenable in the late

Fairchild Aerial Surveys, Inc.

Outerbridge Crossing from Staten Island to Perth Amboy.

Recruits arriving at Camp Kilmer.

spring of 1777 after General Washington moved his troops from Morristown to the southern slope of the Watchung Mountains. After trying unsuccessfully to lure Washington's army out of the hills, Howe broke camp on June 22 and moved on to Perth Amboy and Staten Island. The British burned and pillaged as they went, adding to the suffering Middlesex County had already endured. No savage battles raged over the country, yet more than 100 buildings were burned and the British ransacked 650 other homes.

The county saw little direct warfare after 1777, but Washington brought his troops to New Brunswick after the Battle of Monmouth in June, 1778. Then, on August 29, 1781, the General dramatically and unexpectedly wrote in New Brunswick the orders which took his army to Yorktown for the decisive victory over Cornwallis.

New Brunswick edged to the fore as the county's center and met only token opposition when county courts transferred there in 1778. Elsewhere in Middlesex in the waning days of the eighteenth century, a few potteries began to utilize the rich clay beds underlying Middlesex County soil in a wide

arc from Woodbridge to Cheesequake. Most of South Middlesex depended on huge lumber and timber shipments, although farmers along the Manalapan Creek found that the Indian word for the creek—meaning "good country producing good bread"—correctly characterized the region.

Prosperity in the county did not extend to Queen's College, the struggling little institution the Dutch Reformed Church had established on the banks of the Old Raritan in 1771 (on charters granted in 1766 and 1770). Its beginnings were inauspicious enough, with one tutor, 18-year-old Frederick Frelinghuysen. The first class, in 1774, had one graduate.

At least the small college could move about easily, and it did during the Revolution—first to Millstone, then to North Branch before returning to New Brunswick in 1778. Acute financial pains closed the college from 1795 to 1807, again from 1821 to 1825.

Finally the trustees announced in 1825 that the college would reopen as Rutgers College. "Queen's," they pointed out, had become unpatriotic as a result of the Revolution—but anyone who believed the change had been induced more by the generosity of New York philanthropist Colonel Henry Rutgers than by patriotism wouldn't have been far wrong.

The financial plight of poor Rutgers College failed to loosen the bulging purses in thriving New Brunswick, where more than 5,000 people lived by 1830. Life surged vividly in the town's twenty taverns and many hotels. Down on the river a dozen fast sloops stood by, awaiting grain from Hunterdon, Somerset and Warren counties. Twice a week long lines of massive grain wagons, drawn by as many as six horses, rolled to shipside over the New Jersey Turnpike (Easton to New Brunswick). Often as many as fifty wagons lined up in Water Street overnight while the waterfront erupted in the sound and strife in the taverns and rough hotels for traders. (An early historian said the difference between New Brunswick's trader hotels and its hotels for overland travelers was that "travelers wanted rest.")

Quantities of peaches also cleared through New Brunswick, but that trade centered in Washington (now South River) under the leadership of Samuel Whitehead, Sr. Samuel set out peach trees in the early 1820's and became so successful that farmers for miles around emulated him. From four to six

Old Queens at Rutgers University in New Brunswick.

peach-laden steamers left Washington daily for New York before declining crops ruined the business in the 1850's.

Even more important to all Middlesex, however, were the streams of people crossing between New York and Philadelphia. Perth Amboy, South Amboy, New Brunswick, Woodbridge and Washington all vied for the trade. Competition between steamship companies connecting New York and Middlesex County became fierce, and at county ports stagecoach companies battled without quarter.

South Amboy had a dramatic battle for the business from 1806 to 1833, as Samuel Gordon and Daniel Wilmurt "kept things hot between Amboy and Bordentown" with their rival routes. Particularly intense rivalry flared in New Brunswick, where the "Citizen's" and "Union" steamship lines scrapped for business. Whistling steamers rammed into New Brunswick docks, passengers (who took unto themselves the rivalries of the steamboat owners) risked life and limb by leaping ashore and sprinting for competing stagecoaches. Off they went up Burnet Street in the swirling dust, with as many as twenty-two coaches jockeying for positions on the narrow street.

Down-county Middlesex towns cared little who got the up-county trade first because they got it eventually. Inns in Dayton, Rhode Hall, Cranbury and Kingston catered splendidly to the cross-state transients. The pre-Revolutionary War Kingston House, for example, boasted of having as many as 49 stages waiting out front at once while more than 400 passengers dined or rested inside.

The peach and grain trade and the colorful stagecoach era were doomed by the dawn of the canal and railroad age. Naturally Middlesex became the intermediary—the bridge—when the Delaware & Raritan Canal and the Camden & Amboy Railroad built across the narrowest part of the state in the 1830's. Steamboat operators continued to prosper for awhile, but only until the Camden & Amboy and the New Jersey Railroad (from Jersey City and Newark) joined tracks in New Brunswick in 1839.

Some of South Middlesex benefited from the railroad, notably Jamesburg, and tremendous changes swept over the entire Raritan River area soon after the canal and railroad bridged the county. The Raritan carried the third largest tonnage of any river in the country, but New Brunswick port gained little from the trade passing her wharves.

Voorhees Chapel at New Jersey College for Women.

However, facilities afforded by the canal and railroad led to the quick rise of New Brunswick industry. Young Martin Howell opened a wallpaper factory on Water Street in 1837, using canal water for power; Horace H. Day founded a rubber plant in 1839, and other companies took advantage of the ready supply of raw materials and anthracite coal.

Rubber became a prime industry in Middlesex County, mainly because of Christopher Meyer, who came from Newark in 1839 to set up Day's machinery. While Day continuously poured his money

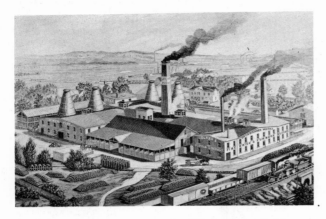

1880 engraving of Salamander Works, Woodbridge.

into the courts to protect himself during a protracted suit for alleged infringements of Charles Goodyear's vulcanizing process, Meyer set up effective competition in Milltown in 1844.

Eventually Meyer controlled Day's plant, too, as well as the Milltown factory and a New Brunswick hard rubber manufactory. Millions of boots, rubbers and the patented "Arctic" overshoes flowed from Middlesex in the Civil War era and immediately after.

At about the same time the big North Middlesex clay industry edged into the industrial picture. Some use of the fine Raritan clay had been made earlier in small local potteries but two Frenchmen finally made clay into big business in Woodbridge in 1825. In that year Michael Lefoulon and Henry De Casse started the Salamander Works, which in twenty years became the state's largest clay manufactory.

John R. Watson set up a fire-brick plant in Perth Amboy in 1836 and James Wood built brick kilns at Sayreville in 1851, although the important "big" names in those communities were Alfred Hall in Perth Amboy and Peter Fisher and James Sayre in Sayreville. Hall located in Perth Amboy in 1845 to make fire brick, but his greatest contribution came in the 1870's when he set up an extensive terra cotta plant.

Quickly Perth Amboy and the nearby area became the terra cotta center of the world, and Middlesex terra cotta is today found all over the world. Fisher and Sayre started their brick plant in 1851 and within twenty years made more than 22,000,000 bricks annually. That, plus the 8,000,000 manufactured each year by the James Wood Company, made Sayreville one of the nation's biggest brick producers.

Rutgers College, meanwhile, continued to struggle in the midst of plenty. The Class of 1862 had thirty-eight graduates, but two years later Civil War vicissitudes cut the number to eleven men and the college again faced serious times. Three significant things occurred almost simultaneously to boost Rutgers toward both academic and economic solidity.

First, the state established on the Rutgers campus the Land Grant College of Agriculture and Mechanics in 1864 (as "The Scientific School"). Secondly, Rutgers in 1865 became non-sectarian. Finally, the intensive scholarship and endowment campaign of Reverend Dr. William H. Campbell raised $144,758 in the closing days of the Civil War. By the 1870's the college began to attract some large endowments, and its reputation was enhanced by the establishment of the State Agricultural Experiment Station at the college in 1880.

In fact, the school had shucked enough of its academic rigidity and its economic problems to encourage some campus lightheartedness. One result was the nation's first intercollegiate football game on the Rutgers campus on November 6, 1869, when visiting Princeton obligingly dropped a 6-4 decision after the rival schoolboys (25 on a side) trampled over one another. Four years later Howard N. Fuller (Rutgers '74) wrote "On the Banks," the school's alma mater.

Middlesex retained a distinctly rural air in the 1870's, even in the "cities." Perth Amboy, despite its brickyards, continued as a quaint village, where visitors came to enjoy the "salubrious sea air." Woodbridge had a reputation as a summer resort. Hundreds of men found employment in the big oyster beds in the healthful Raritan Bay off Perth Amboy. Then the Lehigh Valley Railroad, built from Easton to Perth Amboy in the 1870's, brought huge coal shipments into Perth Amboy and changed it overnight into a bustling industrial town. Population jumped from about 2,800 in 1870 to more than 7,000 in 1880.

Thomas Alva Edison found rural peacefulness at Menlo Park, where in 1876 he set up the first laboratory in America devoted to research and invention. First, Edison devised a "talking machine," which in the fall of 1877 repeated in Edison's own voice four lines of "Mary Had a Little Lamb."

Edison and his men turned to the development of the incandescent light. The search for a workable filament focused, after hundreds of experiments, on ordinary cotton thread, and in October,

1879, a piece of carbonized thread glowed for forty-five hours before the yellow loop dulled to gray. On New Year's Eve, 1879, 3,000 visitors came to Menlo Park on a special excursion to watch a demonstration of the light. Before Edison left Menlo Park for West Orange in 1887, the hilltop laboratory was the site of many other inventions—including an electric locomotive, which Edison operated at Menlo Park.

The rubber and wallpaper industries which buoyed New Brunswick through the nineteenth century began to slip as the twentieth century dawned, but New Brunswick had in the meantime welcomed Robert W. and James W. Johnson, who came in 1886 to establish their pioneer gauze and adhesive tape plant. The Johnsons started in the old Parsons Mill by the river at a time when antiseptic standards were virtually unknown; soon they had America reaching in time of emergency for a "red cross" box rather than a torn-up old sheet or towel.

Perth Amboy's industrial pattern spurted ahead in 1899 after the Raritan Copper Works started to

Menlo Park and Edison's laboratory, about 1880.

refine copper in the city. Within a few years it became the world's largest copper refinery (and today it is still one of the country's biggest). Milltown had a spurt, too, when the Michelin Tire Company bought the old Meyer rubber works in Milltown in 1907 to make automobile tires. Michelin hired 3,000 people before it moved out of the Meyer plant in the late 1920's.

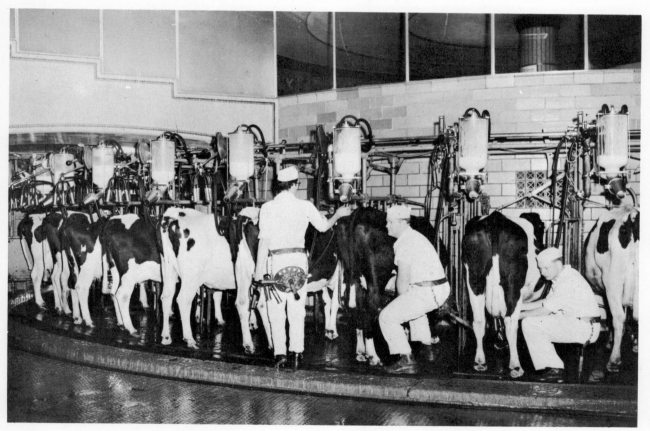

Walker Gordon rotolactor, Plainsboro, milks 1650 cows three times a day.

World War I strengthened Middlesex County industries, of course, and fixed the sharp contrast between the heavily industrial Raritan Bay area and the sparsely settled regions south of New Brunswick and Milltown. Rubber and wallpaper enterprises, long important along the Raritan, moved away but other industries moved into the abandoned plants.

Small industry typifies Middlesex County today. Most of its more than 2,000 widely diversified plants employ fewer than 300 persons and some of them are unique—such as the George W. Helme snuff factory in Helmetta, one of the nation's biggest snuff plants. Chemicals, primary metals, paints, explosives, clay, textiles and drugs are parts of the huge and varied pattern.

The pharmaceutical industry, by way of illustration, employs more than 4,600 persons in New Brunswick alone (split about evenly between Johnson & Johnson and E. R. Squibb). At Parlin, Hercules Powder Company and du Pont have big plants. Piscataway has more than 2,600 employed in the Bakelite Company factory; 2,000 work in Carteret for the U.S. Metals Refining Company; and the New Jersey Shipbuilding Company employs 2,600 at Perth Amboy.

One facet of the Middlesex industrial growth in the last twenty years has been the building of ultramodern, handsomely landscaped structures to house such varied enterprises as Johnson & Johnson subsidiaries, automobile assembly plants and paint manufactories.

Oddly enough, in view of the North Middlesex factory pattern, the county has more than 1,200 farms, averaging upwards of 55 acres apiece in size. The annual value of farm products approaches $9,000,000, with the immense potato farms surrounding Cranbury an important factor (Middlesex is second only to Monmouth in the state in potato production). Several large dairy farms prosper in the southwestern part of the county.

Possibly no county has so neat a division of industry and farming along a more or less fixed line. Just as Middlesex serves in a transportation sense as the span between great cities, so does the agricultural college of Rutgers University bridge the gap between town and country. From the College of Agriculture has come vital aid to the state's multimillion dollar oyster industry, important developments in fruit and vegetable culture, and in mosquito control. The searching in the soil also led to the discovery of streptomycin and neomycin at Rutgers—and to a 1952 Nobel Prize for Dr. Selman A. Waksman, one of Rutgers's most noted sons.

Through all this, Rutgers had moved slowly toward the State University status it achieved in 1945. Establishment of state scholarships in 1890, the founding of New Jersey College for Women in 1918, and the adoption of the name "Rutgers University" in 1924 were important steps along the way.

Fittingly enough, two years after Rutgers became the State University, the state's first Constitutional Convention since 1844 met in Rutgers gymnasium to draft a new State Constitution. Its approval by voters in 1947 bridged a 103-year-old legislative gap.

Transportation agencies continue to make Middlesex County the vital bridge. The county's exceptional railroad and highway facilities made it an ideal location for Camp Kilmer during World War II. Now the New Jersey Turnpike bisects Middlesex in one direction; the Garden State Parkway bisects it in another.

Often, on summer days, traffic stalls completely on the banks of the Raritan. Blame it on geography —and the placement of New York City and Philadelphia in the seventeenth century.

MORE ABOUT MIDDLESEX

Clayton, Woodford, ed., *History of Union and Middlesex Counties, New Jersey*. Philadelphia, Pennsylvania, Everts and Peck, 1882.

Dally, Joseph W., *Woodbridge and Vicinity*. New Brunswick, New Jersey, A. E. Gordon, 1873.

Demarest, William Henry Steele, *A History of Rutgers College, 1766-1924;* New Brunswick, New Jersey, 1924.

Demarest, William Henry Steele, 1863, *The Anniversary of New Brunswick, New Jersey 1680-1730-1930*. New Brunswick, New Jersey, J. Heidingsfeld Co., 1932.

Wall, John P., *History of Middlesex County, New Jersey, 1664-1920*. New York, Lewis Publishing Co., Inc., 1921.

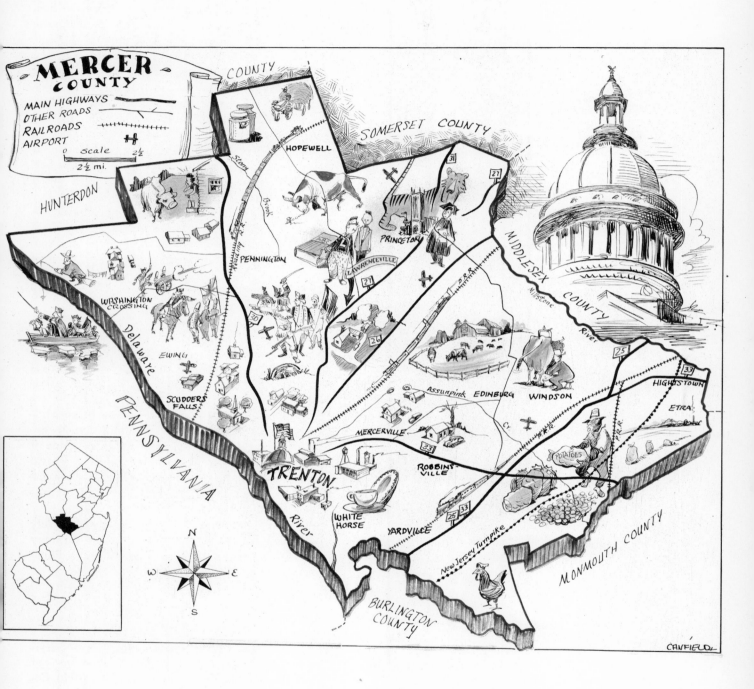

State's lawmakers in session at Trenton.

MERCER

Mercer County, long before her official birthdate in 1838, had a past and a pedigree upwards of 150 years long. Her forebears came from the finest families; prestige and culture and heroics lodged firmly in her background. The wonder was not that Mercer finally was born, but rather that her delivery took so long.

Little bliss accompanied Mercer's actual birth, mainly because it occurred in the "smoke-filled" atmosphere so typical of state capitals. Burlington, Middlesex and Hunterdon counties, on the one hand, and Somerset, on the other, all contributed land (somewhat reluctantly) to form Mercer. Somerset, given assurances of the inviolability of its own territory, joined the majority of the Legislature in severing parts of Burlington, Middlesex and Hunterdon on February 22, 1838, to form Mercer.

Five days later Burlington, Middlesex and Hunterdon, with understandable relish, indorsed a second legislative act—this time cutting off a bit of Somerset to be joined to the brand-new infant called Mercer County. Thus, with extended labor pains and two birthdays, was Mercer born. It should have been easier and more natural.

The region surrounding the state capital had long been unnaturally divided. Residents on the north side of Assunpink Creek (which cuts through the heart of Trenton) went to Flemington for county business, residents on the south side of the creek had to travel to Mount Holly for their county affairs. Princeton had it even worse; Somerset and Middlesex counties split along Main Street. Those on the north side traveled eighteen miles to Somerville to the county seat, while their Middlesex County neighbors across the way had to go twenty miles to New Brunswick to their courthouse.

Moreover, no section of the state had a more homogeneous past. No county had more reason for being. Take, for instance, the colonial heritage. The first settlers had much in common, coming either from old Burlington or across-state from Long Island. Mahlon Stacy gets credit for being the first arrival of record; as early as 1680 he established one of the state's first mills at the Falls of the Delaware. Quaker families took up residence on the banks of Stony Brook at Princeton, Long Island emigrants put down roots near Hopewell and Maidenhead (Lawrenceville), and within twenty years most of the region had been settled.

Colonel William Trent bought an 800-acre farm from Mahlon Stacy in 1714, built a home in 1719, and by donating land induced the county government in 1720 to stay permanently in town. Grateful villagers called the settlement "Trent's Town" (al-

Nassau Hall and front campus, Princeton University, 1856.

though many grumbled that "Stacy's Town" would have been more appropriate).

Unquestionably, however, a decision by the College of New Jersey's board of trustees to move their young college out of Newark in 1754 had more to do with Mercer's early growth than roads or streams or emigrants.

The trustees first approached New Brunswick. "Look," they bargained, "you people can have the college if you'll raise £1,000 and give us 10 acres of land in town and 200 acres of woodland within three miles of town."

New Brunswick residents pondered the bargain, but their Princeton neighbors quickly stepped forward with an offer to meet the terms. Immediately the offer was accepted and work started on a college building; by 1756 the imposing three-story Nassau Hall was ready. Called "the largest stone building in all the colonies," Old Nassau's 60 rooms had a capacity of 147 students (although the college had only 70 students when it transferred from Newark in 1756).

The arrival of the college naturally intensified cultural feelings throughout the region. Six miles away in Hopewell, Reverend Isaac Eaton opened his Baptist Academy the same year the college came to Princeton. Reverend Eaton's academy is the acknowledged birthplace of Brown University, since the academy's first pupil, James Manning of Piscataway, founded Brown University and became its first president in 1764.

Possibly even more vital to the future of the region and of the nation, the College of New Jersey became the center of intense anti-British feeling, particularly after fiery Reverend John Witherspoon arrived from Scotland in 1768 to head the college. Students in 1774 burned tea on the campus after word came of the Boston Tea Party.

Battle of Trenton, Dec. 26, 1776.

McConkey Ferry House, Washington Crossing Park.

Reverend Witherspoon and Richard Stockton became outspoken in support of revolution and their voices found an echo in Hopewell, where John Hart bitterly denounced the British.

Small wonder, then, that Reverend Witherspoon, Stockton and Hart became three of New Jersey's five signers of the Declaration of Independence (Francis Hopkinson of Bordentown and Abraham Clark of Roselle were the others). Small wonder that the state's first Legislature held its first session in Nassau Hall in August, 1776, or that Jersey's first governor, William Livingston, took his inaugural oath in Princeton.

The fires of revolution flickered low early in December, 1776, when General Washington's sadly disorganized army limped through Mercer County and disconsolately crossed the Delaware to Pennsylvania. British and Hessian troops swarmed over Princeton, Trenton, Hopewell and Lawrenceville, showing scorn for the ragged revolutionists and displaying an eagerness to punish the area for its rebellious leadership. Outspoken John Hart fled from his home in Hopewell and hid in the Sourland Mountains. The State Legislature fled to Haddonfield and the College of New Jersey suspended classes.

But even as the gloom deepened, Washington plotted the boldest stroke of the Revolution. Finally, on Christmas night, 1776, scouts brought word from Trenton that the Hessians were deep in their wassail cups. The Continental Army moved across the ice-choked river to McKonkey's Ferry, eight miles north of Trenton. Nine hours passed in the crossing before 2,400 men gathered about Washington on the New Jersey side to hear him order: "On to Trenton!"

Meanwhile, the Hessians dozed drunkenly in Trenton, completely unable to believe the word brought at 8 A.M. that the Continentals had pierced the city's outskirts. Minutes later Washington's army smashed them, killing or wounding 106 Hessians and capturing 23 officers and 886 enlisted men. Up the river road raced Washington's victorious men, across the menacing Delaware to Pennsylvania.

A week later the Colonial troops recrossed the Delaware, this time walking over on the ice. They dug in on the south side of Assunpink Creek to face the now-furious enemy. Three times on January 2, 1777, the British attacked the bridge over the creek, three times they fell back. As darkness fell, Lord Cornwallis called off his men with the offhand comment that "we'll bag the fox in the morning."

Next morning the fox was gone, leaving behind brightly burning campfires and a few wooden cannons to confound the British. The startled Cornwallis heard musket fire far off in the distance near Princeton, but before he could move his cumbersome army into action the fox had swept on. Nassau Hall changed hands three times in bloody battling, with the British finally retaining the hall as Washington withdrew his forces and headed up the Millstone Valley for winter headquarters at Morristown. Behind in Princeton lay thirty dead or wounded Americans, including General Hugh Mercer, for whom the county is named.

Fittingly enough, Princeton served as the capital of the infant nation from June 26 to November 4, 1783, when the Continental Congress convened in Nassau Hall for that period. There news was received of the signing of the peace treaty, there Washington received the thanks of the nation. Nearby, at Rock Hill, the General waited for the official end of the war.

Strong sentiment in New England and elsewhere favored Trenton as the permanent capital of the United States in 1784 and a three-man commission actually met to fix a spot "not more than six miles from Trenton." But the South favored a location at Georgetown on the Potomac River, and when Washington expressed disapproval of the Trenton location in February, 1785, selection of the Potomac site was a foregone conclusion. Nevertheless, yellow fever epidemics in Philadelphia three times drove Federal departments to Trenton in the 1790's, and in 1799 President John Adams and his wife lived temporarily in the town.

Trenton's reverence of Washington continued, of course, despite his disapproval of the place for a national capital. As he passed through town on April 21, 1789, on his way to New York to accept the Presidency, white-robed "virgin's fair and matron's grave" (they so described themselves in song) greeted him at Assunpink Creek beneath a flower-festooned arch which proclaimed in gilt letters: "THE DEFENDER OF THE MOTHERS WILL BE THE PROTECTOR OF THE DAUGHTERS."

The following year the State Legislature fixed the New Jersey capital in Trenton. Work started on the first quaint State House in 1791 (and parts of the original building are said still to exist somewhere in the vastly enlarged and altered State House of today).

Trenton was little more than a village in 1791, with a town pump, a pillory and a whipping post on its streets. Its location astride the New York-Philadelphia stage route aided its growth, and completion in 1806 of a 1,100-foot wooden covered bridge over the Delaware sped travelers on to Philadelphia. Life for the traveler centered at Princeton's Nassau Hotel, where from 1812 to 1836 innkeeper John Joline had more than a hundred horses standing in the immense stables to serve the thirty stages which each day started from the hotel. Inside the old pre-Revolutionary inn, college students downed their grog and carved their initials in the rough furniture.

Institute for Advanced Study, Princeton.

Trenton-Morrisville Bridge over Delaware River.

College students became exceedingly troublesome in Princeton from 1800 to 1820. The burning of Nassau Hall in 1802 was believed to be the work of undergraduates. In an effort to bring discipline to the campus, College President Dr. Samuel Stanhope Smith insisted (among other rules) that students remove their caps and stand silently when within a hundred feet of the president or within fifty feet of any faculty member. Students became even more rebellious, and about 125 of them were expelled in 1806. Dr. Smith's successor, Reverend Ashbel Green, proved to be even a sterner disciplinarian, and violence flared anew. Early on a January morning in 1817 students locked up the entire faculty and set fire to outbuildings, then held Old North Hall for a full day with cutlasses and pistols before the rebellion died. Only twenty-one students were graduated that year.

Development of water power by the Delaware Falls company, digging of the Delaware & Raritan Canal, and construction of the Camden & Amboy Railroad in the 1830's hastened Trenton's change from a charming colonial village to a busy metropolis. Only 20,000 people lived in all of Mercer County when it was created in 1838, but the city on the Falls of the Delaware had 4,000 inhabitants and was on the eve of an industrial spurt which blossomed at Civil War time and came into full flower in the 1880's.

The canal and the C. & A. Railroad shaped the course of all Mercer. Possibly most important, canal and railroad both carefully kept out of the center of Princeton, thus preserving the college town's exclusive residential character. Until 1840 the railroad ran through the southern part of the county, via Yardville and Hightstown, which meant Trenton-bound passengers had to transfer to stages at Yardville. Hightstown, long a prosperous agricultural center, tripled in size within a decade after the coming of the Camden & Amboy —then settled back to the quiet life beneath its towering Baptist Church steeple after the main line switched northward to include Trenton.

Mercer County played an important role in the Civil War. Its industries helped feed the Union war machine, its troops responded early to pleas for manpower. The College of New Jersey (by then generally known as Princeton College) faced another problem. Princeton had long been favored by Southern plantation owners as the place to edu-

128

cate their sons. Accordingly, the war split the campus and when the college closed for summer recess in 1861 half the student body of 300 went home to the South, never to return.

The county's character was fixed by 1870. State officialdom kept the capital city in constant turmoil—particularly through forty years of strife when the Camden & Amboy Railroad held unbridled sway in the State House. Trenton's industry formed a sharp contrast with the extensive oat fields in nearby Ewing Township, the broad farms near the Sourland Mountains and the fertile fields surrounding Hightstown.

Princeton continued to exert profound influence. The educational atmosphere reached out to surrounding communities and encouraged preparatory schools, such as Lawrenceville Classical and Commercial High School, founded 1810; Pennington Seminary, founded 1839; and Hightstown's Peddie Institute, founded 1869.

Post-Civil War days brought Southern sons back to the Princeton campus, and also brought the much-loved Dr. James McCosh, who started a 20-year term as college president in 1868. Before he stepped down he had introduced a system of elective studies, which upset the rigid theory of church-sponsored education and moved Princeton toward campus liberality and university status.

One of the students under Dr. McCosh was young "Tommy" Wilson, Class of 1879, who returned in 1890 as Professor T. Woodrow Wilson and then became university president in 1902. Wilson's campus presidency found him fighting three bitter battles. He won only one—the battle to get the preceptor system at Princeton.

He lost in an attempt to rid the campus of its exclusive eating societies, and was defeated in a fight to have the graduate school as an integral part of the university. His campus losses had much to with his entry into politics. He became governor of New Jersey in 1911, President of the United States in 1913.

While Princeton progressed, industry boomed in Trenton. A Trenton editor wrote in 1882: "The

Wire Division, John A. Roebling's Sons, bridge builders, Trenton.

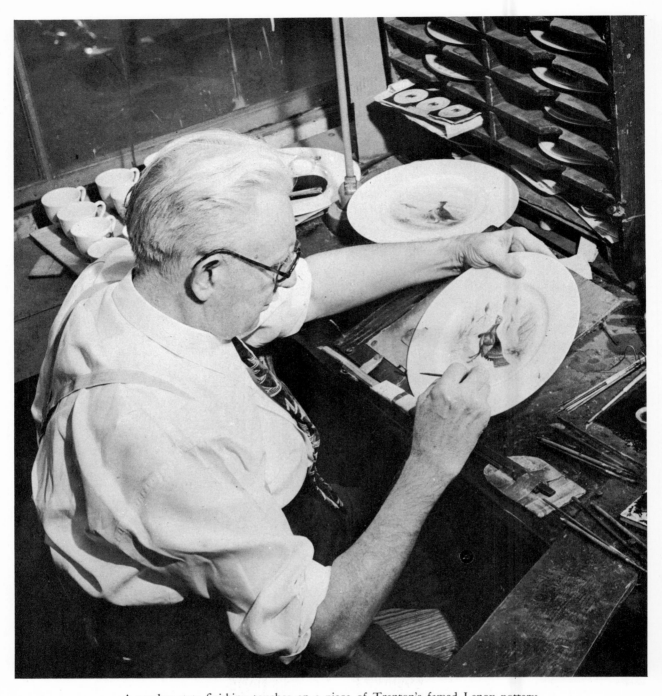

A worker puts finishing touches on a piece of Trenton's famed Lenox pottery.

city has, indeed, been fairly transformed in 20 years from a sleepy, old-fashioned town into a live, wideawake and growing city."

He correctly credited iron, steel, rubber, pottery and wire rope for the transformation. Trenton potteries, started in the eighteenth century, got into full swing between 1850 and 1870. Dozens of potteries operated in Trenton by 1880, making products ranging from white graniteware to the finest

china. From Trenton came, in 1873, the first porcelain sanitary ware in the United States. Trenton potters boastfully called their city the "Staffordshire of America," and some even went so far as to call Staffordshire the "Trenton of England."

Walter Scott Lenox, who learned the industry as an apprentice in Trenton, resolved in the 1880's to perfect American dinnerware. His efforts led to the creamy, richly lustrous ware known throughout the world as Lenox china. Stricken blind and paralyzed in 1895, with his dream about to be realized, Lenox lived to know that Woodrow Wilson bought 1,700 pieces of his china for the White House (where Lenox has been the official dinnerware ever since).

Extensive iron works started in Trenton in the 1830's including the Trenton Iron Works of Peter Cooper and Abram S. Hewitt, which by 1885 covered 11 acres of ground. Trenton's several iron industries employed a total of 3,000 men and produced an annual volume exceeding $5,000,000 in value.

John A. Roebling, founder of the Roebling wire rope company and foremost exponent of the use of wire rope in suspension bridges, transferred his plant to Trenton in 1849. Roebling, who built the suspension bridge over Niagara in the early 1850's, received fatal injuries in July, 1869, while inspecting the site of the Brooklyn Bridge. The Roebling sons completed the Brooklyn Bridge, and put the company on the solid footing which saw it become internationally famed (for the George Washington and Golden Gate bridges, among many things).

Industry naturally pushed residential areas outward, to the western part of Trenton and to Ewing Township and Pennington. Colonel John Kunkel of New York started to develop pasture land in Pennington in 1894, and William P. Howe, Sr., developed nearby fields after 1910. Pennington's muddy streets offered little inducement to newcomers. In 1908 Mayor William Radcliffe had to ask the council to set aside "one place where ladies can get on and off trolley cars without wearing boots." However, a Board of Trade began to "boost Pennington" in 1911, and when town officials paved the streets the Board of Trade found its work easier.

Princeton's shady streets and handsome estates began to attract wealthy retired men in the 1890's (including ex-President Grover Cleveland). Its spreading estates thus have been carefully preserved. In more recent years noted scholars have come to Princeton and environs for widely varied research and cultural activities—some connected with the university, some independent. These include the Westminster Choir School, the Rockefeller Institute for Medical Research, the Institute for Advanced Study, the James Forrestal Research Center and many other schools and research centers.

Naturally State House activity always has been vital in Mercer County, yet it has seemed superimposed rather than an integral part of the county.

That stems largely from two reasons—because legislative sessions are held in the evenings and because rapid transportation facilities in and out of Trenton speed legislators homeward after the sessions. Trenton, accordingly, has not become the social center of the state in the manner of most state capitals. Indeed, there is good cause to doubt that it is even the political fulcrum of New Jersey, since decisions made (or taken apart) in State House caucus usually stem from instructions carried by legislators from their local constituencies (or local party bosses).

As a matter of fact, Mercer is important in its own right, over and above State House business. No Jersey county has a more noble colonial heritage (and it is unlikely that any area in the colonies played a more vital part in winning independence). Mercer's educational assets are nationally known. Trenton's industry justifies the claim that "Trenton Makes—the World Takes" because of the diversity and extent of its more than 300 manufacturing plants. Mercer's population has spurted 150 per cent since 1900 (95,300 to 230,000), yet, surprisingly, Mercer stands eighth in the state in value of agricultural products—because of the extensive potato fields and dairy farms surrounding Hightstown and the dairy farms north and west of Princeton.

Obviously, most of Mercer County's personality existed long before its 1838 dual birthdays. The proof of Mercer's right to county status has been found in the easy way parts of four counties have fitted together since. On the basis of Revolutionary War history alone, the county's components belong with one another. On the basis of compatability, they are one. To repeat: The wonder is not that Mercer was born, but rather that delivery took so long.

MORE ABOUT MERCER

Collins, Varnum L. *Princeton Past and Present*. Princeton, Princeton University Press, 1931 (Revised 1945).

Schuyler, Hamilton, 1862, *The Roeblings: A Century of Engineers, Bridge Builders and Industrialists*. Princeton, New Jersey, Princeton University Press, 1931.

Stryker, William Scudder, 1838-1900, *The Battles of Trenton and Princeton*. Boston and New York, Houghton Mifflin Co., 1898.

Trenton Historical Society, *A History of Trenton, 1679-1929*. Trenton, 1929.

Woodward, E. M., *History of Burlington and Mercer Counties, New Jersey*. Philadelphia, Pennsylvania, Everts and Peck, 1883.

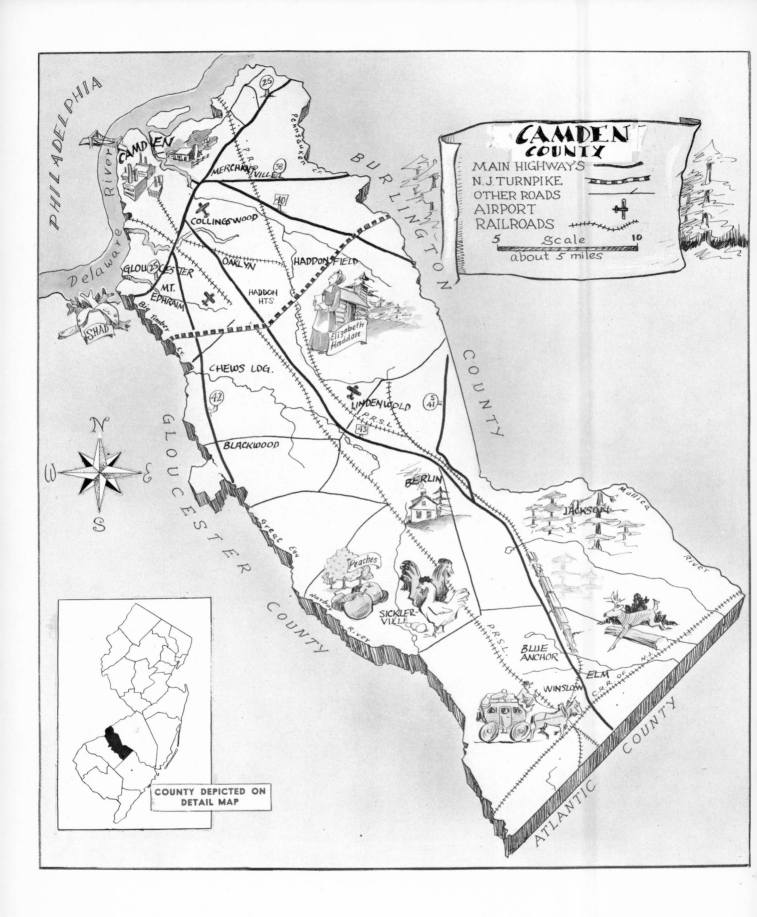

PHILADELPHIA

Delaware River

CAMDEN

25

MERCHANTVILLE

Pennsauken Ck

38

BURLINGTON

40

COLLINGSWOOD

P.R.R.

OAKLYN

HADDONFIELD

GLOUCESTER 25

MT. EPHRAIM

HADDON HTS

Elizabeth Haddon

Big Timber Ck

SHAD

CHEWS LDG.

42

LINDENWOLD

S 41

P.R.S.L.

43

BLACKWOOD

GLOUCESTER COUNTY

Great Egg

Harbor River

Peaches

SICKLER-VILLE

BERLIN

BLUE ANCHOR

P.R.S.L.

WINSLOW

ELM

C.R.R. OF N.J.

JACKSON

Mullica River

BURLINGTON COUNTY

CAMDEN COUNTY
MAIN HIGHWAYS
N.J. TURNPIKE
OTHER ROADS
AIRPORT
RAILROADS
5   Scale   10
about 5 miles

N
W   E
S

ATLANTIC COUNTY

COUNTY DEPICTED ON
DETAIL MAP

CAMDEN

Vivid colors vied with somber tones on the canvas of time as history painted Camden County's portrait. Certainly the background sketched in by the Quakers was quiet enough, yet highlights twinkled—in the romance of remarkable Elizabeth Haddon and in the Celtic enterprise of Mark Newbie's "Patrick's Pence."

Soon the painting became lurid as Philadelphians crossed the river to frolic and gamble in Jersey. However, just as highlights brightened earlier Quaker somberness, now the less volatile residents on the Jersey side insisted firmly that their towns would not be painted permanently red. Walt Whitman touched in pastel contrast after the Civil War, at the same time that industrial giants added body and vigor to the canvas.

Always, however, history painted against a shadow—cast from across the river by Philadelphia.

So all-pervading was the Philadelphia influence, in fact, that Camden city was known merely as "Cooper's Ferry" for its first century. Right from the time William Royden was granted a license in 1688 to run a "very needful and much wanted" ferry across to Philadelphia, the ferries seemed to run "to" Philadelphia rather than "between" towns.

William Cooper arrived in what is now Camden in 1681 and built a home on land he called "Pyne Poynt." Soon after Royden established the ferries, Cooper bought them and built up the cross-river trade, although few had chosen to settle on the Jersey side. Exceptions were the Irish Quakers, who ventured up Newton Creek in 1682 to found towns now known as Collingswood, Woodlynne and South Camden.

One of these was enterprising Mark Newbie, who filled his sea chests with a quantity of half pence struck in Dublin forty years earlier to commemorate a religious war. The coins, known as "Patrick's Pence" because of a likeness of St. Patrick on one side, were not legal tender in Ireland, but in America they were valuable. Soon after his arrival Newbie secured a bank charter from the Assembly and issued the coins, making the Dublin opportunist the country's first banker.

Others settled Gloucester Point at the mouth of Big Timber Creek, close to the spot where a Dutch colony had mysteriously vanished in the 1620's. The disappearance of those twenty-four Dutchmen set ashore by Captain Cornelius Jacobsen Mey in 1623 rivals the story of Roanoke's Lost Colony. Mey built Fort Nassau for the colony before he left, yet when another Dutch ship sailed to the spot in 1631, nothing remained.

Determination marked all early Quakers, but gracious, courageous Elizabeth Haddon was most de-

Hotel and fisheries of "Duke" William J. Thompson.

133

Air view of Camden, home of the famous "Big Four"—soup, ships, pens, and "talking machines."

termined of all. Elizabeth, only eighteen years old, came alone to America in 1701 to develop the 500-acre plantation purchased in 1698 by her London Quaker father, John Haddon. She rode on horseback through the woods to the Haddon acreage on Cooper's Creek, where in a hut in a forest clearing the young Quaker miss settled down to live. Her zeal was not alone due to the pioneer spirit; her heart was in America, along with young Quaker Missionary John Estaugh, who had arrived a few months before.

Eventually John arrived in New Jersey from a Virginia preaching tour and Elizabeth met him. John showed great delay in coming to the point, so Elizabeth (in the words of Longfellow in "Tales of a Wayside Inn") finally whispered to the missionary on the way to Quaker meeting:

"I have received from the Lord a charge to love thee, John Estaugh!"

John spoke for himself soon after, of course, and they were married in her home in 1702. Three times the Estaughs traveled home to London, yet always they returned to Haddonfield. John died on a preaching trip in the West Indies in 1742; Elizabeth lived on to the age of eighty.

Romance brought 21-year-old Betsy Griscom across the Delaware River, too. Betsy, demure in a Quaker bonnet, slipped over to Gloucester Point in 1773. In famous old Hugg's Tavern she stood side by side with John Ross, serious harness maker's apprentice, and heard a justice of the peace marry her "out of meeting"—and to the son of an Episcopal rector at that!

The marriage was kept secret for a year, but in 1774 the Quakers heard of the union and read the young wife out of the faith. Three years later Betsy Griscom Ross sewed thirteen stars on America's first flag.

Just before the Revolutionary War Jacob Cooper had forty acres laid out in a town plot he called Camden, in honor of the powerful English champion of constitutional liberty, Charles Pratt, first Earl of Camden. Cooper visualized six streets north and south, intersected by Cooper and Market streets,

General view of harbor in Gloucester, Armstrong Cork in foreground, Philadelphia in upper left.

Indian King Tavern, built in 1750, Haddonfield.

but no one paid much attention. "Cooper's Ferries" remained the town name.

The Revolution found Camden County (then still a part of Gloucester County) playing a legislative rather than an aggressive role. There were a few skirmishes, because Cooper's Ferries and Haddonfield were important outposts of Philadelphia. "Mad" Anthony Wayne, Count Pulaski and Lafayette strode the streets of Haddonfield with their troops. However, Haddonfield will be remembered as the meeting place in 1777 of the New Jersey Legislature, driven out of Trenton by the Hessians. Meeting in the Indian King Tavern (built in 1750), the Legislature approved the powerful Council on Safety, approved bills involved in the design and preparation of the Great Seal of the State of New Jersey, and enacted a bill substituting "state" for the word "colony" in certain public documents.

Cooper's Ferry also had distinguished visitors in 1777 when the trustees of Princeton College were driven southward by the Hessians. The trustees convened on the Delaware banks to award degrees to the Class of '76.

Philadelphia really discovered its Jersey neigh-

bor after the war. Excellent ferry service lured hundreds across the river, among them winsome Dorothea (Dolly) Payne, who frequently visited at the Indian King in Haddonfield. A Quaker with charm, beauty and vivacity, Dolly married John Todd in 1791 and became a 21-year-old widow in 1793 when Philadelphia's yellow fever plague took her husband. The next year she met and married young James Madison and went on to renown in Washington as Dolly Madison.

Many Philadelphians headed for Gloucester Point, particularly the aristocratic Fox Hunting Club, which gathered there from 1766 to 1818 to chase foxes through Jersey meadows. Later the famed Fish House Club met in a river-front cottage at Delair (north of Camden), and for years farmers from all over the state gathered at Gloucester Point for a tremendous picnic and day-long fishing expedition.

Cooper's Ferries and Gloucester Point suffered diminished importance when the county seat of Gloucester was moved to Woodbury late in the eighteenth century. Out in the eastern regions of the present Camden County several important stage stops grew up: Blue Anchor, where the 1740 inn was a favorite stopping place; Winslow, with its noted "Sailor Boy" tavern; Mt. Ephraim, where Ephraim Albertson kept a top-notch place on the King's Highway; Chew's Landing, where travelers stopped in the two-and-a-half-story pre-Revolutionary War hotel and heard tales of John Chew, war hero; Blackwood, where Uriah Norcross centered his big stagecoach business; and Stratford, where a white horse pictured on a swinging sign gave the road to Absecon its familiar name of White Horse Pike.

Most noted, however, was Long-a-Coming, fifteen miles from the Delaware and astride the pike from Camden to Mays Landing and Somers Point. Good-natured disagreements arose concerning the origin of the name. Some attributed it to sailors who struggled through the forests, hungry and thirsty, until they found a spring near the spot. One drank deeply, then turned and exclaimed: "Wonderful, but sure long-a-coming!" More prosaically, other insisted the name described the slowness of the stagecoaches.

The spring story has good possibilities because Long-a-Coming (now Berlin) is near the ridge where four of South Jersey's most important streams arise. Water from springs on "The Divide" flows eastward to the Atlantic Ocean—in Mullica and Great Egg Harbor rivers—and westward to the Delaware, in Pennsauken and Big Timber creeks. All four streams are part of Camden County's borders.

Cooper's Creek took the first stride toward independence in 1828 when leaders cut themselves off from Newton Township and officially adopted the name "Camden" which Jacob Cooper had given his real estate dream in 1773. It wasn't much of a town—only 1,143 inhabitants—but its proximity to Philadelphia gave the promoters hope (even though one "segar-box" was enough to hold all the mail the new-born Camden received in a day).

Engagingly enough, the gayer Philadelphians were partially responsible for the incorporation of the town. First they flocked over to floating bath

Stratford's eighteenth-century White Horse Hotel, gave name to busy modern pike.

houses near Windmill Island, to the consternation of the modest passengers abroad the ferryboats. Then they frolicked in John Johnson's Vauxhall Gardens (where John's rum toddies were often too strong for weak heads) and Gottleib Zimmerman's Columbia Gardens. All-night reveling made the sterner folk resolve to set up their own government—and their own Police Department.

Sterner laws failed to squelch the Philadelphia sporting set; they simply went elsewhere. The Philadelphia and Camden Race Course, built in 1835 on White Horse Pike near Haddon Heights, welcomed them. Spring and fall meets drew the best horses in the land—and some of the worst people. Betting on the horses cleaned out many a farmer in the neighborhood, and what the horses didn't take the confidence men did.

Drunkenness, gambling and debauchery hastened the track's demise. Despite the pleas of the promoters that they existed only to improve the breed, opposition persisted. Finally, after a great crowd gathered in 1845 to watch Fashion ("The Queen of the Turf") defeat Peytona in a heralded match, the track closed in 1847—much to the improvement of humans.

Agitation of a more important nature swept through the area at the same time, as leaders insisted that Camden County be cut away from Gloucester County. The coming of the Camden & Amboy Railroad to Camden in January, 1834, made the river town thrive. Many opposed a break from Gloucester County, but on March 13, 1844, Camden County was born. Long-a-Coming became the first county seat, but after prolonged political maneuvering county government moved permanently to Camden in 1848.

Camden began to grow. Streets were sliced through cornfields for new homes; hundreds of wagons loaded with South Jersey produce, South Jersey bog iron and Philadelphia-bound shoppers rumbled through town headed for the bustling steam ferries. Camden's principal business continued to be ferrying, with big boats constantly shuttling back and forth, carrying produce to Philadelphia or bringing passengers back to the railroad terminals. There was even hope that Philadelphia families might see the advantages of living in rural Camden County, now that transportation was so good.

Suddenly, on the night of March 15, 1856, that hope died. More than a hundred persons crowded aboard the ferry New Jersey that night before the

Hay and Company's glass works at Winslow.

boat eased out into the ice-clogged Delaware and headed slowly for Camden. In midstream fire broke out near the smokestack. Billowing smoke drove the pilot and engineer from the bridge, leaving the flaming ship to drift helplessly in the river. Ice hampered the rescuers, and the next morning Camden counted forty-eight dead on the New Jersey. Understandably, Philadelphians lost their enthusiasm for living in Camden County.

Civil War time found the county well established, however. Railroads cutting through the forests to Atlantic City encouraged glass manufacturers to start or expand business in Atco, Waterford and Clementon. Near Winslow, J. L. Mason made his famous fruit jar from 1856 to 1862. Real estate men laid out paper cities along the tracks in efforts to lure city people into the salubrious country, only to have the Civil War check their promotions.

A "railroad" of a different nature focused attention on Camden during the Civil War—the "Underground Railroad," the name given to the system used to help slaves escape across the state to freedom. Camden was an important underground point and tradition says that escaping slaves sometimes hid in the cellar of Haddonfield's Indian King Tavern. A few of the freed slaves eventually found their way to Snow Hill (now Lawnside), a town set up by Abolitionists in 1840 for emancipated slaves, but most of the fugitives headed for New England or Canada as quickly as possible.

The middle of the nineteenth century marked Camden's emergence as a manufacturing city of note. Richard Esterbrook came from England in 1858 to establish the Esterbrook steel pen factory, the first of its kind in the United States and forerunner of the Camden business which today produces 200,000,000 steel pens annually. Nearby, Joseph Campbell and Abram A. Anderson started to pack fancy peas and tomatoes in 1869. Soon the name "Campbell" became nationally known. However, it remained for John T. Dorrance, who joined the company in 1897, to conceive the line of condensed soups for which Campbell's is today universally recognized.

Other businesses and industries came before 1880: lumber yards, tanneries, worsted mills, hat makers, iron works, machine works, chemical and dye plants, silver platers and porcelain teeth makers. Still, as Philadelphia prepared its centennial celebration in 1876 (from which Camden hoped to gain business), Camden newspapers carried complaints that cattle ran at large in the Second Ward, that the absence of streetcars on Sundays ruined business, and that street lights were doused on nights "when the moon was supposed to shine," whether nature cooperated or not.

Across Newton Creek, Gloucester town experienced an economic resurgence in 1844 when David S. Bowen, Philadelphia dry goods merchant, started textile manufacturing in the big four-story Washington Mills. Population jumped from 200 in 1840 to 5,347 in 1880. The town enjoyed that prosperity, but its views were split on William J. (Billy) Thompson, shad fisherman, hotel owner and sporting man, who arrived in 1869 to revive the gay era.

"Billy" made his start in shad fishing, then opened a hotel specializing in shad toasted on a white oak plank. Extensive advertising lured people from all over the world to eat Gloucester planked shad. Attempting to make certain that transportation was convenient for his customers, Thompson tried to buy the ferryboats but the owners refused. Just to add insult to injury they stopped running boats after midnight.

Thompson retaliated by importing the steamboats *Sylvan Dell* and *Sylvan Glen* and running them twenty-four hours a day. He built a race track in 1890 and became enmeshed in a state-wide controversy which led to strong antiracing movements in the 1890's. Racing was outlawed in New Jersey and the downfall of the "Duke of Gloucester" was swift. First "Billy's" power vanished, then

Armstrong Cork, McAndrews & Forbes Co., and Southwork Manufacturing plants, Camden.

Where Walt Whitman lived in Camden for eight years.

his wealth, and he died in Ireland in absolute poverty.

The hustle and bustle of Camden after the Civil War suited Walt Whitman, the "Good Grey Poet," who came to live with a brother in Camden in 1873, soon after he suffered a paralytic stroke.

Whitman's Camden period was the happiest of his life. He lived to see a transformation of public opinion regarding his writings and his days were productive and pleasant. He revised "Leaves of Grass" for five new editions between 1876 and 1892, and wrote "Specimen Days and Collect" in 1882-83. After he moved to 330 Mickle Street, Camden, in 1884 Whitman enjoyed the company of new-found friends. Facing death in 1892, he described himself as "a little spark of soul dragging a great lummox of a corpse-body to and fro." Friends buried him in a simple rough-cut vault in Harleigh Cemetery. The vault bore the inscription which Whitman wrote himself: "For that of me which is to die."

Whitman died at a time when Camden began to emerge as a great city, described by an 1890 writer as "crystallizing the life of Southern New Jersey and offering a thousand streams of influence and succor to its giant companion on the west side of the Delaware."

Chance brought Camden one of South Jersey's greatest boons in 1894 when a customer stepped into Eldridge R. Johnson's repair shop with one of the crude talking machines of the time. Johnson studied it and recognized its potentialities. He substituted a flat disc record for the cylinders perfected by Edison and began manufacturing machines. Johnson incorporated Victor Talking Machine Company in 1901, the year the little fox terrier listening to "His Master's Voice" was born. Victor became the largest producer of phonograph records in the world long before Johnson sold out to a syndicate in January, 1927, for a reputed $28,000,000 and 240,000 share of RCA stock.

Camden's "big four"—soup, pens, talking machines, and ships—was rounded out in 1899, when the New York Shipbuilding Company started to build its works in Camden. Shipbuilding started on November 27, 1900. Ships for both World Wars slid down the New York ways—including the *Idaho* and the *Saratoga*. The great transatlantic liners *Manhattan* and *Washington* were among peacetime vessels built in the plant.

Industrial growth naturally led to the emergence of a large local working class, one of whom was Peter J. McGuire, who fittingly enough started his earnest quest for an eight-hour day in the 1870's in

Fifth tee at Pine Valley's world-famed golf course.

the city which bore the stamp of Walt Whitman's democracy. In 1881 McGuire helped Samuel Gompers found the American Federation of Labor, and McGuire's insistence on a holiday for labor led Congress to establish Labor Day in 1894. "The Father of Labor Day" is buried near Pennsauken.

Proud city fathers called Camden "The Biggest Little City in the World" in 1915 promotions. If only, they said wistfully, there was a bridge to Philadelphia.

Actually, Camden leaders had been saying that as far back as 1816, but not until July 5, 1926, did the dream come true. That day President Calvin Coolidge dedicated the 8,536-foot-Delaware River Bridge linking the Delaware River cities. Four years in the making, the $40,000,000 span was the longest suspension bridge in the world at dedication time.

The bridging of the Delaware might well have cast Camden even more sharply into Philadelphia's shadow, yet strangely the bridge seemed to set Camden free and in new-found equality rub the shadow from the portrait. That was partially be-

cause Philadelphia commuters began to come across the bridge to find home sites in Camden County. Industry attained new prosperity. County population increased sharply' to three times in 1950 what it was in 1900. Camden became New Jersey's fifth largest city, independent and alive to its responsibilities and potentialities.

Outward from the river the highways each year bear hundreds of thousands of Philadelphia vacationists across the state to Atlantic City and Cape May, a continuation of a 150-year-old tradition. The old stagecoach stops are mainly gone, yet the highways bear the old names—Black Horse and White Horse pikes. Near the site of old Long-a-Coming, just off the main road to Atlantic City, is Pine Valley, the golf course whose sandy fairways and tricky greens have resisted the par-breaking efforts of the country's top golfers.

Much of Camden city's past is swallowed up in the industrial growth, although many narrow streets still show its ferry-town beginnings. Heritage lives on, however, in places like Haddonfield, where

Homes of Camden and Philadelphia commuters are ranged in neat rows on Camden's outskirts.

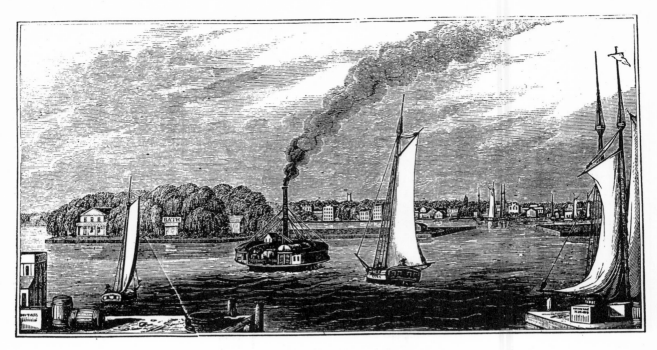

Camden, from Walnut Street ferry, Philadelphia, 1840.

some of the charm and simplicity of Elizabeth Haddon and the winsomeness of Dolly Madison can be felt in a visit to Indian King Tavern.

All in all, Camden has sat for an attractive portrait.

MORE ABOUT CAMDEN

Boyer, Charles Shimer, *The Span of a Century*. Camden, New Jersey, Centennial Anniversary Committee of Camden, N. J., 1928.

Camden County Anniversary, 1681-1931. Two hundred and fiftieth anniversary. Camden Chamber of Commerce, Camden, N. J.

Clement, John, *Revolutionary Reminiscences of Camden County*. Camden, New Jersey, S. Chew and Sons Co., 1876.

Haddonfield, N. J. The two hundreth anniversary of the settlement of Haddonfield, New Jersey, celebrated October 18, 1913. Publication Committee, Haddonfield, N. J., 1913.

Prowell, George R., *The History of Camden County, New Jersey*. Philadelphia, Pennsylvania, L. J. Richards and Co., 1886.

The GARDEN SPOT

We call New Jersey "The Garden State," and we mainly mean four South Jersey counties on the western rim of the thick Pines.

That would be Burlington, Gloucester, Salem and Cumberland counties, where the loamy soil grows vegetables at the mere dropping of a seed. One-third of all New Jersey farms are in those four counties, and while The Garden Spot spills over into Monmouth County and parts of other counties, its principal domain is the Southern Delaware River banks.

This is the Garden Spot . . .

Where Burlington County farmers speed their dew-fresh products from field to market; where Salem tomatoes add zest to flavorful South Jersey catsup; where Gloucester County has ever been noted as "The Philadelphia Garden Patch"; and where Cumberland County's Seabrook Farms has developed one of the biggest agricultural enterprises in the country.

This is the Garden Spot . . .

Where early Swedes and Finns and Quakers turned to the soil and found their reward; where intensive use of greensand marl a century ago saved the fields, and where the growing of vegetables has always been THE way of life.

This is the Garden Spot, where 70 per cent of all New Jersey vegetables are grown; where 75 per cent of all Jersey tomatoes are picked; where 95 per cent of all the state's asparagus is raised. This is a land where glass manufacturing got its start, where oystering pays off, and where tremendous new industries are moving into the lower Delaware River region. This is where today's gardens and tomorrow's industrial progress meet.

But, for now, it is still The Garden Spot . . .

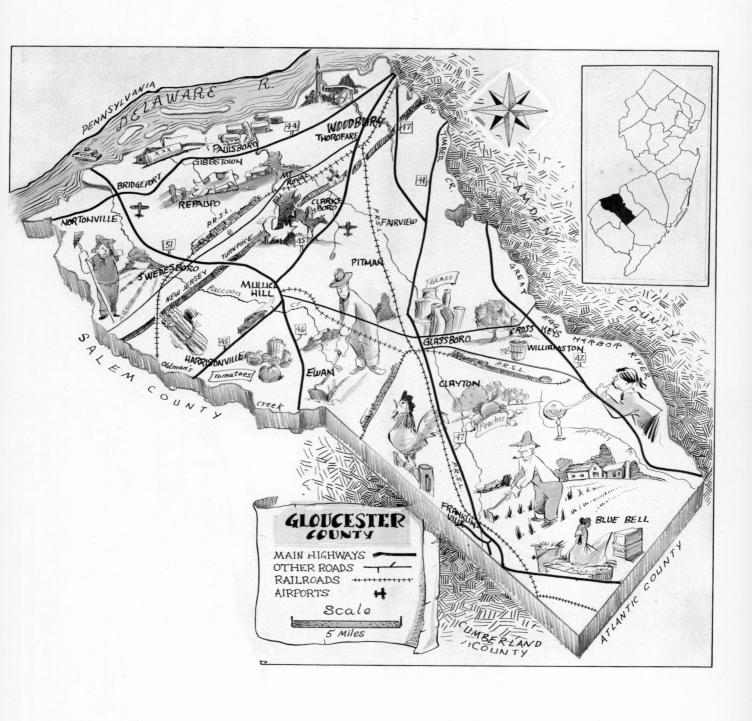

Part of the "Garden Patch of Philadelphia."

GLOUCESTER

Possibly the most "English" of all New Jersey county names is Gloucester, yet logically that South Jersey agricultural county might well be "Stockholm" or something equally Scandinavian. Long before English Quakers came, Swedes and Finns occupied the county creek banks, but the name "Gloucester" indicates what happened: the English moved in and moved ahead; the amiable Swedes moved over.

Except for Swedesboro on Raccoon Creek, the apparent Swedish story is gone from Gloucester, but it lives on in the strong influence the Swedes had in making the county an area of relatively small farms. Today only a handful of its 1,900 farms are more than fifty acres in size. Swedes led the way to intensive cultivation, to the truck gardening which as early as 1870 earned Gloucester a still-meaningful nickname—"Philadelphia's Garden Patch."

"New Sweden" began in 1638 on the west bank of the Delaware River near what is today Wilmington, in a region also claimed by the Dutch. For years the Dutch and Swedes struggled as fiercely as limited manpower on both sides permitted, and eventually both lost, because in 1664 England accepted the Dutch surrender of the Delaware River valley. Significantly, neither the Dutch nor the English paid the slightest attention to Swedish claims.

Not that the Swedes cared much by that time. Rocky soil near Wilmington resisted their husbandry, so they slowly drifted across to the Jersey side of the Delaware—as individuals, not in colonies—to break the rich soil. Since many of them were indentured servants who had left their masters, they worried little who ruled the land, as long as they farmed it.

Swedish centers arose, particularly along Raccoon Creek (although as a later historian pointed out, Swedish settlements were merely scattered farms, "held together by the gossiping propensities of Swedish matrons"). Cordiality between Swedes and Quakers existed from the time the first English colonist arrived in the late 1670's; Swedes acted as interpreters when the Quakers bought land between Timber and Oldman's creeks from the Indians—and no one remembered or cared that other enterprising Indians had long before sold the same land to other Swedes.

One of the early Quakers, William Penn, showed great interest in the English colonization and in 1681 seriously considered the present site of Paulsboro for the center of his vast holdings. He decided the land was too low, however, and a year later turned to the higher west bank of the Delaware River to found Philadelphia.

Swedesboro, as an artist saw it in 1844.

147

All West Jersey at the time revolved around Burlington, but soon the Swedes and Quakers resented the long trip to the West Jersey provincial capital. Accordingly, on May 28, 1686, representatives met at Arwames (now Gloucester city) and organized Gloucester County. Many historians maintain that the representatives formed the county themselves, without action or permission of the provincial Legislature, thus making Gloucester the only county in New Jersey deriving its existence from the direct action of its people. However, other historians insist that the Legislature gave at least tacit approval to the new county.

"Old" Gloucester was a sprawling county, embodying all the present Camden, Atlantic and Gloucester counties—nearly 1,200 square miles, or about one-seventh of the state. Atlantic's founding in 1837 took away 613 square miles and Camden's founding in 1844 took away another 225 square miles, leaving "New" Gloucester only 330 square miles.

Repaupo and Mullica Hill became centers of

Swedish life until the completion of the King's Highway to Raccoon (Swedesboro) shifted influence there in 1702. Quaker life centered in Woodbury, founded in 1683 by a member of the Wood family from Bury, England. Slowly the Quaker influence came to dominate the county.

Old-time Swedes fought to keep themselves and their children "Swedish." Establishment of the Swedish Lutheran Church in Raccoon in 1703 helped (even though the first minister, Lars Tollstadius, possessed such dubious character that in 1706 he was "bound over" to Burlington Court for getting Ole Persson's daughter into difficulties). A Repaupo school set up in 1715 perpetuated old-country language and customs for years; but "Swedishness" couldn't last.

Young Englishmen found young Swedes attractive, and vice versa, and nature took it from there. By 1750 the assimilation was so complete that few even complained when their town name of "Raccoon" was anglicized to "Swedesboro." The following year the church minister agreed to keep

Kings Highway, which dates back more than 250 years, is the main street of Swedesboro.

Attractive, busy street in Woodbury.

records in English rather than Swedish. Thus expired "New Sweden."

Gloucester County assumed a two-fold importance in the Revolutionary War: its "garden patches" attracted food-seekers from both armies and its strategic position just below Philadelphia made it an obvious spot for river-dominating fortifications.

Continental land agents bought a large plot of land at Billingsport on the mouth of Mantua Creek on July 4, 1776—the first land purchased by the just-born United States of America. The infant government quickly built a fort at Billingsport, and in 1777, when Philadelphia's fall seemed imminent, the army threw up Fort Mercer on the bluff at Red Bank, directly across from South Philadelphia.

Four hundred ragged and despairing Rhode Island volunteers waited behind Fort Mercer's crude walls for the attack they knew must come after the fall of Philadelphia. Finally, on October 22, 1777, 2,000 Hessians struck under cover of a river barrage from the 64-gun *Augusta* and the 18-gun *Merlin*. Colonel Christopher Green cautioned his American troops to hold their fire until the Hessians reached the walls.

A hail of musket fire and grape shot cut the Hessians viciously. They withdrew, then charged again, only to become panicky in the face of the murderous fire. Their disorderly flight left 400 dead and wounded under the walls, including their mortally wounded commander, Colonel Donop.

Meanwhile, American guns mounted on barges sank both the *Augusta* and the *Merlin*, but not before shot from the British vessels peppered the side of James Whitall's farmhouse near Fort Mercer. Inside the house, Mrs. Anne Cooper Whitall sat calmly spinning while the battle raged outside. Suddenly a cannon ball blasted through the side of the house and hurtled past Mrs. Whitall into the far wall. The imperturbable Quaker picked up her wheel, went into the cellar—and continued to spin. Later, as she bound up the wounds of the Hessians, she scolded them for coming to America to butcher the colonists.

Continental troops abandoned both Fort Mercer and Billingsport within a few weeks, however, and the British held full sway over the lower Delaware, enabling Lord Cornwallis's foraging party to exploit Gloucester's gardens (whenever bold "Mad" Anthony Wayne didn't beat him to the harvests). Cornwallis stayed in Woodbury briefly, from November 21-24, in the home taken from Patriot John Cooper, brother of Anne Cooper Whitall.

Woodbury's emergence as Gloucester's leading town began in 1787, when the decrepit old county buildings in Gloucester town burned. The following year the cornerstone for a new courthouse was laid in Woodbury and county government moved to Woodbury to stay.

The village at the head of navigation on Woodbury Creek prospered even then. It took justifiable pride in its progressiveness: in its Free school, started by the Quakers in 1773; in its famed Woodbury Academy, opened in 1791; and in its Gloucester County Abolition Society, one of the nation's first such groups when founded in 1793.

America's first airborne trip came to an end in a field near Woodbury in 1793, when Jean Pierre François Blanchard stepped from a balloon after a leisurely trip from Philadelphia. The smiling Frenchman bore a letter from Washington and told the cautious few who ventured near of the tumultuous sendoff Philadelphia's sophisticated populace had given less than an hour before.

Blanchard was diverting (if a bit frightening), but far more vital to Gloucester County's growth were the Stangers, seven German brothers who came from Caspar Wistar's Salem County glass works in 1775 to start the glass industry which boomed in

Reminder of Glassboro's vanished glass industry.

many parts of Gloucester for more than a century.

Settling down in the dense forest at what is now Glassboro, the seven Stangers built a successful glass factory and naturally enough accepted as much Continental money as they could get. Unfortunately, they had more brains than luck, since when Congress announced in 1780 that forty Continental dollars equaled only one gold or silver dollar the Stangers learned the sad meaning of "not worth a Continental." They went to debtors' prison and their glass works passed into the control of Colonel Thomas Heston.

Eventually the Stangers returned, some of them to work for Heston and some to begin other plants. The Stanger success prompted other glass ventures —at first in Malaga, Williamstown and Clayton, and later in Woodbury in the 1880's. All disappeared because of cheaper competition elsewhere, but while they lasted their owners prospered (partially because they owned almost everything in their glass villages and took back in trade what they paid out in wages).

Gloucester County's pre-Civil War social life centered in the many taverns scattered over the area, such as Clarksboro's "Death of the Fox" Inn, where sportsmen gathered to chase the elusive Reynard; the White Horse Tavern, which gave Five Points the name "Hell Town"; George Sheat's hotel in Bridgeport, where men gathered to down some grog before watching the horse races in the village streets, and the Williamsport Tavern, where boastful hunters met.

Inevitably tavern talk got around to Jonas Cattell, half-historical, half-legendary Gloucester figure whose life spanned almost a century, from 1758 to 1854.

When he was fifty years old Jonas outran an Indian in a race from Mount Holly to Woodbury. Once he walked eighty miles to Cape May, delivered a letter, and returned with an answer the next day. He loved fox hunting, but he traveled on foot, and the horses, riders, hounds and foxes were always more tired than Jonas. Those feats had a strong element of fact in them, but such old hunter's tales as his wrestling a 15-foot sturgeon in the Delaware prompted the disbelievers to declare that Jonas's imagination was as broad and his tongue as stretched, as his legs were swift.

Woodbury attracted hundreds of surrounding farmers on Saturday afternoons in the 1820's—to drink a little "Boston Peculiar" (New England Rum), to wrestle and pitch quoits and to watch

Bridgeport terminal of the Delaware River Ferry to Chester, Pa.

the militia drill (armed with everything from 1776 flintlocks to cornstalks). Gaiety took a back seat in 1825, however, to the talk that Camden challenged Woodbury's right to retain the county seat. Bitter wrangling engulfed the county that year before Woodbury won a victory at the polls (and, according to some, precipitated Camden County's secession in 1844).

Firmly established as the county seat, Woodbury rejoiced even more in 1831 when the 75-year-old dam across Woodbury Creek below the town was broken. Built in 1766, the dam long had hamstrung the village at the head of navigation. Thus, when two sloops sailed through the broken dam, crowds cheered and cannon roared a welcome. An orator enthusiastically pointed out that the tide which "ran out 75 years ago finally has run back."

Five years later a railroad stretched down to cement Woodbury's destiny to Camden and Philadelphia. Nevertheless, Gloucester grew slowly, mainly because of poor roads. The county's first turnpike was not built until 1848, at a time when the turnpike movement was nearly a half-century old elsewhere in New Jersey.

A strong temperance movement swept over Gloucester in the two decades before the Civil War. Paradoxically, a bottle made in Glassboro for the 1840 Presidential campaign of William Henry Harrison helped to bring the word "booze" into common use. Shaped like log cabins, supposedly symbolic of Harrison's humble beginning, the bottles were filled by a Philadelphia distiller, E. C. Booz. Soon they became known as "Booz" bottles, popularizing the word "booze," which had been used as early as 1812 by Parson Weems.

In view of its long-time belief in the abolition of slavery, Gloucester naturally stood solidly behind the Union cause in the Civil War. Mullica Hill even sent an all-Quaker company into active service. Immediately after the war a pressing religious fervor swept Gloucester, resulting in the establishment during the 1870's of huge camp meeting grounds at Pitman and Malaga (both of which still exist, by the way).

Two centuries of agricultural dominance passed before two men—one a home-town boy and the other from across the river—gave Gloucester its first large-scale industrial impetus.

George G. Green, son of a county farmer, started things on a big scale when he returned to Woodbury on Thanksgiving Day, 1872, with his new bride. He had been away several years, proving himself as a Civil War veteran, a salesman and a druggist. Now he was back to buy and run his father's small patent medicine business.

The Green medicines long had been known locally. "Green's August Flower" cured dyspepsia (and so on) and "Boschee's German Syrup" cured illnesses of the chest (and so on). George G. Green scoffed at "cure-alls" and "modestly placed his medicines before the public." He gave away 10,000,000 free samples of "Boschee's" and 2,400,000 samples of "August Flower." Five million almanacs went forth from Green's each year to advertise the products.

Hundreds of Woodbury residents secured work in the spreading Green enterprises and George prospered greatly. He built a huge hotel in Pasadena, California, and a big summer home at Lake Hopatcong. George G. Green became one of South Jersey's biggest men; in Woodbury he was all.

The town's biggest night took place annually when Green's nineteen salesmen came home to a meeting at Green's house (to which they wore high silk hats and swallow-tail coats). Each year, before the Greens left for Pasadena, the family's private "palace car" stood on a siding and all townsfolk were invited to go through at their convenience.

(Eventually the patent medicine business declined; today several smaller concerns occupy the big Green factory and only a handful of employees work in the Green company.)

Out on the Delaware River, where shad fishing had brought wealth and health to scores of fishermen, big business grew, too. At Gibbstown, Lammot du Pont of the noted Wilmington du Pont enterprises bought a farm in 1880 and built the largest dynamite plant in the world.

For months Lammot and his cousin William, construction boss, rowed almost daily across the wide Delaware to watch the progress of the new plant rising amid the surrounding cornfields. Du Pont initiated features at Gibbstown which, with only minor changes, are standard practice in the

South Jersey tomatoes shipped from Swedesboro to one of South Jersey canning plants in 1923.

Sweet potatoes are an important crop in Gloucester.

explosives field today. Ironically, Lammot du Pont died in March, 1884, in an explosion at the plant.

Some years after, in 1902, the du Pont company opened its Eastern Laboratory at Gibbstown, the beginning of the company's research program and said to be the first industrial research laboratory in the country. Among hundreds of other developments, the first commercial production of TNT was initiated at Eastern Laboratory.

The last half of the nineteenth century saw agriculture reach maturity, particularly in the eastern section of Gloucester where liberal uses of fertilizer turned sandy soil into rich farmlands. Fittingly enough, many of the farms spread over acres of former forest land, which the defunct glass industry had cleared to obtain timber for use as charcoal in its plants. Elsewhere in the pine regions the glass and bog iron industries were blamed for ruining the land; in Gloucester, farmers made the clearings blossom.

Gloucester's growing pains, which included a new $75,000 courthouse started in 1885 and a new $10,000 span built to replace the covered bridge over the creek in 1891, resulted in a minor revolt

in 1890. Angered by the extravagance of the freeholders in boosting the county tax collector's annual salary from $250 to $500, the people elected a majority of Democrats to the Board of Freeholders in 1890, the only Democratic board in Gloucester's history.

How Gloucester grew, yet remained rural, appears in these headline-making items from 1890 to World War I: 1891, John Blake, owner of the Pole Tavern, killed his 1,157-pound hog after a weight-guessing contest which excited all of South Jersey; 1892, Swedesboro got the first mile of stone road in New Jersey under a new state law; 1893, little Woodbury was seventh among New Jersey cities in postal revenues because of the huge volume of mail from Green's Laboratories; 1900, Postmaster Jessup was soundly denounced by merchants because he suggested free home mail delivery (which would mean the end of afternoon window shopping, merchants said); 1900, Dr. Buzby sold his three horses in Swedesboro and bought an automobile; 1911, New Jersey had only twenty miles of turnpike road left, seventeen of them in Gloucester; 1915, the county bought the seven-mile Woodbury-to-Mullica Hill toll road for $25,000.

Since 1900 Gloucester's population has almost tripled, from 31,905 to more than 92,000 in 1952. Still, the county's outlook is essentially rural, although Woodbury's life is attuned to its heavy percentage of commuters, who go daily to Camden or Philadelphia, or who work for du Pont or one of the big oil companies in the industrial area stretched along most of the county's Delaware River border.

Today there is speculative stirring over what the future holds for Gloucester now that the National Steel Company has purchased 2,800 acres of farmland between Thorofare and the Delaware River for a modern steel plant. The county knows that an additional 6,000 acres of farmland back from the river will be needed for houses for the workers. Experts say that that is just the beginning, predicting that subsidiary plants will come and more farmland will disappear.

However that may be, right now Gloucester is still a thriving garden patch; more than 51 per cent of its total area is under cultivation, producing vast quantities of peppers, asparagus, tomatoes, cucumbers and cantaloupes. Gloucester leads New Jersey in all those categories and its total farm income exceeds $14,000,000 annually. Tomatoes, asparagus and sweet potatoes abound in the areas around

Swedesboro and Mullica Hill; peach orchards surround Glassboro.

If industry ever crowds agriculture out, or confines it, Gloucester will be strangely different.

Ever since those first Swedes poked up Raccoon Creek 300 years ago the land has been meant for the plow, reserved, in a way, as a garden patch, while elsewhere cities grew—and ate.

MORE ABOUT GLOUCESTER

Cushing, Thomas, and Sheppard, Charles E., *History of the Counties of Gloucester, Salem and Cumberland, New Jersey*. Philadelphia, Pennsylvania, Everts and Peck, 1883.

Federal Writers' Project, *The Swedes and Finns in New Jersey*. Bayonne, New Jersey, New Jersey Print Co., 1938.

Mickle, Isaac, *Reminiscences of Old Gloucester, or Incidents in the History of the Counties of Gloucester, Atlantic and Camden, New Jersey*. Philadelphia, Pennsylvania, T. Ward, 1845.

Record of the 250th Anniversary of the Formation of Gloucester County. Woodbury, N. J. Gloucester County Freeholders, 1936.

Stewart, Frank H., *Notes on Old Gloucester County, New Jersey*. Woodbury, N. J., Constitution Company, 3 vols. (1917, 1934, 1937).

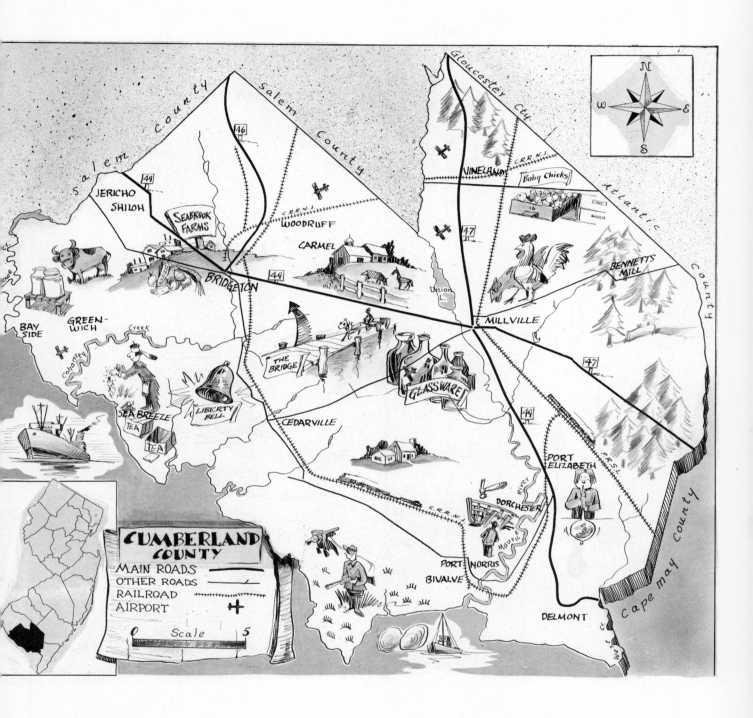

The oyster fleet tied up at Bivalve.

CUMBERLAND

Cumberland County's prosperity fits as naturally and easily as a tailor-made suit. Everything about the county—rich soil, equable climate, navigable streams, teeming oyster beds, even its fine sand—made the good life inevitable. There's nothing of the *nouveau riche* about Cumberland either; too much oldfashioned charm lingers for that.

Those who know Cumberland best insist that it is "tidewater country," closer in outlook and tradition to Maryland and Delaware than to the rest of New Jersey. The interesting corollary is that two of Cumberland's vital towns (Bridgeton and Millville) are at the head of navigation, yet are deep in the county interior. In fact, the twisting Cohansey Creek and the serpentine Maurice River have been vital keys to unlocking Cumberland's riches—and to preserving her "tidewater" character.

The broad mouth of the Maurice enticed Swedish settlers off Delaware Bay in the 1630's (and tradition says Swedes named the river after the ship *Prince Maurice*, which burned in the river at a spot known as "No Man's Friend"). Swedish settlements near Dorchester and Leesburg disappeared soon, probably before Quaker colonizer John Fenwick envisioned "Ye Greate Streete" of Greenwich on the Cohansey in the 1680's.

Fenwick's fancy of a street a hundred feet wide and two miles long came into being a year after his death in 1683. Settlers from New England built on 16-acre plots along "Ye Greate Streete" and immediately opened trade with the outside world, particularly with the village of Philadelphia, founded by William Penn in 1682.

Up creek, Richard Hancock, Fenwick's surveyor, built a sawmill in 1686 where Bridgeton now stands, but his interest was timber, not town-founding. Across the Cohansey from Greenwich, Connecticut colonists arrived in the 1690's to establish New England Cross Roads and Fairton.

Cohansey, as all of the region surrounding the creek came to be known, enjoyed good harvests, to the extent that a legislative act in 1695 authorized annual Greenwich fairs in April and October. Philadelphia traders and their ladies found the fairs worth sailing up Cohansey Creek to visit and the twice-yearly event continued uninterrupted until 1762.

Just as the Cohansey united interior and coast, it divided settlers on the east and west banks until those near Hancock's sawmill in 1716 built the bridge that gave the settlement the name "Cohansey Bridge" or merely "The Bridge."

"The Bridge" it remained, too, after the Legislature sliced away about half of Salem County to form Cumberland County on January 19, 1748. even when the county seat was moved from Greenwich to "The Bridge" in December, 1748, the ap-

Millville, 1840, view of manufacturing plants on south side.

157

pellation remained unchanged. Indeed, the first courthouse had been built and burned and a second courthouse constructed before the hamlet finally called itself Bridgetown in 1765.

Cumberland prosperity centered in Greenwich as the town rolled toward a 1774 date with immortality. Largest town in Cumberland and boasting a port good enough to carry on trade from Philadelphia to Boston, Greenwich seemed a logical place for Captain J. Allen to drop anchor from his brig *Greyhound* in the gathering dusk of December 12, 1774. Captain Allen, knowing that his cargo of tea would be unwelcome in Philadelphia, guessed that it might be safe in Greenwich, particularly since Dan Bowen was willing to store it in his cellar.

Townspeople, aware that the tea had been unloaded, buzzed angrily but generally agreed to wait on a decision from Bridgetown. Then, on the night of December 22 a little band met in the home of Richard and Lewis Howell near Shiloh, disguised themselves as Indians, and headed for Green-

wich. They stole through Greenwich's darkened streets, removed the tea to an open field, and destroyed it in a roaring fire which lit up the village and indelibly marked Greenwich's place in time.

Naturally there were protests from financially interested nonpatriots, and seven of the tea burners were brought to trial in April, 1775. Sheriff Jonathan Elmer, brother of one of the "Indians," summoned a sympathetic jury, foremanned by Daniel Elmer, Jonathan's nephew, and it was not surprising that the burners were found not guilty. That trial, incidentally, involved at least three New Jersey citizens who later became outstanding. Richard Howell, one of the burners, became governor of the state in 1792 and was succeeded by Joseph Bloomfield, counsel for the defendants, in 1801. Sheriff Elmer was elected one of New Jersey's first two U. S. senators.

Reputedly the tea burners were led by Reverend Philip Vickers Fithian, along with his cousin, Joel Fithian, and Andrew Hunter. Philip kept copious

Lane toward Cohansey Creek, Greenwich, where patriots destroyed sloop *Greyhound*.

Cumberland County courthouse, Bridgeton.

journals—of his Princeton College days, of his travels in Virginia, of his love for Elizabeth Beatty, and of his life as an Army chaplain in the early days of the Revolution. His death of camp fever in 1776 cut short his brilliant existence, but his journals (published by Princeton University Press in 1900 and 1934) make him live on.

Half of Cumberland's population by Revolutionary War time lived west of Cohansey Creek in one-sixth of the county area. A stage route from Greenwich to Philadelphia began in 1774, via Roadstown—and skipping Bridgetown. Out along the Maurice River a few settlers had established Mattock's Landing (now Mauricetown) in the 1730's, and Lucas Peterson built a solitary house at Shingle Landing (now Millville) in 1750.

Agriculture dominated Cumberland life well before the strife with England and naturally the county became looked upon as a wartime food supplier. General Washington declared that if it hadn't been for the provisions sent by Cumberland and Salem counties to feed his troops at Valley Forge he would have had no army to continue the war. Patriotic feeling ran high, even though the war little touched the county, and the reading of the Declaration of Independence from the courthouse

steps in 1776 called for prolonged pealing of Bridgetown's own Liberty Bell.

Bridgetown had special cause for grief in 1780 when word came of the sinking of the schooner *Gov. Livingston* off the Capes of the Delaware. Bridgetown's patriots had built the ship and sent her across the seas on only one successful voyage before a British frigate ended her glory days.

As the eighteenth century waned Cumberland grew but slowly. An "actual count" showed only 8,248 persons living in the county in 1790, with about 300 of those in the county seat. Considerable up-county wheat cleared through Bridgetown and Greenwich for Philadelphia, but local residents had to be content with once-weekly mail service. On the Maurice River, life centered about Port Elizabeth, established in 1785 by Mrs. Elizabeth Clark Bodeley, Salem widow.

James Lee, a wandering Irishman whose ability to establish industry exceeded his interest in continuing it, saw gold in the inexhaustible quantities of fine sand surrounding Port Elizabeth and brought glass-making to Cumberland in 1799. He set up the Eagle Glass Works in Port Elizabeth that year, then in 1806 started making window glass in Millville. From those beginnings Cumberland has become New Jersey's principal glass center. (Bridgeton got its first plant in 1830 and Vineland welcomed a plant in the 1870's).

Millville's growth started in 1803 when Joseph Buck laid out a town and built himself a fine mansion on the corner of Main and High streets. Later several entrepreneurs banded together as the Union Company and dammed the river to form Union Lake as a source of power to run their mills.

Downstream, Joseph J. ("Coffee") Jones, son of a wealthy Philadelphia coffee merchant, bought hundreds of acres near Jonathan Dallas's Ferry and renamed the village "Port Norris" after his son Norris Jones. "Coffee" tried raising sheep and did well until an 1812 storm killed thousands of his animals. He prospered in the lumber industry but discouragement overcame him when the British captured his wood-ship *Plow Boy* in the War of 1812 and demanded $1,000 ransom. Soon "Coffee" disposed of his real estate in a lottery and moved away, leaving only his son's name in memory.

Bridgetown acquired a bank—the first in South Jersey below Camden—in 1816 and in the same year had the "w" dropped from its name when the bank issued notes bearing the apparent typographical error, "Bridgeton." Residents liked the shortened form (or else felt it would be easier to change the town name than a bank note).

Coincidentally with the coming of the bank, hard times hit the predominantly agricultural county. That summer of 1816 was the noted "cold summer," when frost touched the fields often during July and August. Men wore their "great coats" in the fields at harvest time, and shook their heads in dismay when they reaped scarcely enough grain to supply seed for the next spring. Financial distress struck the county; hundreds migrated to Ohio.

Cumberland soil led the way back. In 1825 a county fair report declared, "it was manifest that increasing agricultural spirit would speedily supersede the toilsome and unprofitable labor of cutting timber." Bridgeton, with a new name and booming nail and glass factories, especially moved along —so much so that Millville's 1837 bid for the county seat stunned Cohansey people.

Bridgeton beat back the effort in a public referendum, but Millville threw the controversy to the Board of Freeholders for final decision. There a

4 to 4 vote prolonged the debate. Finally, without advance warning to Millville, "Columbia Township" was born—and lived only long enough to cast a deciding vote for Bridgeton before lapsing quietly back into Hopewell Township.

Regular steamboat service between Bridgeton and Philadelphia started in 1845 but it had difficulty competing with the railroad from Camden which rolled into Millville in 1859 and into Bridgeton in 1861.

By then Cumberland had thrown itself wholeheartedly into the Civil War. It could boast that no other county in the nation lent the Union cause more men, in proportion to population, than Cumberland.

The county sent off its famed Cumberland Greys in the summer of 1861, after a vigorous flag presentation ceremony in which the principal speaker punctuated his remarks by thumping the floor with the flagstaff—so often and so enthusiastically that the out-spread wings of the handsome golden eagle atop the staff broke off. Later, news of the fall of

Sand pit near Mauricetown supplies sand for glass works in Bridgeton, Millville and Vineland.

P. J. Ritter Company, Bridgeton, producers of tomato products.

Richmond sparked a tremendous torchlight parade, led by Professor Dorville's Band and highlighted by the singing of the "Star Spangled Banner" by young ladies seated on the window sills of the Female Seminary.

Letters from home to the Cumberland Greys unquestionably carried mention of a fellow named Charles K. Landis, Philadelphia lawyer and banker. Up in the unpromising woodlands of Millville Township the man of vision bought 32,000 sandy acres of straggling pines and scrub oaks, all well "charcoaled over." About fifty people lived in the vast territory on the morning of August 8, 1861, when Landis drove a stake to found his "town"— Vineland.

Most of them felt like the native who sidled up to Landis and asked: "What are you doing, friend?" Landis replied: "Founding a town." The native warned nearby workers that Landis was addled.

He was, in a way—for 1861. He dreamed of a model way of living in Vineland (which he quite frankly admitted would help him sell his real estate). Landis visualized a town a mile square in which would be centered industrial, governmental and cultural pursuits. Surrounding lands were for agriculture, particularly vineyards. For his town he turned to New England, for his farms he turned to Italy. In the marriage of New England sagacity and thrift with Italian zeal and way-with-the-land his dream came true.

Landis planned brilliantly. All streets were at right angles to one another, with principal streets 100 feet wide, all others 60 feet wide. He sold acreage in five-and-ten-acre plots to avoid speculation and to encourage self-ownership. Houses had to be set back 75 feet from the street in the country, 25 feet in the city. Every property owner was required to plant shade trees and grass beside the roads.

An oasis grew in the sand land. By Christmas, 1862, 75 settlers and a fiddler rallied to a celebration; by 1864 more than 1,000 acres had been sold, and by 1869, 6,500 persons lived in the Landis tract (which had been divided into Vineland and Landis Township in 1864). Interestingly enough, in this grape-growing region, nearly all residents agreed with Landis that liquor should not be sold—and Landis fought through the Legislature a bill for local option. Landis, no teetotaler, merely felt liquor was poor business.

One Vineland resident, Dr. T. B. Welch (a dentist and a staunch Methodist) had even stronger feelings about alcoholic beverages—he felt it was wrong to use fermented wine for Communion. He introduced unfermented grape juice in his own church, offered it to others. Demand (both spiritual and secular) grew to the extent that the Welches gave up den-

This 1865 engraving showed quick Vineland growth.

tistry for grape-squeezing. Before the family moved its business to Westfield, New York, in the 1890's, the grape juice concern was well on the way to its present $15,000,000-a-year income.

At about the same time that Welch's conscience prodded him into a new venture, Captain Edmund Stites of Newport catapulted Cumberland's oyster beds into wide prominence when he made the first commercial shipment of oysters from Bivalve in 1870. Maurice River fishermen had long known of the importance of oysters—starting in 1846 they transplanted seed oysters from natural beds to save the industry—but it took mass shipments to give oyster farming lasting significance.

Cumberland's pattern of growth was set by 1900. That year Charles K. Landis died, content that Vineland fulfilled his hopes (even if grape growing had given way to truck gardening, glass making and chicken raising). Glass manufacture moved to the forefront in Bridgeton and Millville. Bridgeton had become a bustling county seat, where old houses contrasted with new growth and where the town's three far-famed nineteenth-century private schools (West Jersey Academy, Ivy Hall Seminary and South Jersey Institute) closed their doors in favor of broader public education.

Education in Cumberland also reached out to the less fortunate, when Reverend S. Olin Garrison founded Vineland Training School for the mentally retarded in 1888. The school has now achieved a world-wide reputation for clinical therapeutics and research. Among other things, the Binet intelligence scale was introduced to this country at the school

Main Street in Vineland. Broad streets date back to founding by Charles K. Landis in 1861.

Planting time at Seabrook Farms.

in 1908, and as early as 1914 its representatives had been invited to twenty-six other states to discuss the school.

Another of Cumberland's remarkable young men, Charles F. Seabrook (even then known as "C. F."), was nineteen years old in 1900. His fertile mind kept visualizing schemes beyond the reach of his father's 57-acre farm. "C. F." bought out his father in 1912 and organized Seabrook Farms, Inc. He tried everything—overhead irrigation, mechanization, cold storage—and slowly built his farm to 3,000 acres by World War I. He induced a New York firm to build a canning plant on his property in 1922 and just eleven years later his experiments with frozen foods resulted in Seabrook's first consumer pack.

Today Seabrook Farms is far and away the biggest agricultural enterprise in New Jersey, and one of the largest in the world. It owns land in excess of 19,000 acres, and nearly a thousand South Jersey farmers lease their lands to Seabrook or sell the company products from another 40,000 acres. Seabrook has led the way to making Cumberland one of New Jersey's prime agricultural counties, particularly in the use of mechanized equipment and modern methods in the fields.

Sharing the phenomenal twenty-century rise of

Seabrook and Cumberland farming in general is Vineland's poultry industry. Farmers in 1900 grew chickens only to round out their diets. Even the establishment in 1905 of the Vineland Co-operative Poultry Association had only minor commercial overtones. That group consisted mainly of sportsmen interested in exhibiting their prize poultry.

However, the founding of the Vineland Co-operative Egg Auction in 1931 focused attention on what had happened in the northeastern section of the county. Since 1934 the auction has sold more than $50,000,000 worth of eggs; at the present it boasts of being the largest egg co-operative in the world.

Vineland today is the poultry center of the East ("the egg basket of the nation," the prideful say). Millions of eggs are laid in Vineland nests, millions of baby chicks are hatched and sent to far-off farms. Statistics are startling—one farm can hatch 1,800,000 baby chicks at a time; another hatches over 8,000,000 annually. Small wonder that Cumberland's annual poultry income is over $9,000,000.

Cumberland tops the state in many agricultural categories, with nearly $22,000,000 annual income from all farm products. Cumberland is first in the amount of irrigated land, first in acreage and production of vegetables, first in the amount of farm products sold co-operatively, first in the number and volume of fruit and vegetable processing plants. One-sixth of Cumberland's population is engaged in agriculture on the county's 2,300 farms, and more than half of the county's acreage is tilled.

Yet Cumberland's economic success depends on more than the farmer. The glass industry, with smaller plants now largely consolidated into larger systems, is of supreme importance. Owens-Illinois Glass Company, owner of the Bridgeton works, turns out 300,000,000 glass bottles annually. Kimble Glass Company in Vineland is one of the nation's largest producers of scientific laboratory glass, and Armstrong Cork Company produces heavily in its Millville glass plant.

Oysters do their share—to the extent of about $6,000,000 annually. More than a hundred boats hover over the oyster beds in season, with payrolls running more than $70,000 weekly. Boatbuilding is important along the Maurice River, and during World War II vessels ranging up to 165 feet in length slid down the ways at Leesburg and Dorchester. Moreover, the $2,000,000 sand industry finds good digging close to the Maurice River.

Thus, Cumberland has achieved the success

Heart of Seabrook Farms in Cumberland County.

nature intended for it. The greenness of its fields impress; the breadth of Vineland surprises a first-time visitor (particularly since the July 1, 1952, merger with Landis Township made Vineland the largest city—in area—in New Jersey). Millville and Bridgeton wear a mantle of success tinged with old-time color. Oyster fleets make the Maurice River as picturesque as it is economically vital.

Today and yesterday merge in Cumberland. Particularly is that typified in Greenwich on the Cohansey. There Ye Greate Streete dozes contentedly in the knowledge that its moment in history is secure. There dwell citizens who are proud of Cumberland's present well-being, yet at the same time treasure every detail of the tea-burning.

There, in fact, is Jersey's Tidewater Land.

MORE ABOUT CUMBERLAND

Bridgeton, N. J. *Historic Bridgeton, 1686-1936*. Bridgeton, New Jersey, Bridgeton Evening News, 1936.

Cushing, Thomas, and Sheppard, Charles E., *History of the Counties of Gloucester, Salem, and Cumberland*. Philadelphia, Pennsylvania, Everts and Peck, 1883.

Elmer, Lucius Q. C., *History of Early Settlement and Progress of Cumberland County*. Bridgeton, N. J., George Nixon, 1869.

Landis, Charles K., *The Founding of Vineland, New Jersey*. 1903.

Sickler, Joseph S., *Tea Burning Town*, New York, Abelard Press, 1950.

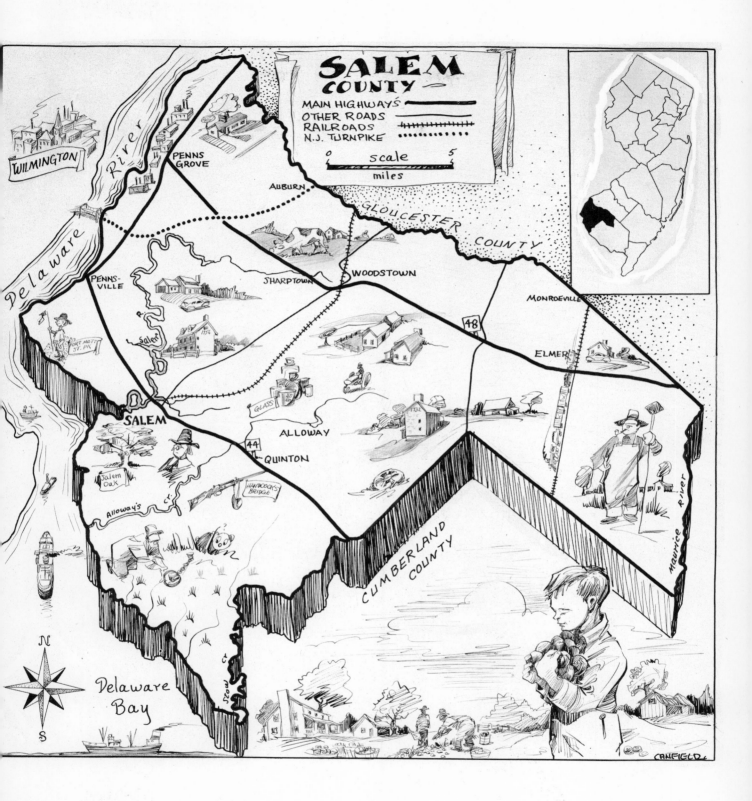

A herd of Holstein cattle roam the pasturelands of a Salem County dairy farm.

SALEM

John Fenwick gazed intently inland as the English ship *Griffin* dropped anchor in a pleasant cove off Delaware Bay in the early spring of 1675. Across the marshes occasional wisps of smoke curling through the trees bespoke a few earlier arrivals scattered through the vast area that Fenwick had secured in 1673 from Lord Berkeley.

At least Fenwick *thought* the £1,000 he had given Berkeley bought him the province of West Jersey. Now, after two years of trouble and litigation, Fenwick couldn't be sure. He expressed his troubled mind when he stepped ashore.

"Its name shall be Salem," said Fenwick, thinking of the Hebrew word for peace.

For Fenwick, "Salem" was as much a prayer as an expression of the tranquility of the land. Peace had been Fenwick's desire since his days as a major in the army of the ill-fated Oliver Cromwell. He embraced the Quaker faith after he left the army and listened with interest when people spoke of the new lands across the Atlantic Ocean. Thus, when Lord Berkeley offered to sell half the province of New Jersey, Fenwick grasped the chance. The price was £1,000 and 40 beaver skins annually.

Soon the English courts studied Fenwick's purchase, investigating allegations that Edward Byllynge had used Fenwick as a front man in the purchase. Young William Penn, a Quaker like both Fenwick and Byllynge, sat in arbitration on the dispute, and decided in favor of Byllynge and his creditors. Fenwick lost all but an area embraced by the modern Salem and Cumberland counties (not a small piece of real estate, at that).

Fenwick wrote Penn bitterly, but Penn urged him to put aside his rancor. "Fall closely to thy business," Penn advised, "lest thy grandchildren be in the other world before the land thou hast allotted be employed."

So, Fenwick fell closely to his business in Salem. He bought the land from the Indians for the usual guns and shot, rum and assorted articles of clothing. He laid out a wide street from the wharf on Salem River and saw his loved ones comfortably housed. He planned villages at Cohanzick (Greenwich) and Finn's Point.

Many more English Quakers joined the colony, lured by Fenwick's word pictures. Among other things, Fenwick assured prospective buyers that "if there be any terrestrial Canaan, 'tis surely here, where the land floweth with milk and honey."

As settlers pushed outward they learned the story of the Swedes and Finns who arrived before 1640. They found traces of the New Haven Puritans who had unsuccessfully attempted settlement in 1641 along Salem Creek (twenty-five years before establishment of the colony at Elizabethtown, Union County).

Already, however, time had dimmed memories

Engraving of Woodstown in 1840.

167

of the thirty-year struggle of the Dutch and Swedes for control of the Delaware River. Governor John Printz, bustling, able 400-pound Swedish leader, and the fort he had built at Elfsborg Point in 1643, were fading into history and legend. The story persisted that mosquitoes swarming over the marshes drove the Swedes from Fort Elfsborg before 1655—something Dutch guns couldn't do.

John Fenwick had no time for legends. His English financial troubles returned to plague him in America. Many of his colonists began to entertain grave doubts concerning Fenwick's right to sell them land. Finally, in 1682, he conveyed to William Penn for ten shillings "and other valuable considerations" all his land except 150,000 acres.

Salem never meant peace to John Fenwick. When he died in December, 1683, he must have considered himself a failure. After all, for a man who once owned half of New Jersey, the 150,000 acres he had left seemed like a mere garden patch. His visions of building a great estate for his children evaporated; there was not even a son to carry on his name.

Fenwick's most lasting memorial is probably the fact that it was he who interested William Penn in America.

Had he not been sickened by his financial difficulties, Fenwick would have been overjoyed by the growth of Salem County. Mills sprang up along the numerous streams in the land of peace. Boats sailed up sinuous Salem Creek in sufficient numbers to enable it to become an official port of entry in 1682—a real plum for the little village.

Farming dominated the "terrestrial Canaan." In May, 1682, the first of Salem's famous country fairs was held. Solemn Quakers at first ruled that during the fair, and for two days before and after, all persons were exempt from arrest. But such latitude induced evil—a 1698 law pointed out that "foreigners do flock in from other parts and do sell liquor by retail." That must stop, said the law. Only local folk could sell liquor and, just to keep everything honest, the law provided that any one who reported a "foreigner" selling liquor could keep half the confiscated stock.

Gun emplacements and dugouts at Fort Mott, now a state park.

Marshlands on Delaware Bay side of Salem County.

The land of peace had its violent crime and even more violent punishment. Salem, New Jersey, matched even the cruelest of the notorious Salem, Massachusetts, punishments when, in 1717, a young Negro slave woman was burned at the stake as an accomplice in the murder of her master.

Otherwise things moved placidly along in the days before the old Fenwick territory lost half its area by the establishment of Cumberland County in 1748. By then Salem County had several scattered villages, most of them along the winding creeks, which during most of the county's early days served as the only dependable highways. Many of Salem County's old houses still face the creeks, commemorating the days when the boat rather than the cart served to link settlers with other parts.

Most important of the early outposts was Wistarburg, the glass-making village started in 1739 by Casper Wistar of Philadelphia. Wistar bought a large woodland tract and built a cordage pot and glass house, a general store, houses for workmen and a mansion house. He paid a sea captain £58 to transport four experienced glass workers from Holland to show him how to convert the fine Jersey sand into splendid Wistar glass.

Wistar products quickly gained fame after Casper started production in 1740, and prominence of the glassworks continued unchecked when Casper's son Richard took over after his father's death in 1752. In addition to making exceptional glassware, Wistarburg also trained many glassworkers who then put their knowledge to good use in establishing other South Jersey glass manufactories.

The German immigrants who came to Wistarburg helped advance religious freedom in Salem County. Catholics who worked for Wistar celebrated mass (probably the first formal mass in New Jersey) in June, 1744, in the nearby home of Matthew and Adam Kiger. German Lutherans at the glass works established a church four years later at Friesburg. Other Protestant faiths followed, with all of the religious groups finding a relatively liberal climate among the Quakers.

Salem's long-time reputation as a garden spot attracted the attention of both the American and British armies during the Revolution, with the foraging activities of the two armies erupting sharply in 1778.

First, General "Mad" Anthony Wayne landed at Salem on February 19, seeking cattle (which some farmers promptly hid in the swamps). Undaunted, Wayne and his men collected upward of 300 head in forty-eight hours and started overland to Valley Forge via Haddonfield and Trenton. Wayne marched his troops between the cattle and the river, to "amuse the British."

The British were not easily amused. After Salem beef helped relieve the wretched plight of the men at Valley Forge, Colonel Charles Mawhood and Major John Graves Simcoe spread over the county in March to "chastise the rascals" (in Mawhood's words). American troops fell back to a thin line along Alloway's Creek, concentrating on three bridges at hamlets known as Hancock's, Quinton's and Thompson's (Alloway).

A bitter, indecisive skirmish at Quinton's Bridge on March 18 turned back the British. Three days later Major Simcoe led a group of 300 assorted Hessians, Tories and hangers-on against the home of Judge William Hancock at Hancock's Bridge. Some of Simcoe's 300 troops even knew personally the thirty men sleeping in the house on the morn-

ing of March 21 when the British force surrounded it.

Sentries at front and rear doors died quickly and quietly from bayonets thrust into their backs in the darkness. Then Simcoe's raiders rushed the house, aroused the sleeping men and chased them into the attic. Blood flowed over the attic boards as the helpless Americans died under savagely wielded bayonets. Simcoe withdrew his troops, satisfied with the night's work; the fortunes of war shifted elsewhere—but darkened blood stains remained on the boards of Hancock's house to recall the murderous night.

After the war quietude returned sooner to Salem County than to most regions. Wharves along the creeks buzzed with activity, mills spun busily, traffic picked up over the high road leading to Cooper's Ferry (Camden). Above all, the farmers worked.

How they worked! So much so that without warning the weary soil quit producing in the late 1790's. Bewildered farmers sadly watched wizened crops in the fields. Families left the homes ancestors

Hancock House, where British massacred thirty Americans in a savage raid on March 21, 1778.

Muskrat trappers near Clinton examine drying skins.

had built a century before and headed west in the Great Migration. Onward they went seeking the milk and honey—to Ohio, West Virginia, Indiana, on across the Mississippi River.

Leading the march was Zadock Street of Salem city. In 1803 Zadock founded Salem, Ohio; a dozen years later Zadock and son Aaron founded Salem, Indiana; and in the 1820's Aaron founded Salem, Iowa. The cross-country trail finally ended in 1844 at Salem, Oregon. (Interestingly enough, a Salem, Oregon, citizen wrote the mayor of Salem, New Jersey, in 1916, suggesting that all of the country's other twenty-five Salems change their names in deference to Salem, Oregon. Salem, New Jersey, laughed the laugh of an old, old grandfather.)

Discovery of extensive marl beds in the northern part of the county checked the migration before the middle 1820's. Salem farmers again ruled supreme, with Colonel Robert Gibbons Johnson of Salem city in the forefront. Colonel Johnson, wealthiest man in the county in those days, owned many farms but, like many farmers of the day, lived in town while others worked his land.

Colonel Johnson imported the tomato in 1820, at a time when most farmers considered the rich, red fruit at least worthless (and possibly even poisonous). Tradition declares Colonel Johnson had to eat one of the "love apples" on the courthouse steps to get his fellow-farmers to consider the tomato as edible. Highly progressive Colonel Johnson helped organize an agricultural society, reintroduced fairs to the county, and in his spare time wrote a creditable history of Salem County.

Throughout the nineteenth century Salem County farmers particularly distinguished themselves by the immense cattle and pigs they raised. Judge William Clawson of Woodstown fattened many hogs to over a thousand pounds in the 1850's, while Charles Clark of Pilesgrove in 1860 raised fifty-two hogs averaging over five hundred pounds each. Later, Clark Pettit of Hedgefield Farm had the largest herd of breeding hogs in the world.

Greatest of the overstuffed livestock specimens, nevertheless, was the first of note—the famous ox Job Tyler shipped from Salem wharf to Philadelphia in 1823. A special steamer came down from Philadelphia to bring the ox up-river, and a band led an impromptu parade through Philadelphia streets from dock to market. The ox merited the honors, because when dressed he yielded 2,111 pounds of beef, 365 pounds of tallow and 176 pounds of hide—2,652 pounds overall!

Job Tyler's water-borne ox also focused attention on Salem County's growing steamship prominence. Steady service, started before 1830, prospered for sixty years. Salem, Alloway, Sculltown, Pedricktown and Quinton's Bridge all spurted from increased steamship business. Penns Grove attracted thousands over by steam ferry from Wilmington for recreation, thousands more to attend the rousing camp meetings in the nearby groves.

Shipbuilding attained importance, particularly at Alloway, where the Reeves brothers started in 1824 to cut planks and timber for Philadelphia shipyards. Seven years later they launched their first boat and in 1844 they built their first steamboat. Many canal boats and sidewheel steamers slid down the ways at Alloway before the Civil War.

Salem County's proximity to the South, as well as the militant antislavery feelings of its Quaker settlers, made it play a prominent role in the drama leading up to the Civil War. As early as 1835 a group of Salem city people forcibly took away from a Philadelphia agent eight naked slaves who were being led on chains through the city streets. The agent received rough treatment, much to the indignation of editors in the City of Brotherly Love, whose thoughts lingered on the agent rather than the slaves. Twenty years before the war broke out hundreds of slaves crossed the Delaware River to Elsinboro Point and started northward to freedom on the Underground Railroad.

One of the county's daughters, Miss Cornelia Hancock of Lower Alloway's Creek, gave Salem County reason for pride at the Battle of Gettysburg, where she was the first woman nurse to arrive on the field of battle. Closer to home, tales of horror seeped back to the Salem mainland from Fort Delaware, the Confederate prison camp on Pea Patch Island in the Delaware River. Finally, in the waning days of 1863, dozens of corpses came to the mainland each day from the Fort, where 12,000 Confederate prisoners occupied space intended for 2,000 men.

Fort Delaware deserves a place in the annals of infamy. Dr. S. Weir Mitchel of Philadelphia, a Federal inspector of hospitals, wrote in 1863: ". . . there are a thousand ill . . . there are 20 deaths a day from dysentery and the living have more life on them than in them . . . thus a Christian nation treats the captives of the sword. . . ." Underfed, miserably treated and given the scantiest of medical attention, Confederate prisoners died horribly. Nearly 2,500 of them found Salem's peace only in the cemetery at Finn's Point.

The year of 1863 was a year of destiny for Salem County, because, in addition to the heroics of Miss Hancock and the wretchedness of Fort Delaware, it

DuPont's plant at Deepwater.

Finn's Point, where Confederate dead are buried.

was the year the railroad finally inched down from Camden. The railroad did two things: it switched the county's main focal point from Wilmington to Philadelphia, and it brought a resurgence of the old Salem glass industry.

Salem Glass Works, founded by H. D. Hall, J. D. Pancoast and J. V. Craven in 1862, became one of the largest hollow glassware manufactories in the world within ten years after the railroad came. John Gayner opened his glass works in 1874, and at about the same time an oilcloth maker, an iron foundry and two canning companies made Salem city's economy boom. The city population jumped to nearly 5,000, including scores of retired farmers and more than a hundred active farm operators who preferred to live in the city.

Glass also became vital to Quinton in 1863, although not until 1893 did the railroad supplant Alloway's Creek boats. Quinton's "golden age" lasted until 1908. For forty-five years 3,000,000 feet of the finest French plate glass in the nation came annually from Quinton Glass Works. Western competition killed the plant eventually, but Quinton at least had the distinction of being one of the last places in the East to make window glass.

As the nineteenth century waned, farmers in

Pilesgrove and Pittstown townships happily applied marl and reaped their rewards. Shad fishermen pulled thousands of fish from the Delaware. Tomato growers found increasing public demand for their "love apples." Noted ice cream makers, particularly John Bruna, made Salem County ice cream famous throughout South Jersey and as far away as Washington, D. C.

Then, one day in 1890, the du Pont company bought land at Carney's Point and announced plans to make smokeless powder. Most Salem historians call that du Pont decision the most important event in the county since the first arrival of the Swedes and Finns 250 years before. Du Pont's first guncotton left Carney's Point in 1892, while smokeless powder for sportsmen was produced in 1894. The Spanish-American War boosted production somewhat, but World War I really boomed Carney's Point.

More than 25,000 men came to the Point in World War I to help make 900,000 pounds of smokeless powder daily. Farmers and fishermen left their plows and nets—most of them never to return, because at war's end most of them transferred to the "dye works" at Deepwater. The war had cut off German dyes, forcing this country to find substitutes. Du Pont produced them and stayed on in full production, slowly changing to widely varied chemical production.

"Old Salem" gave way a little before the industrialization. The two glass factories in Salem city were joined by a big H. J. Heinz canning house in 1906. Floor-covering plants moved into the county. Population increased. Old mud and oyster shell roads disappeared under blankets of macadam. Residential areas like Woodstown and Pennsville grew rapidly. Intensive farming made the fruitful soil produce wonderfully—and the coming of Seabrook Farms to neighboring Cumberland County opened undreamed-of new markets for Salem farmers.

Somehow, though, despite the changes, Salem County has emerged charmingly as the place where John Fenwick's "milk and honey" declarations and his prayer for peace blend nicely with glass manufacture and the chemical works at Deepwater. More than 2,000 people work in the two glass plants in Salem (one is now part of the Anchor-Hocking Company, the other is still called Gayner's), another 7,000 draw weekly checks from du Pont. Out along the Delaware, near Deepwater, the generating plant of the Atlantic City Electric Company supplies power to most of the counties in South Jersey.

Farming continues a prime way-of-life, with the county's more than 1,400 farms annually producing more than $7,000,000 from field crops alone (with tomatoes a major item), and well over $13,000,000 each year from all farm products.

The immediate years ahead bid fair to change Salem's outlook (already the Deepwater Bridge and the New Jersey Turnpike seem to be switching the county's axis from Philadelphia back to Wilmington, where it was in the beginning). Industry is an increasingly major economic factor. Hundreds of new residents are bringing new customs into the county—unlike the days when Salem had the reputation of being way off the beaten path.

Yet, what can really change Salem? Scattered throughout the county are at least 150 old brick houses predating the Revolution. Salem city's venerable streets are lined with enough handsome old houses to bring joy to an antiquarian. Salem's ancient oak makes believable the humorist Robert Burdette's declaration that the tree is "four years older than the Atlantic Ocean."

Even the county's towns commemorate the names of original settlers of 250 years ago, as town names in few other counties do—such as Pedricktown, Pilesgrove, Quinton, Hancock's Bridge, Woodstown, to name just a few. Out in the marshes surrounding Hancock's Bridge dozens of muskrat trappers still make good livings in a continuation of almost 300 years of trapping in the swamplands.

Above all, Salem seems truly to mean peace in 1953. Since the beginning most men have found relatively tranquillity there, even though the man who named it Salem never found on earth the peace he so much wanted.

MORE ABOUT SALEM

Cushing, Thomas, and Sheppard, Charles E. *A History of Gloucester, Salem and Cumberland Counties.* Philadelphia, Penna. Everts and Peck, 1883.

Johnson, R. G., *An Historical Account of the Frst Settlement of Salem in West Jersey.* Philadelphia, Pennsylvania Orrin Rogers, 1839.

School children of Salem County, *A Story of Salem County.* Salem, New Jersey.

Shourds, Thomas, *History and Genealogy of Fenwick's Colony.* Bridgeton, New Jersey, George F. Nixon, 1876.

Sickler, Joseph Sheppard, *The History of Salem County, New Jersey.* Salem, New Jersey, Sunbeam Publishing Co., 1937.

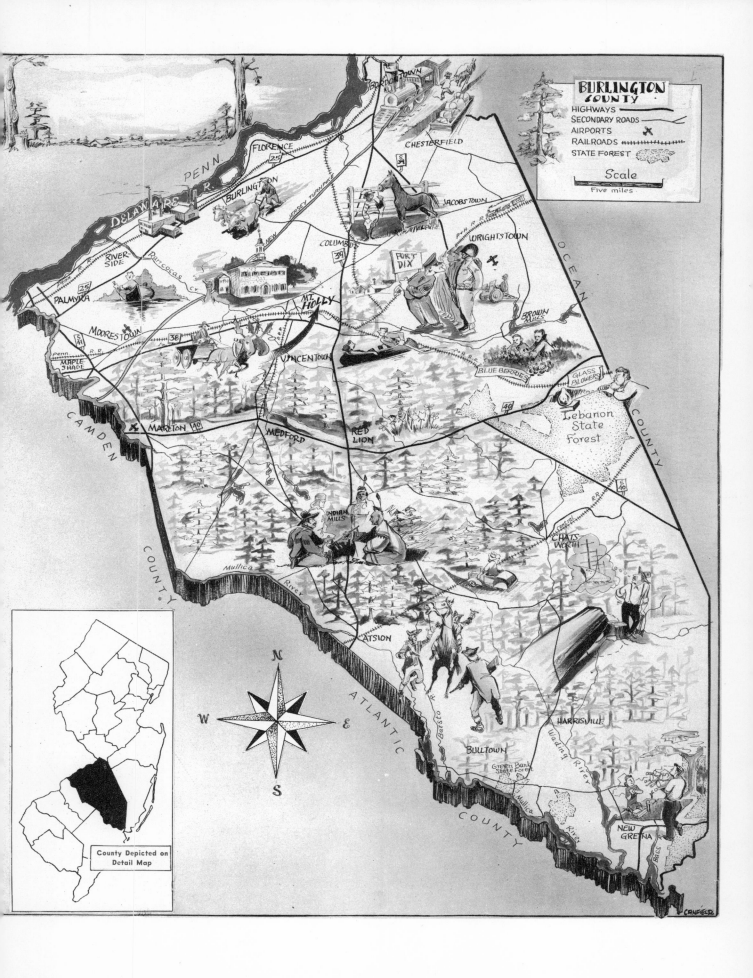

The pine country on Route S40. The bend in the road marks the Burlington-Ocean County line.

BURLINGTON

Nature decreed from the start that Burlington County's personality would be split between the verdant brightness along the Delaware River banks and the piney gloom stretching eastward ten miles inland from the river. The Quakers who first set foot in the colony learned that in 1677; it always has been a dominant factor in the county's growth.

More than a thousand square miles were granted the first colonizers by the West Jersey Proprietors in 1676. Since then the county-makers have whacked away at Burlington's borders, cutting off a chunk to help make Hunterdon in 1713, slicing away another bit in 1838 to make room for Mercer, and, finally, chopping off a section on the Atlantic Ocean side in 1891 to add to Ocean County.

Nevertheless, Burlington remains New Jersey's largest county and one of its least settled. Through the years it has easily absorbed the vast schemes of iron makers, paper makers, charcoal burners and glass manufacturers. Three state parks (and parts of two others) have been cut from its pine vastness, and Fort Dix has been accommodated without Burlington's even drawing a deep breath. Burlington can adjust to anything; adjustment has been its forte from the first.

Adjustments were necessary, for example, for the hardy Quaker souls on the good ship *Shield of Stockton*, who fastened their ship's rope to a giant sycamore on the banks of the Delaware on a gloomy December evening in 1678. The ship's company walked ashore on the ice the next morning to join the Friends who had laid out the village in 1677, and quickly set about to make homes in caves or in rude lean-tos for the rest of the winter.

The village grew rapidly, and not the least of the changes was the adoption of the name of Burlington in place of the former name of New Beverly. New settlers soon followed, attracted both by the lush land and by the liberties granted in the "Concessions and Agreements" of the West Jersey Proprietors. In 1681, after West Jersey became a separate province, the Colonial Assembly designated Burlington city as the West Jersey capital and official port of entry.

Settlers pushed outward. Thomas Farnsworth went eight miles up the Delaware in 1682 and founded Farnsworth's Landing (now Bordentown) on a breeze-swept bluff. Rancocas Creek was an invitation to the interior; Friends went up its placid waters soon after the establishment of Burlington and founded Bridgetown (now Mount Holly) on the flats beneath a holly-covered hill. Thomas Olive opened a gristmill in 1678 and John Wills, son of Burlington's first physician, started a famous gristmill on the Rancocas in the 1690's. Until Andrews's mill was opened at Tuckerton in 1704, men on horseback struggled all the way across the state from Little Egg Harbor to Wills's Mill. The cross-state visitors brought news of scattered bands of settlers

Burlington County farm scene in the 1880's.

working their way from the Atlantic Ocean up the Mullica, Wading and Bass rivers to sink their roots in Burlington's eastern edge.

Quickly it became established that Burlington County's destiny was linked with Philadelphia's. The county's harvests were welcomed by the city, and the county's future was cast in the straight line which, linking New York and Philadelphia, ran straight through the towns of Bordentown and Burlington.

True, New Jersey might be slated to be "like a barrel tapped on both ends," but Burlington County had no intention of being caught in the drainage.

Roads of a sort twisted across the state, around the northern edge of the pine barrens, linking Burlington and Bordentown with Perth Amboy (capital of East Jersey). River packets from Philadelphia to Burlington or Bordentown, and from Perth Amboy to New York, soon appeared and by the 1730's boat-stagecoach trips were firmly established —although advertisements of their punctuality,

their speed and their comfort often were far superior to the service, until 1771, when the noted "Flying Machines" cut the cross-state trip to thirty-six hours.

Revolutionary War time found Bordentown and Burlington on a sound basis and both cities had their share of gentlemen who argued that all this prosperity was due to the King. Some were vehement in their pro-Crown arguments. William Franklin, illegitimate son of Benjamin Franklin and governor of New Jersey, was forced from his aristocratic Green Bank estate in Burlington and lost his Royal governorship rather than agree with the patriots. Reverend Jonathan Odell, rector of Burlington's old St. Mary's Church, wrote fierce satires on America. Both chose to remain Tories and both ended their days in foreign countries.

Despite such defections, Burlington welcomed the Provincial Congress of New Jersey in 1776 and sent off to Philadelphia the five delegates who signed for the state the Declaration of Independence, including its own keen-witted and sharp-tongued 38-year-old Francis Hopkinson of Bordentown.

Crosswicks Meeting House dates back to 1692. Oak in yard is 300 years old.

1789 home of venerable Mount Holly fire company.

Hopkinson predicted the Revolution in a 1774 essay, "A Prophesy," and later in life he designed the Great Seal of the United States and aided in the design of the Stars and Stripes. Still, some of his lasting fame came for his merry jingle satirizing "The Battle of the Kegs."

The "kegs," filled with gunpower, were launched with the ebbing tide on a January night in 1778. The hope was that the floating mines, vintage 1778, would strike British ships anchored at Philadelphia. Only one of the kegs exploded, killing four men, but it created panic in the fleet. Flint-happy Redcoats for days fired at everything floating in the river. Hopkinson's 22-verse tongue-in-cheek jingle extolled such "bravery."

Despite its strategic location, Burlington County suffered no major Revolutionary War battles, although foraging parties and minor skirmishes kept the county embroiled throughout the war. A band of 400 Hessians invaded Burlington city in December, 1776, and a punitive naval expedition was sent against Bordentown in May, 1778 (in retaliation, it is said, for Hopkinson's unappreciated poetry). The ships returning from Bordentown fired on Burlington, first taking the precaution to warn small boys off the bank!

Mount Holly was the scene of a clash when the iron works and other properties were destroyed, and English soldiers slaughtered steer in the old Friends Meeting House in 1778. At Crosswicks a minor engagement ensued when Continental volunteers sought to destroy a bridge on June 23, 1778, to delay Hessian soldiers.

Thomas Paine, who fired colonial imaginations and lagging patriotism with his "times that try men's souls" writings, found peace in Bordentown from 1783 until he traveled to Europe to become embroiled in the French Revolution. He wrote longingly of Bordentown while in France, but when he returned he found that few of his old friends cared to see the author of "The Age of Reason." He was literally run out of town by a mob of jeering pursuers.

Adjacent houses in Burlington city welcomed famous-to-be sons in the 1780's, when James Lawrence was born at 459 High Street in 1781 and J. Fenimore Cooper was born at 457 High in 1789. James Lawrence, who went into the Navy, won immortality for his plea, "Don't give up the ship!" as he lay dying after a sea battle with the British in the War of 1812. The Coopers moved away when J. Fenimore was a year old, but Burlington rightfully gains some glory from the great early American novelist.

At the war's end Burlington farmers turned back to the soil. One of them, Charles Newbold, decided something better than the crude tilling of the soil was imperative. He patented the nation's first cast

Lake Absegami boat basin, Bass River State Forest.

iron plow in 1797, but overcame only with difficulty the prejudices of farmers' who feared Newbold's invention would poison the soil.

The county had grown so by 1796 that the county seat was moved to Mount Holly—a splendid choice. The new county seat had a deep heritage, even by 1796. It pointed with quiet pride to John Woolman, the intense Quaker who fought slavery and wrote brilliantly. It discussed with satisfaction the famed Indian Missionary John Brainerd, who preached in Mount Holly from 1767 to 1775 and spoke courageously against the British in 1776.

One of Brainerd's joys, incidentally, was the nation's first Indian reservation, established in Burlington County in 1758 at Edgepelick or Brotherton (now Indian Mills). Brainerd taught school there among the Indians he loved before accepting a call to Mount Holly. Soon, however, the vanishing tribe of New Jersey red men found life in the reservation lonely and departed the state forever in 1802 for greener pastures at Oneida, New York.

Eastward from Mount Holly the great pine lands stretched afar, covering two-thirds of the county and spreading far off into adjacent counties. Charles Read penetrated the forest in 1766 to set up iron works on the Mullica River at Batsto, but it was General Washington's good friend, Colonel William Richards, who made the works productive during the Revolution. Elsewhere iron forges and furnaces prospered at the dawn of the nineteenth century, combining the bog iron dug from the swamps with the seemingly unlimited charcoal timber to turn out quantities of iron pipe, firebacks, Dutch ovens and other iron goods. Burlington at one time had more than a dozen iron works within its borders.

Out along the Delaware, Bordentown had a burst of excitement in 1816 when Joseph Bonaparte, exiled King of Spain and brother of Napoleon, bought 1,500 acres of land at Point Breeze and developed an elaborate estate. A special act of the Legislature was required to sell him the land and the passage of the act earned New Jersey the sobriquet of "New Spain." Joseph liked Bordentown so well that in 1824 he unhesitatingly turned

Clara Barton School, Burlington, operated briefly by founder of the American Red Cross.

Pickers in a cranberry bog near Chatsworth.

down a commission from Mexico offering him the throne, but eventually he returned to France in 1839. Joseph's nephew, tall, handsome Prince Napoleon François Lucien Charles Murat, caused local sighs of despair when he eloped with Caroline Fraser, the belle of Bordentown.

Bordentown's river quaintness changed forever in the 1830's. First, Isaac Dripps put together the "John Bull" in 1831 and prepared the locomotive for travel across the state to South Amboy on the Camden & Amboy Railroad. In 1834 the Delaware & Raritan Canal was completed to link Bordentown and New Brunswick. The railroad established big shops in the city, and the canal terminal required lodging places for somewhat ungenteel canal mule drivers and their mules. Many of the aristocrats refused to compromise; they moved out.

Culture continued vital to the county, nonetheless. The Quakers had established a school in Burlington as early as 1682, and a library had been started in that town in 1758 under charter from King George II. Burlington County's cultural pride also embraced Clara Barton, a quietly determined miss who reached Bordentown in 1851. Aroused by

the lack of schooling for the poor, she established in a one-room building a free school, one of the first in America. When townspeople insisted that she be supervised by a male principal she resigned and went elsewhere, to found the American Red Cross.

Not exactly cultured, but certainly fascinating, was another Burlington character, Hezekiah B. Smith, who arrived from New England in 1865 to convert an abandoned thread mill on Rancocas Creek into a thriving machine manufacturing center. Modestly he renamed the surrounding village Smithville.

Smith, simple and proud of his humble beginnings, affected a Quaker hat and shawl. Nevertheless he lived the life of an industrial prince, maintaining a gambling casino in town and a well-filled liquor cellar. Smith manufactured the high-wheeled Star bicycle, among other things. He took out more than forty patents and was at times experimenting with models of flying machines and steam wagons.

Hezekiah created a sensation with the trained bull moose he imported to pull his carriage when he campaigned for Congress, and with his Smithville

Brass Band. Smithville mourned with Hezekiah in 1881 when his young "wife" died. His death in 1887 brought Smithville up short, however, because at will-reading time his true wife and five children suddenly appeared from Woodstock, Vermont, where Hezekiah had deserted them. Thus, Smithville learned for the first time that Hezekiah, for all his glittering, was not pure gold.

Such diversions as Hezekiah B. Smith to the contrary, however, concern over the pine land continued. The bog iron mining industry collapsed before the Civil War. Glass works prospered for a time at such places as Lebanon and Herman, but they were gone by 1870. A paper mill started at Harrisville reached its peak in the 1880's, only to fold in 1892.

Lumbermen and charcoal burners found wealth of varying proportions in the Pines, but they combined their businesses with a wanton disregard for the facts of forest life. They cut and burned and they failed to realize that their actions and the horrendous forest fires which raged freely and fre-

quently were dooming the great white cedars. Soon the cedars were no more and the straggling pine and scrub oak growth which replaced them was incapable of sustaining any sizable enterprise.

Nature lent a hand at this point by beckoning men to cultivate the wild cranberry bogs in the forests. By the middle '80's the Pines were producing half the nation's crop (and today only Wisconsin and Massachusetts grow more cranberries than Jersey's pine bogs). It remained for Miss Elizabeth C. White, daughter of one of Burlington's earliest cranberry growers, to awaken the county to the potentialities of cultivating swamp huckleberries. Still alive today at Whitesbog, Miss White ranks as one of the nation's foremost blueberry pioneers.

Population has been declining in the Pines for years. Dr. John W. Harshberger in his *Vegetation of the New Jersey Pine Barrens* called the area in 1916 "one of the wildest, most desolate portions of the United States." He told of traveling as far as ten miles without seeing even a house, much less

Fort Dix, where millions of soldiers have been trained and processed since World War I.

Intersection of Broad and High Streets, in the center of Burlington.

a human being. He pointed out that the sparse population had contributed to the county some of the nation's most personalized locale names—Mt. Misery, Ong's Hat, Mary Ann Forge, Bozarthtown, Martha Forge, Apple Pie Hill—highly suggestive of the people who had passed through or had stopped and had been remembered. Above all, Dr. Harshberger definitely called attention to the unique and diversified flowers, trees and plants thriving in the so-called "Barrens."

Just before World War I Miss Elizabeth C. Kite, a social worker from the Vineland Training School, startled the state with a report on sordid conditions in the woodlands. She told of illiterates living in squalor, of people like "The Squire"—who elected himself "the law" and for a flat fee of fifty cents "gave writin's" ranging from a marriage license to a "divorce writin'." Miss Kite claimed that the worst conditions in the Pines were in Burlington County, and a direct result of her work was the establishment in 1916 at New Lisbon of Four Mile Colony for the mentally retarded.

Miss Kite traced the origins of the Pineys (a name given pineland inhabitants) back to the "Pine

Robbers" of Revolutionary War times. They were joined through the years by Tories, by Hessian deserters, by people who sought religious freedom, or who desired just plain independence. There were some disreputable people, of course, but mainly the Pineys sought merely to be left alone. Unfortunately that desire, not unpraiseworthy in itself, also included a lack of responsibility toward others, which meant that schools were not built, roads were not maintained, and man was a law only unto himself.

Arguments about the merits and faults of the Pineys have raged throughout the years ever since Miss Kite's report. Authorities concede today that the people of the Pines are (and always have been) more shy and reticent than mean. Many of the Pineys were drawn from the forests to work in constructing Fort Dix in World War I and in rebuilding it in World War II. Many of them have found work on the state highways cutting through the forests. They work as guides, as skilled forest hands in the state forests at Lebanon, Green Bank and Bass River, and as workers in the cranberry bogs. Significantly, during World War II Selective Service found few shirkers among the Pineys—and if ever there was a spot in which to dodge the draft, it's the Pines.

The pinelands continue to be a problem in present-day Burlington County, nonetheless. Only about one-tenth of Burlington's population lives in the great stretch of land covering more than two-thirds of the county. Ownership of much land is unknown and taxes have been unpaid for years on many properties. The sprawling estate acquired by Joseph Wharton in 1876 occupies tens of thousands of acres where the state would like to establish a state forest and potable water supply.

Elsewhere in Burlington there is the good life. New industries are spreading along the Delaware River front in the continuing migration of manufacturers to the lower Delaware. Burlington's agricultural production remains high—with 13 per cent of all New Jersey farm acreage within the county. Burlington grows one-third of all sweet corn produced in the state, ranks first in blueberry and cranberry production, and has more than a half-million peach and apple trees. Its tomato, potato and truck garden farms yield heavily and its chickens and cows each year rank in production among the top three or four counties in New Jersey. Agriculture means a $17,000,000 annual income to Burlington.

Burlington is modern and growing (population up from 97,013 in 1940 to 135,910 in 1950), and the New Jersey Turnpike will speed its growth. Yet, in towns like Bordentown and Burlington and Mount Holly, much of the past remains preserved in the old buildings, in the spirit and in the traditions. It comes as no surprise, for example, that the West Jersey Proprietors still continue to meet in Burlington every April 13 to conduct business. It seems fitting and natural that Mount Holly's 200-year-old Fire Department should be the nation's oldest.

Out in the pines, few people stop. Yet who can resist the hint of excitement in the sandy roads leading through the forests, possibly to a ghost town in the underbrush? Or who would deny the beauty of the white birches and the colorful laurel intermingling with the pines and scrub oaks? Nature, at least, knows there's a future in the Pines.

MORE ABOUT BURLINGTON

Devery, Elizabeth C., *The Story of Four Mile Colony*. New Lisbon, New Jersey, New Jersey State Colony, 1939.

Ewan, Nathaniel R., *Early Houses in Burlington County, N. J.* Moorestown, New Jersey, N. R. Ewan, 1938.

Schermerhorn, William E., *The History of Burlington, New Jersey*. Philadelphia, Penna., J. D. Scott, 1876.

Woodward, E. M., *History of Burlington and Mercer Counties, New Jersey*. Philadelphia, Pennsylvania, Everts and Peck, 1883.

Woodward, E. M., *Bonaparte Park and the Murats, 1879*. Trenton, New Jersey, MacCrellish and Quigley. 1879.

The JERSEY SHORE

Everybody knows the Jersey Shore . . .

They know of wonderful beaches, of suntan lotions, of beach umbrellas, of boardwalks, of souvenirs. They know of traffic jams on roads heading in and out. They know of Miss America and Mrs. America, and conventions and gaiety. Sure, that's the Jersey Shore.

This, too, is the Jersey Shore . . .

Where Southern aristocrats rocked on Cape May verandas until the Civil War sent them home, where Diamond Jim Brady and others of like mind made Long Branch gay. Where Presidents and Governors and Congressmen bathed in the dashing surf, a spray away from the commoners who came down in wagons. Where a railroad from Camden turned a sandy wasteland called Absegami into glittering Atlantic City.

This is the Jersey Shore . . .

Where winter turns vacationland into ghost town, with boardwalk stands silently braving the icy gales of a January storm. Where ships once beached and broke up on the desolate sands, and where federally-supported lifesaving service was born. Where summer's welcoming waves turn into winter's savage surf.

This, then, is the Jersey shore, all things to all men. A land of magic, a land of wistfulness, a land of excitement, a land of mood. This is a land where today erases yesterday and prepares for tomorrow.

This is the Jersey Shore . . .

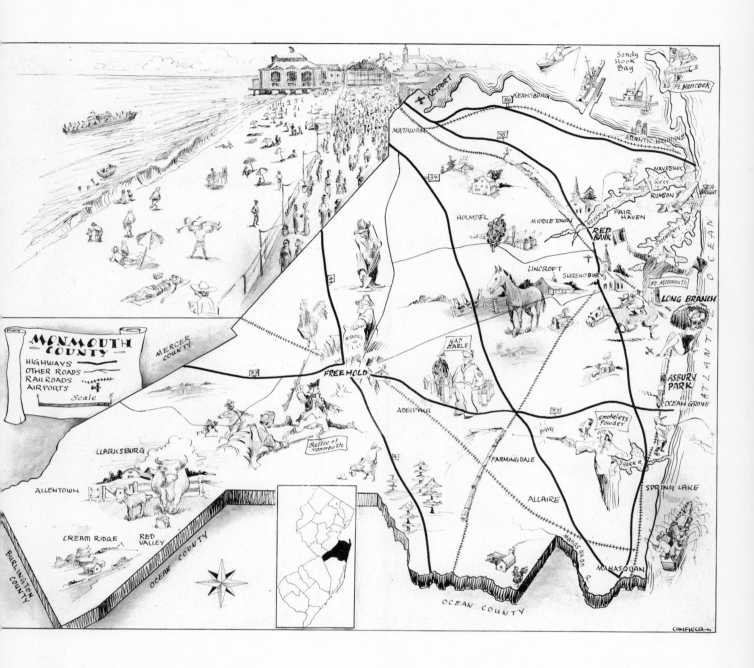

Boats in Navesink River indicate sea-going outlook of Monmouth County.

MONMOUTH

Many stars crowd the stage in the unfolding of the Monmouth County drama, yet credit for pointing the story in a definite direction must go to two unidentified bit players, the Irishman who recognized greensand marl in the soil near Freehold in 1768, and the Long Branch woman who took in surf-loving boarders in 1788.

In all truth, the players who preceded and followed the Irishman and the boarding-house proprietor embodied far more dash and excitement. Nevertheless, in capitalizing on the natural resources of Monmouth County, the anonymous characters firmly set the pace of the Monmouth story, for what they did resulted in a long and happy marriage of resort and farm.

It took more than a century to set the stage for the state's first extensive use of marl and the first Long Branch boarding house. Prosperity came easily after the first settlers drifted over from Gravesend, Long Island, in 1664 to settle huge plantations in Middletown and Shrewsbury. Some of the Indians grumbled a bit; Richard Hartshorne had to guarantee them the right to pick beach plums on Sandy Hook before they sold him vast acreage on the Atlantic Highlands.

Middletown and Shrewsbury had prominence enough in 1675 to warrant being established as the "County of Nevysink" with loosely defined borders. By then Colonel Lewis Morris had acquired control of New Jersey's first iron works, started in 1674 on the "Falls of Shrewsbury" by James Grover. Morris bought 3,540 acres on the Shrewsbury River "to dig, delve and carry all such mines for iron as they shall find." He called his plantation Tintern Manor, which local usage corrupted to "Tinton" and then "Tinton Falls."

Influence naturally followed the state's first ironmaster, so when Monmouth became one of East Jersey's first four colonies in 1682, Morris had it named Monmouth after his native Monmouthshire, Wales. East Jersey Proprietors looked fondly on Monmouth; in the 1680's it was the wealthiest county in the province of Jersey, and consequently paid the most taxes. Already Monmouth was known as "a great resort for industrious and reputable farmers."

A boatload of Scotsmen stranded on the Jersey coast made their way inland to near Freehold in 1685, some Dutch traveled across Raritan Bay from New York in the 1690's, and French Hugenots settled in the county in 1700. Meanwhile, a few

Rushing to Long Branch amusements in the 1890's.

189

Old engraving of the Twin Lights of the Navesink.

plot to the county for thirty shillings, thereby proving his business acumen; the building of the first courthouse in 1715 made his own holdings increase tremendously in value.

Bordered on the north by Raritan Bay and on the east by the Atlantic Ocean, Monmouth County naturally looked upon the waters as its main transportation arteries. Such exceptionally broad and well-protected streams as the Shrewsbury, Navesink, Shark and Manasquan rivers made ocean commerce thrive. Navesink Highlands and Sandy Hook had lighthouses on them before the Revolution, with the beacon on the Hook (built in 1762) being one of the oldest in the country.

Down-county (called "Upper" Freehold, oddly enough), gristmills hummed busily on Doctor's Creek at Allentown and Imlaystown and on Crosswicks Creek at Waln's Mills long before the Revolution. Scows laden with flour went down the Crosswicks to Philadelphia, since Lower Monmouth (or Upper Freehold) naturally looked to the west for its trade.

Early in the eighteenth century a big New Eng-

settlers pushed westward to Allentown and Imlaystown. Thus, settlements were widespread enough to warrant the choice of a centralized county seat late in 1713 at Monmouth Court House (Freehold).

A few weeks later one John Reid, who must rate with Monmouth's more enterprising residents, bought land where county fathers had decided the new courthouse would be. Generously he sold a

Loading potatoes at F. H. Vahlsing farm, Robbinsville.

Modern resort hotels, Ocean Grove.

lander named Mordecai Lincoln came to Upper Freehold Township, where he married Hannah Salter, daughter of wealthy landowner Richard Salter. They set up housekeeping near Mordecai's forge at Fillmore and reared a family. One of their sons, John, became the great-grandfather of President Abraham Lincoln.

Historians who recorded the discovery of marl on Peter Schenck's farm near Freehold in 1768 forgot to get the name of the discoverer. Listed simply as "an Irishman," the anonymous agricultural benefactor recognized the greensand marl from having used it in "the old country." Tried on nearby fields on the Irishman's say-so, the marl produced "extraordinary results." Quickly its usage enriched surrounding farms and gave the region its name, "Marlboro."

Monmouth suffered cruelly during the Revolution, both from small bands of British troops who slipped in from the sea and from Tories who banded together on Sandy Hook or hid in the forests. Further woes came from the pine robbers, who as often as not struck at either side. Jacob Fagan and Lewis Fenton gained notoriety as bandit leaders, while General David (Black David) Forman hunted them down mercilessly and "hung them without waiting for superfluous ceremony."

That strictly local pattern of warfare exploded on June 28, 1778, when General Washington's army finally caught up with General Clinton's British troops in the fields west of Monmouth Court House (Freehold). Washington held a slight advantage in troops but Clinton had superior position in the thick woods and extensive marshlands.

The chance of a full American victory vanished at the outset when General Charles Lee disobeyed Washington's orders to attack. Washington faced the sulky Lee on the battlefield and in his anger "swore 'til the leaves shook in the trees." What motivated Lee has never been made clear, but he was court-martialed and dismissed from service for his actions. Meanwhile, the battle raged all day without decision before Clinton slipped off and escaped over the Highlands.

Both sides suffered severe losses in the indecisive action, from the deadly June heat as well as from enemy fire. The heat brought to the fore an American heroine of legendary proportions—red-haired, freckle-faced Irish Molly Hays, who had followed her husband John to the battlefield from Carlisle, Pennsylvania. Under the hot June sun Molly carried water from a nearby creek to the parched soldiers. An enemy bullet wounded John, whereupon Molly, so legend has it, took his place at the cannon and earned immortality for herself as "Molly Pitcher."

One shocking war episode remained for Monmouth. Captain Joshua Huddy of Colt's Neck, captured at Toms River in March, 1782, faced charges that he had killed Tory Philip White. Evidence proved Huddy had been in a British prison when White was shot, but a British company executed him on the gallows at the foot of Navesink hills. Huddy's death outraged and stunned even British leaders.

War-time bitterness subsided quickly in Monmouth, however, possibly because of the remarkably deep roots of the county's churches. Shrewsbury, for example, had New Jersey's first Quaker meeting house, built in 1682. The state's first Baptist congregation was organized at Middletown in 1668. Christ Church, Middletown, and Christ Church, Shrewsbury, were both organized in October, 1702, while St. Peter's Church, Freehold, traced its beginnings back to 1695. Old Tennent Church was built in 1751, and Bethesda Methodist Church at Adelphia, founded in 1780, was the state's oldest regularly constituted Methodist Church.

A few wealthy men came to Monmouth's shore and built summer homes after the Revolution, the most noted being U.S. Senator William Bingham of Philadelphia, who entertained lavishly at his residence at Rumson Neck. However, it remained for an unidentified old lady in charge of a palatial mansion at Long Branch to open the shore to summer "renters." Elliston Perot of Philadelphia persuaded her to rent him the building in 1788, on condition of providing the beds and the food.

Other Philadelphians begged the privilege of sharing the big old house with the Perots and this gave one Mr. McKnight an idea: He bought the mansion for $2,000, invited the best families of

Commercial fishing boats at Elberon.

Old Tennent Church, built in 1751.

Philadelphia (no rabble, mind you) and quickly cleared $40,000 in his investment. Another accommodation, conducted by Messrs. Herbert and Chandler, advertised in 1792 "a good stock of liquors and everything necessary for the entertainment of ladies and gentlemen."

Long Branch vied with Cape May by 1800 for the patronage of Philadelphians, many of whom made the long trek across the state in wagons that were returning to the shore after their owners sold loads of fish in Philadelphia or Trenton. Farmers along the Monmouth coast opened their homes to paying guests, aware that cultivating summer visitors offered far better prospects than digging their thin beachfront soil.

Long Branch gained particular attention for its discreet bathing regulations. When a white flag went up only ladies bathed; when a red flag went up only gentlemen tested the surf. Strangers often went on the beach at the wrong times (through ignorance, of course), and one day in 1819 a wag hoisted both flags together, "which created some awful squinting and no little confusion."

Inland from the sea, untroubled by red or white flags, farmers spread marl over land once considered worthless, and nature responded. Monmouth farms by 1840 were "under the highest state of cultivation." Many farmers began growing Irish potatoes in the 1840's, and yields were so great that the invention of a mechanical potato digger by Thomas Stout of Keyport in 1853 met a pressing need.

All Monmouth throbbed with transportation hopes and plans in the two decades preceding the Civil War. Steamers had provided the logical link with New York from the late 1820's on, with vessels touching at Sandy Hook, Keyport, Matawan, Oceanport, Red Bank, Eatontown Landing and Long Branch. Many of them brought in summer visitors, of course, but farm trade provided stability.

Oceanport's steamers also relied on products from James P. Allaire's Iron Works in Howell Township from 1822 to 1846. Allaire, New York iron-maker, bought the Howell Township works from an owner who had established it soon after the start of the nineteen century. The works prospered for two decades and its products enjoyed wide distribution until Allaire & Company abandoned it in 1846.

Red Bank and Keyport both grew rapidly after steamers started touching their docks in the 1830's. Red Bank, called "the most rapidly increasing village in the state except for Keyport" in 1840, carried on a brisk trade in vegetables, wood and oysters. Keyport, established in 1830, hoped for great importance when promoters began to build a cross-state plank road from Keyport to Florence in 1852. Only short stretches were built, however, before the impracticability of the wooden highway became apparent.

Farmers indorsed railroad ventures, getting behind the Freehold & Jamesburg Railroad in 1853 and the Raritan & Delaware Bay Railroad in 1854. Branch railroads pushed out to big marl beds at Squankum and Marlboro. A short line carried farm produce from Freehold to Keyport piers. Finally, the building of the New York & Long Branch Railroad in the late 1860's and early 1870's ended the farmer's dependence on the seaports.

The N.Y. & L.B., rolling down over the sandy wastes, slowly changed the character of the shore by making it possible for vacationists to come in as easily as farm produce went out. With the exception of Long Branch, the North Jersey shore was little frequented before 1870, except by those who could afford to stay all summer.

Take, as prime examples, Ocean Grove and Asbury Park. Only one family lived at Ocean Grove in July, 1879, when twenty people pitched their tents on eleven acres of beachfront purchased for fifty dollars. The following year twenty-six members of the Ocean Grove Camp Meeting Association each put up twenty-five dollars to buy more land, which the Association auctioned off on June 1, 1870, for $1,500.

The notion of a religious seaside resort "free

from the dissipations and follies of fashionable watering places" caught on with a rush. Sixty cottages were built by the end of 1871; by 1875 lots purchased for $50 at the 1870 auction brought $1,500.

James A. Bradley, New York City brush manufacturer, bought the first lot at Ocean Grove, but his thoughts dwelt on the briar-covered acres across the lake to the north. Not a soul lived on that stretch of beach in 1870, and the asking price of $90,000 for 500 acres seemed ridiculously high. Bradley bought, nevertheless, and named his wilderness Asbury Park after Bishop Francis Asbury. The first hotel was built in 1873 and eight large hotels and hundreds of smaller boarding houses covered Bradley's Folly in 1878.

Railroad statistics for Asbury Park and Ocean Grove in 1883 illustrate the quick transition from wilderness to resort. As many as 103 trains brought 8,000 people in one day and a total of 600,000 people visited the two towns between June and September, 1883.

Summer resorts of widely varying natures sprang up in the county. Many of them, particularly in the region of the Highlands and the Navesink and Shrewsbury rivers, became highly exclusive. However, until the late nineteenth century, farmers continued to make Wreck Pond near Sea Girt their destination on the second Saturday in August in celebration of "Beach Day" (many of them traveling great distance in wagons, wearing bathing suits under their overalls and pinafores). That area grew less bucolic, however, after the Governor and his staff began visiting Sea Girt every August to review National Guard troops.

As early as the summer of 1884 Guardsmen held rifle practice on the north side of Manasquan Inlet, but it was not until 1890 that a large Sea Girt tract was set aside by the state as a National Guard reservation. Men trained there for three wars, although Jersey Guardsmen were sent to other camps during World War I and II and the Sea Girt camp was employed for the training of Army specialists.

Gustav Kobbé's 1889 guidebook had this comment on other Monmouth shore resorts: Spring

The boardwalk at Asbury Park is a modern attraction of the 80-year-old resort.

Trotters at Freehold Raceway.

Lake, "a resort conspicuous for elegance"; Elberon, "laid out with much taste"; Monmouth Beach, "its great charms are privacy and refinement"; Rumson Neck, "on all sides there is evidence that it is controlled by people of wealth and taste"; Sea Bright (where foreign cricket teams and great tennis players always visited), "one of the gayest resorts on the coast."

Long Branch boomed particularly. President Grant for a time made Long Branch the nation's summer capital. Presidents Hayes and Harrison stayed at the old Elberon Hotel and President Garfield came home to die in Long Branch after he was shot in 1881. President Wilson also stayed in Long Branch in later years.

The tone of the resort changed considerably in the 1890's, as flamboyant characters made Long Branch a playground. Quite obviously, the red and white bathing flags had long since vanished. Phil Daly ran his gambling house even on Sundays, and such as Lillie Langtry, Diamond Jim Brady and Lillian Russell found the resort to their fancy. The sporting set thought Long Branch wonderful, but Kobbé's guidebook declared that the place probably repelled as many as it attracted. Be that as it may, Long Branch remained one of the country's most noted resorts throughout the nineteenth century.

Monmouth Park, in nearby Eatontown, lured the Long Branch crowd after racing started in 1870, but by the 1890's that, too, had fallen under a cloud. The park had rocky days until 1878, when a new group took it over. Then the racing season was increased from four days in 1878 to twenty-five days in 1888, and purses jumped in those years from $12,600 to $210,850. Indignation against state race tracks in the 1890's closed them all. However, a new Monmouth Park, this one in Oceanport, now draws the faithful.

Monmouth County's reputation for fine horses dated to colonial days. As far back as 1840 the Lairds of Colt's Neck trained horses, with the little mare Fashion becoming nationally famous. Joe Laird, who rode Fashion, became known as the "best jockey of the North." Noted stud farms grew up in the Eatontown-Tinton Falls-Scobeyville-Holmdel region (where, incidentally, many splendid horse farms still exist).

Few of New Jersey's counties had their characters so firmly set at the turn of the century as Monmouth. By then farming had become predominant, although marl had largely given way to more balanced fertilizers. Monmouth had become "The Shore" to North Jersey, as the result of improved railroad transportation. Changes in the county since then have been largely a matter of degree rather than kind.

Throughout Monmouth's long life the sea has been the background for most of the action, bringing pirates, colonists, enemy troops and vacationists (more or less in that order). Sandy Hook lighthouse and Navesink's twin lighthouses blinked security to vessels on the Atlantic's swelling surf. Still, through the years ships have smashed upon Monmouth's shores—such as the *New Era*, which broke up in December, 1854, off Deal Beach, with a loss of 500 lives, and the *Morro Castle*, whose burning hulk drifted to rest at Asbury Park in September, 1934.

Bootleggers came by sea, too, in the Thirsty Twenties. Atop the Highlands, in a home formerly owned by Oscar Hammerstein, illicit liquor salesmen erected one of the nation's most powerful radio stations. They supplied customers from Maine to Florida before a 1929 raid broke up the ring (or, at least, moved it elsewhere).

Manasquan Inlet also had its visitations by bootlegging operators during the prohibition period. However, the wide waterline dividing Monmouth and Ocean counties is better known as a haven for private and public fishing boats and the start of the important Inland Waterway stretching all the way to Florida. Noted artists and writers have made their homes on the borders of Manasquan Inlet and a parade of celebrities, most notably Robert Louis Stevenson, made their way to the old Union House which stood in what is now Brielle.

Sandy Hook's exposed position has made it a logical spot for fortification. A fort was started there before the Civil War, but by the 1890's it had not been finished. Then the Hook reverberated to the sound of a proving range. The smokeless powder which Hudson Maxim developed at Farmingdale in 1893 was tested on the Hook. Since then Fort Hancock has served the nation in peace and war, and the advent of the Korean war interrupted plans for making the Hook a state park.

Monmouth population has grown from 82,037 in 1900 to more than 225,000 today. Since 1940 the growth has been especially great, with more than 65,000 new residents moving to Monmouth in the last decade. The result has been to move Monmouth toward an "all-year" status, which in no way hurts the annual welcoming of millions of summer visitors.

Industry has made only slight inroads in Monmouth County, although Long Branch, Red Bank and Freehold have some industrial standing. The largest industry continues to be the long-established Karagheusian rug plant at Freehold, where more than 2,000 persons are employed.

Farming, however, is *the* money-maker in Monmouth. Each year the county vies with Cumberland for state dollar-farm leadership. Monmouth has an impressive list of agricultural firsts: in number of farms (2,530), in Irish potatoes (with about one-third of the state's total acreage), in poultry and poultry products, in products of orchards, vineyards and planted nut trees. Down in Upper Freehold dairies range through the aptly-named Cream Ridge section. Potato fields, truck gardens and chicken ranches spread everywhere.

All Monmouth comes uniquely together for a midsummer visitor, particularly if he goes by way of Englishtown and Freehold. He sees wonderfully preserved old homes and churches, "Molly Pitcher's Well," potatoes, chickens. He lolls on the beach, and after enjoying the sea, he stops at a roadside truck garden stand to enjoy the products of the soil.

In a way, that stop at the stand celebrates the "marriage" of the Irishman who discovered the richness of the soil and the boarding house lady who became aware of the richness of the surf.

MORE ABOUT MONMOUTH

Ellis, Franklin, *History of Monmouth County, New Jersey*. Philadelphia, Pennsylvania, R. T. Peck and Co., 1885.

Leonard, Thomas Henry, *From Indian Trail to Electric Rail*. Atlantic Highlands, N. J., The Atlantic Highlands Journal, 1923.

Lewis Historical Publishing Co., *History of Monmouth County, New Jersey, 1664-1920*. New York, Lewis Historical Publishing Co., 1922.

Salter, Edwin, *A History of Monmouth and Ocean Counties*. Bayonne, New Jersey, E. Gardner and Son, 1890.

Stryker, William Scudder, 1838-1900, *The Battle of Monmouth*. Princeton, New Jersey, Princeton University Press, 1927.

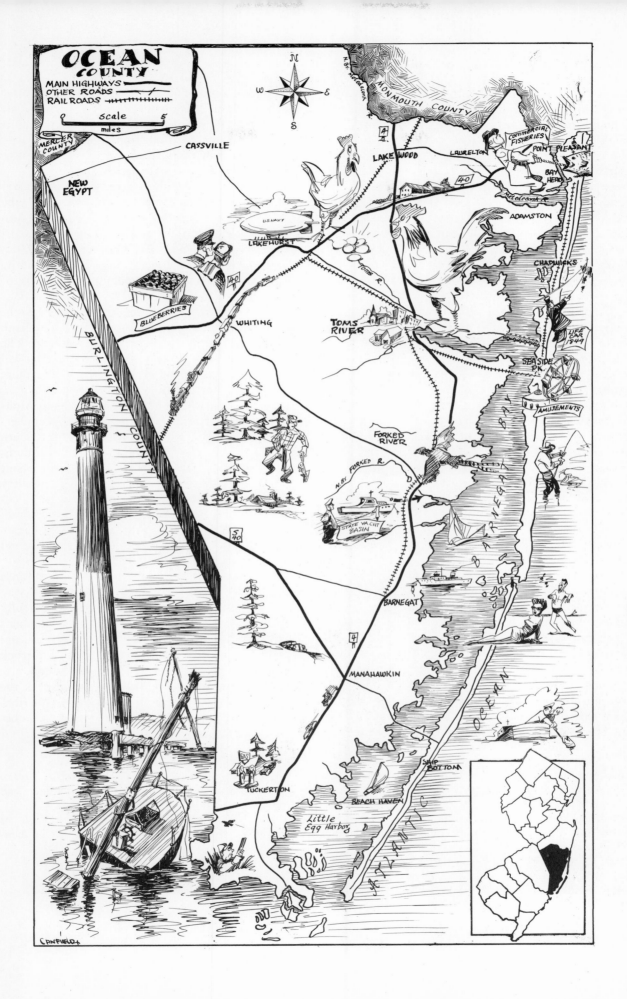

Barnegat Light, known to thousands as "Old Barney."

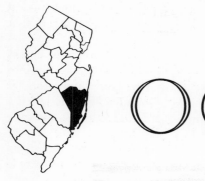

OCEAN

County fathers waisted little time in naming Ocean County after its separation from Monmouth on February 18, 1850. Simply and directly they titled their land in appreciation of their dependence on the sea, and if in their hearts some of them also meant to recognize the moody savagery and winsomeness of the surf, so much the better.

There was no casting about to pay tribute to some English nobleman. Too many diversified nationalities had sifted into Ocean by 1850 to make such a name logical. Besides, with a coastline of 50 miles and 150 years of sea-linked memories, why anything but Ocean? All the county's rich past—and hope for the future—went into that name.

Henry Hudson took a look at Ocean County's beachfront in 1609 and, to the eternal delight of county publicists, his ship's log spoke of this being "a very good land to fall in with, and a pleasant land to see." Captain Cornelius Jacobsen Mey, the much-traveled Dutchman, took a much closer look in 1614 and bestowed two names which have partially withstood the anglicizing tides of time—Barende-gat ("Inlet of Breakers") and Eyre Haven ("Egg Harbor").

Nomadic fishermen and whalers put in to Barnegat or Egg Harbor bays after Mey's visit, and mingled with Indians who frequented the shore looking for sea food. Occasionally a ship flying the Jolly Roger dropped anchor off the coast (to bury treasure, the excitable say). Other ships foundered on the shoals and cast their passengers upon the sands.

Most of those early arrivals stayed without the formality of buying the land, possibly reflecting that English noblemen had no more right to split up land sight unseen than they to settle, sight seen. Captain William Tom, English official from Newcastle, Delaware, looked over the land in about 1673, and for his trouble has had Toms River—creek and town—named after him.

However, Henry Jacobs Falkinburg of Schleswig-Holstein became the first settler of record, because he bought 800 acres from the East Jersey Proprietors in 1698 near what is now Tuckerton. At about the same time Mordecai and Edward Andrews, Quaker brothers from Oyster Bay, Long Island, bought land nearby. Edward built the first gristmill on the Jersey coast in 1704, powering his stones with water from a pond created by South Jersey beavers.

Many others came before 1720, representing vary-

Sad shipwreck aftermath, as 19th-century artist saw it.

199

ing nationalities and creeds. Most of them wished merely to be left alone, and they were. And they left others alone. A minister who toured the coast had this to say about the settlers in Ocean in 1750: "Some are decent people, who have lived in better places; but those who were born and bred here have neither religion nor manners." In all fairness, his writings also revealed a rather meager record of conversions, which surely colored his observations.

Indeed, as far as religious intensity is concerned, two Quaker missionaries from Tuckerton—Ann Gauntt and her niece, Ann Willet—attained greater fame than the bitter itinerant preacher as they toured North Atlantic states from 1728 until the Revolution. Moreover, Ocean County in 1770 gave rise to the Universalist Church in America, at Good Luck where Thomas Potter had erected a church in 1766.

Potter waited patiently for a preacher who would reflect his own liberal views of a universal God. Then, in 1770, John Murray, stranded when an English sloop went aground nearby, came to Potter's home seeking food. Murray and Potter talked, learned that each believed in a just and loving God (in a day when most religious leaders looked upon God as stern and harsh). Murray agreed to stay and preach in Potter's church—and the Universalist Church in America grew from that spot on the barren Jersey coast.

Sawmills dotted the county's numerous creeks before 1760, and dozens of sailing vessels set out into the open sea from Toms River or Tuckerton by 1770. Steady streams of fish-laden wagons left the coast to trundle through the forests across the state to Mount Holly and Philadelphia.

The nature of their occupations and their personal characteristics made these coastwise people willing to undertake war with England or with any one else who threatened their freedom. Privateering became a way of life, where the chance of a profit may have helped induce some to undertake risks in the name of patriotism. Toms River and Tuckerton assumed importance after the

Boat basin, Point Pleasant.

Coast near Barnegat City.

British blockaded larger ports. Privateers slipped out of Barnegat Bay and Little Egg Harbor to attack the King's shipping, then slipped back in to sell their captured cargoes. Many of the supplies found their way to Philadelphia via the sandy roads through the pine barrens.

Toms River had additional unique Revolutionary importance as the site of saltworks established by the Continental Congress and the State of Pennsylvania. Congress spent £6,000 (about $30,000) to set up its works, while Pennsylvania expended £400. Many other private works flourished along the coast, since both the manufacture of gunpowder and the flavoring and preservation of food demanded huge quantities of salt.

A windmill pumped salt water from Barnegat Bay to vats at Toms River, where evaporation under the hot sun permitted workers to collect the salt. The British considered the salt manufactories vital, too, and in 1778 sent an expedition of 135 men to burn the government works at Toms River.

Not more than 2,000 people lived in Ocean County at the end of the Revolution. Trade revived quickly (if, indeed, it ever stopped). President Washington signed papers making Tuckerton the port of entry for thirty miles of coast from Barnegat Inlet south to Brigantine Inlet. Tuckerton's harbor business spurted and its shipbuilders assumed importance. An 1823 visitor reported the harbor full of ships and the place "rich in money," with taverns and boarding houses full and hundreds of men cutting timber for the shipbuilders.

One of Tuckerton's shipbuilding families, the Shrouds, built the *Lorainer*, said to be the first brig (or brigantine) ever made. The two-masted, square-rigged vessel won attention as one of the most popular sailing types ever built.

Elsewhere, at Waretown, Toms River, Barnegat and Forked River, shipbuilders pushed forward with their whaleboats, oyster boats and smaller craft for coastwise shipping, leaving the larger vessels to Tuckerton. Ocean County masters sailed the world and the little boy who didn't dream of growing up to follow the sea was rare.

Another important early facet of the county's economic welfare started modestly in 1789, when David Wright lit the fire in his iron furnace near what is now Lakehurst. An extensive works followed at Staffordsville in 1797 and by 1812 other forges hummed near Laurelton (Butcher's Forge), near Lakewood (Washington Furnace), on Bamber Lake (Ferrago Furnace) and on the headwaters of Cedar Creek (Dover Forge).

At first the ironworks depended on local bog ore, but later ships brought in iron ore from the Fishkill region on the Hudson River. Butcher's Forge made water pipe for New York City and mule teams hauled quantities of iron across the state from Dover Forge to Philadelphia. Ferrago Furnace turned out bar iron in what authorities called "one of the best planned and built forges in New Jersey."

Ocean's ironworks had disappeared by Civil War time. Possibly the most important contribution of the forges was the fact that William Torrey, Sr., and Joseph W. Brick came seeking fortunes in iron and stayed to bring new life to the pines.

Torrey bought 27,500 acres of woodland surrounding the old Wright Forge in 1841 to make charcoal on a large scale. He built a railroad to Toms River, using wooden rails and mule-drawn

charcoal-carrying cars. Years later Torrey and his sons, William and John, stood up to the powerful Camden & Amboy Railroad monopoly and demanded a charter for a railroad across South Jersey. They won the right to start the Raritan Bay and Delaware Railroad in 1856. Completion of the railroad in 1860 helped open the pinelands to outside interests.

Joseph Brick, meanwhile, rebuilt the old Washington Furnace in 1833 and saw it thrive before his death in 1847. His family carried on and the area became known as Bricksburg (now Lakewood) in his honor. In addition, the pretty lake which powered Brick's works was given the name of Carasaljo—combining the first syllables of the names of Joseph W. Brick's three daughters, Caroline, Sally and Josephine.

Elsewhere in the pines, John Webb—best known as "Old Peg-Leg John"—drained a swamp near Cassville in 1845 and grew cultivated cranberries which netted him high sums in Philadelphia (where sailing masters thought cranberries prevented scurvy

Commercial fisheries, Long Beach Island.

Horses and carriages are familiar sight on streets of Pineland winter resort at Lakewood.

on long voyages). Webb's success prompted neighbors to engage in cranberry planting of their own.

Nevertheless, despite the activities in the pines, life centered on the coast. Actually, fear of the sea haunted coastal folk as much as love of the surf lured them. The treacherous shoals of Barnegat pounded ships to pieces and flung their cargoes and their dead and dying passengers on the sands. Hulks of ships destroyed by the moody ocean littered the beaches. Truly the coast from Point Pleasant to Little Egg Harbor merited its reputation as the most dreaded shoals north of Hatteras.

Congress took official notice in 1834 by building the original Barnegat lighthouse. Sullenly the ocean fought back, licking away at the sands until the beacon toppled into Barnegat Inlet in 1856. Immediately Congress appropriated $60,000 for a new light, built in 1857 and 1858 under the direction of Lieutenant George Gordon Meade, U. S. Army engineer who later won fame as General Meade at the Battle of Gettysburg. F. Hopkinson Smith, author and playwright, worked on the lighthouse as an engineer, and in his spare time started to write a seaside classic, *The Tides of Barnegat*.

The cruelty of the ocean struck young Dr. William A. Newell with full force during a visit to Long Beach in 1839. Out on the beach at the height of a summer storm, young Dr. Newell watched the Austrian brig *Perasto* break up on a sand bar only 300 yards from shore. His horror mounted as, one by one, the captain and crew of the *Perasto* drowned in the surf, with watchers powerless to help.

"If only a rope could be tossed that 300 yards," Dr. Newell thought. As he mourned the dead he conceived the idea of tossing a line to stricken ships by means of a shortened blunderbuss. Elected to Congress in 1846, Dr. Newell offered a resolution in 1848 which laid the foundation of the United States Lifesaving Service, forerunner of the present U. S. Coast Guard rescue stations. The sum of $10,000 was appropriated to provide surfboats and ropetossing equipment along the Jersey coast, and, fittingly enough, the country's first two nationally supported lifesaving stations were built in Ocean County.

At about the same time Joseph Francis of Toms River, noted boatbuilder, also sought means to snatch victims from the sea. In 1843 he built the first corrugated metal lifeboat and a year later invented the lifecar. The lifecar and Newell's idea of a rope fired from a gun merged on January 12, 1850, at Chadwick's on Squan Beach, where the Scottish barque *Ayrshire* struck a sand bar after she foundered in a blinding snowstorm.

John Maxen used Newell's system to fire a lifeline over the barque, and Joseph Francis's lifecar brought all 201 passengers safely ashore. Maxen, first man ever to throw a lifeline over a helpless vessel, received a gold medal. Congress honored Francis by striking a medal in his honor, said to be the most massive gold medal ever awarded by that body.

So, with thoughts of gallantry at sea fresh in their minds, the county's founding fathers naturally chose "Ocean" for their land after it split from Monmouth County in 1850.

Other decisions came less quickly. For example, economy-minded freeholders coldly rejected a budget of $2,000, then settled on $1,800 as sufficient for Ocean's 10,032 inhabitants. A courthouse

commission chose Hudson County's building as a model, but agreed that Ocean courthouse must be "smaller and less ornate." Completion of the building on June 13, 1851, satisfied most, although some grumbled that $9,956 was too much money to spend on a courthouse.

Despite the sparse population of the new county, Ocean saw one of its sons, Dr. George F. Fort of New Egypt, elected governor in 1850. Three years later another Ocean gubernatorial candidate, Reverend Joel Haywood, lost by only 3,782 votes, while in 1856 William A. Newell's election as the state's first Republican governor brought joy to Ocean County, which felt that Newell's lifesaving activities made him at least an adopted son.

A cranberry craze swept the county in 1863. Everyone who had money or could borrow it started growing cranberries. Swampland became priceless, even pine barrens brought $100 an acre. The craze killed itself; as soon as the vastly expanded bogs bore fruit, cranberry prices collapsed. When cranberry growing settled down to a sane

United States Navy's lighter-than-air craft base, Lakehurst.

Ciba States Ltd., pharmaceutical plant, Toms River; first major industry in Ocean County.

existence, growers formed one of the state's first farmer co-operatives at Bricksburg.

Scores of families came to Bricksburg in 1866 when the Bricksburg Land & Improvement Company assured them that the soil grew fruit trees in profusion. Two New York Stock Exchange brokers bought 19,000 acres of land there in 1879, built the Laurel House, changed the town's name to Lakewood—and wisely decided to capitalize on the pine trees rather than the apple trees.

Men of wealth followed in search of the healthful pine air; Lakewood assumed prime importance as a winter health resort. Many estates flowered among the pines, the most noteworthy being those of George Jay Gould and John D. Rockefeller.

Out along the coast, shipping by boat gave way to shipping by rail in the 1870's. Fishing, clamming and oystering zoomed in economic stature, however, and for years a standing joke in the State Legislature was to call any bill dealing with oysters or clams an "Ocean County bill," a tacit recognition of the importance of oystering and clamming to the county.

Seaside resorts followed the railroads in the 1870's. Point Pleasant Land Company started selling lots in 1870, the same year that a group of Philadelphia Quakers founded Beach Haven. Sea Side Park began as a Baptist religious resort in 1876, and a Methodist camp meeting came to Island Heights in 1878. Bay Head, started in 1883, became very fashionable, luring bathers from as far away as Washington. A railroad on Long Beach in 1885 provided the potential for more resorts.

Ocean County was fully resort-minded by 1900. Seaside towns broke away from larger townships to insure use of taxes to build up local resort facilities. Barnegat Bay became a prime hunting and fishing ground for sportsmen, with Forked River, Waretown and Barnegat vying for the trade of gentleman gunners and anglers.

Staunchly Republican Ocean County received a left-handed gift from the Democratic Legislature in 1891. The Democrats wrote off Ocean County as impossible to convert, but reckoned they had a chance in Burlington. Accordingly, they cut Little Egg Harbor Township (and its Republican votes) away from Burlington and added the township to Ocean.

World War I brought a chemical warfare proving ground to Lakehurst to train troops in handling poison gas. The camp became a Navy lighter-than-air craft base after the war, and the first American-built dirigible, the *Shenandoah*, made her maiden flight from Lakehurst in 1923. After a series of crashes, the ill-fated dirigibles fell into complete disfavor on May 6, 1937, when the German airship *Hindenburg* burned in midair at Lakehurst with a loss of thirty-six lives. The Navy still uses Lakehurst, of course, in its blimp program.

Right after World War I varied groups of immigrants started to arrive in Ocean County, notably the White Russians, who settled near Cassville, and the Scandinavians, who found work in the county's pound fisheries. A writer pointed out in 1923 that the county's "old Anglo-Saxon flavor is disappearing."

Agriculture, which had been confined to the cranberry bogs and the blueberry patches—plus a small area surrounding New Egypt—moved rapidly ahead in the 1920's. By 1925 the Toms River district had become known as one of the nation's most progressive poultry centers. Today, poultry products mean $14,000,000 annual income to Ocean County, second only to Monmouth.

More than 400 new chicken farms have been started in the county since 1945. Significantly, Ocean has some of the largest chicken ranches in the state, many of them being more than 3,000 acres in area, but the average size is less than 20 acres. New chicken farms constantly are being started, many of them operated by displaced persons who find in Ocean County both the room and the incentive to live.

Now past its hundredth anniversary (which it tub-thumped for a full year in 1950), Ocean is New Jersey's fastest-growing county, with a population today of about 65,000. That's a big jump since the 1950 figure of 56,622—and even the 1950 figure was an increase of 52 per cent over 1940. County leaders say 10,000 new homes are being built annually, and add that eight out of ten new homes are being built for year-around living.

Ocean has the lowest industrial employment in the state, but the county is optimistic, mainly because of the $5,000,000 plant which Ciba States, Ltd., has built on the banks of the Toms River between the towns of Lakehurst and Toms River. Nevertheless, 82 per cent of the county is still undeveloped and the feeling persists that Ocean actually has more future than past.

Fishing and clamming are still important sources of income, but when Ocean thinks of its sea today it thinks mainly of resort income (which the county claims is $150,000,000 annually). Large scale development has yet to hit much of the coast; Long Beach, for example, still has long stretches of primordial charm. Above all, 10-mile-long Island Beach, just south of Seaside Park, is still betwixt-and-between conversion into a state park.

There's an air of excitement in Ocean County. People talk hopefully of reclamation of the hundreds of thousands of acres of pine land. The sea still splashes on the sands—usually as a gentle, inviting host; sometimes as a violent reminder of its awesome power. Bones of wrecked schooners no longer litter the beaches, but memories of days when they did linger on.

"Ocean" is every bit as good a name today as it was in 1850. Today fortunes still follow the sea—and the fact is that a boarding house is worth far more (in dollars only) than a brig or schooner ever was.

MORE ABOUT OCEAN

Fischer, William H., *Biographical Cyclopaedia of Ocean County, New Jersey.* 1899.

Salter, Edwin, *History of Ocean and Monmouth Counties.* Bayonne, New Jersey, E. Gardner and Son, 1890.

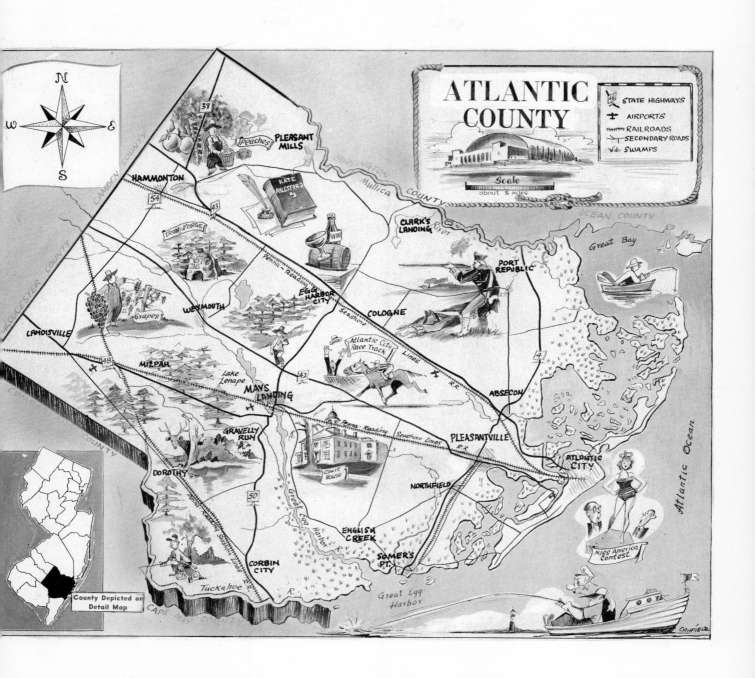

Boardwalk, Easter Sunday, Atlantic City, 1950.

ATLANTIC

Weariness showed in the stranger's face as he reined his horse to a stop in front of Ann Riseley's tavern in Absecon on a bright May day in 1820, yet his vibrancy and his spirit were apparent to those on the tavern steps. As the stranger dismounted one of the loungers spoke up:

"Where you fixin' to go, Cap'n?"

The horseman smiled as he replied, "I aim to stay right here." Dropping his saddlebags to the ground, he introduced himself as Dr. Jonathan Pitney, lately from Mendham in far-off Morris County. The welcome was spontaneous; if there was one thing needed in this sandy stretch at the edge of the Pine Barrens it was a doctor. Absecon was glad he aimed to stay.

Dr. Pitney soon realized something which the oyster fishermen at Leed's Point and the saltmakers on nearby Absegami Island failed to grasp—that here on the edge of the rolling Atlantic Ocean was an earthly paradise. Here among the unpopulated sand dunes was health and here was wealth. No one begrudged Doc Pitney the notion in 1820, so forty years later when they called him "The Father of Atlantic City" no one begrudged him the title, either.

Dr. Pitney's coming from the mountainland to the north excited wonder and curiosity along the beach. Few came overland, for through the years the ocean had been the thoroughfare which brought strangers to the coast; the Mullica, Great Egg Harbor and Tuckahoe rivers had been the avenues which led inland to the thick pine forests.

Early in the 1600's bold men had come to hunt whales off the coast. Eric Mullica later led a tiny band of Swedish colonists up the river which bears his name. Eric Mullica had come to stay. Considerably less interested in colonization were fellows like Blackbeard and his ilk, who found the countless bays and coves to the west of Absegami Island made to order for anyone seeking to elude pursuers.

Deep in the pine forest back from the coast there was great activity as Philadelphia entrepreneurs exploited the bog iron they found in the swamps. One of the earliest of the iron men was Charles Read, who came to the shores of Lake Nescochogue in the 1750's. He built a manor at Sweetwater (now Pleasant Mills) and lived in feudal splendor.

Down along the Great Egg Harbor River another bog iron dynasty began in 1754, when Samuel Richards arrived at Weymouth to take over 86,000 acres of woodland and swamps (greater than the area of all of Essex County). He acquired title for $28,000 dollars—about 33 cents an acre.

Six years later, in 1760, George May sailed up the Great Egg Harbor River and opened a store

Early view from a beach pavillion, Atlantic City.

to supply vessels which put in for timber at the head of the tide. Soon, of course, he was also exchanging Weymouth bog iron for salt, rice and indigo from the Carolinas. By the time of the Revolutionary War May's Landing was a place of great prosperity, and a humming shipbuilding business added to its vitality as a trading center.

The iron men helped Continental troops with products from their forges, yet the embryonic Atlantic County's greatest roles in the Revolution were played by its sailors. The same bays which had so nobly served the whalers and the pirates also proved splendid ports of call for privateers, who slipped out into the ocean to maul British shipping. The privateers did much for the cause, and well enough for themselves too, of course, with sales from captured Royal vessels.

Finally the British decided upon punitive action. They set 800 British regulars ashore at Chestnut Neck in October, 1778, and swarmed over the thin breastworks of the village defenders. The routed Colonial forces retreated up the Mullica River to make another stand, certain that the British would try to destroy the inland ironworks. Chestnut Neck fell to the British torch and the triumphant Redcoats set out after the iron.

Meanwhile, ninety woodland volunteers grabbed muskets and marched to within earshot of the British sentries. Daybreak found the Continental "Johnny Raws" (untrained troops) dispersed through the woods, waiting for drums to signal a British move. Before the sound of the rolling beat had died in the forest dawn, the woods were filled with a deadly rattle from the muskets of the nondescript Americans.

"We just cut loose and gave 'em hell," one of the farmers declared later.

Completely stunned, the invaders fell back, then fled in confusion. A second volley made the retreat a rout; the British were driven forever from the South Jersey pines.

Great was the rejoicing in the forest that night, particularly at the Read Mansion, where Charles Read's daughter, the gay Honoria, presided over the celebration. The mansion reflected not only the joy of the moment, but also the broader joy of the Reads, their happiness in the prosperity they had found in this woodland.

Not everyone shared the jubilance of the Reads. Such a dissenter was handsome Joe Mulliner, leader of a band of forty rogues who lived in the forest and never let pass an opportunity to steal from the

Boardwalk, Easter Sunday, Atlantic City, 1903.

rich. As if to excuse Joe—a good talker and a good mixer—some said he was "a regular Robin Hood, stealing from them as had, and giving to them as didn't."

Secretly Joe loved Honoria Read, a passion he shared with every male in the area whether rich or poor. In the summer of 1781 Honoria distributed invitations to a splendid party. Understandably from the viewpoint of the Reads, Mullinger was not included. On the day of the party he kidnaped Honoria and held her until late evening, long enough to ruin the party. But justice triumphed; soon after Joe was captured and hanged for his crimes.

(Long after, in 1855, Charles Peterson used the life at Sweetwater as the basis for the first truly New Jersey novel, *Kate Aylesford, or The Life of the Refugees.* Today the Read house, still standing, is known as Aylesford Mansion.)

By 1800 inland bog-ironworks neared peak production. Forges prospered at Weymouth, Gloucester, Etna and Walker's Forge. The Weymouth holdings at the time Dr. Pitney came to Absecon in 1820 serve well to tell the story. The vast tract was split into centers of 20,000 acres apiece, each subdivided into 10 divisions to provide for constant forest growth.

Eight large wagonloads of charcoal were fed into the maw of the 30-foot-high furnace each day. Two men at the top of the furnace dumped six baskets of charcoal every few minutes over the iron melting below. Huge bellows driven by water power kept the blast hot enough to send a stream of molten metal running out the bottom and into molds where stove parts, iron pipes and hitching posts were cast. Philadelphia's first water pipes came from Weymouth in 1801 and many a hitching post in that city bore the big "W" of the woodland iron empire. Sometimes iron markers were cast for graves, and enough of these still remain in Atlantic County to confirm the boast that bog iron was "non-rusting."

Other industrialists joined ironmasters in seeking fortunes in the forests. William Coffin built a glassworks in 1812 on a tract he named Hammond Town for his son, John Hammond Coffin. William Lippincott built a cotton textile factory at Sweetwater and named it Pleasant Mills. Later, Coffin & Company followed Lippincott and established another

glassworks in the village. Gloucester Furnace was producing 800 tons of iron, mostly "country" castings (sashweights, etc.) by 1834, only slightly less than Weymouth.

Nevertheless, there was nothing about this thinly-settled country to cause Gloucester County to protest when the State Legislature carved 613 square miles away from Gloucester on February 7, 1837, to set up Atlantic County. Nor was there cause for dissension in the new county when Mays Landing—with its three taverns, four stores, one Methodist Church and twenty-five or thirty houses—was chosen as the county seat. The new county started building its brick courthouse in 1838.

Possibly the least attractive spot of all Atlantic County was the coast, particularly the off-shore island which had been the haven of pirates and squatters until Jeremiah Leeds acquired legitimate title to land and moved there early in the nineteenth century. Only one hand was needed to count the houses on the island when Dr. Pitney first visited there in 1820.

July Fourth is the height of the season at Atlantic City.

Moody scene near Mays Landing, where once a busy shipyard thrived.

A few hardy sportsmen found their way to the beach, where bird life was so plentiful that Jeremiah Leeds could tell of killing forty-eight "squawks" with one blast of his mighty gun. Most of the hunters stayed at the boarding house which Jeremiah's widow, Aunt Millie, opened in 1838.

Others, the younger set, were more likely to head for "Uncle" Ryan Adams's place. Those beach parties came in boats, and as they rounded Rum Point they hoisted flags to their mastheads. That was enough to move Uncle Ryan.

"Aunt Judith," he would call, "Folks a-comin'. Set some food on."

The guests undressed among the dunes (until Uncle Ryan built them crude—and airy—bathhouses out of brush) and "down to the beach they danced to strains of Fisher's hornpipe, discoursed by a single fiddle." At high tide they bathed, and "the hilarity of the occasion culminated when the young men carried the blushing and screaming maidens to the tops of steep sand hills and, tying their feet together, rolled them down to the water's edge."

Still, anyone who seriously wanted to frequent the Atlantic County coast went to Somers Point,

"quite a good place of resort for the Summer, with boarding houses for the accommodation of strangers."

No one ever visited Somers Point without learning of gallant Master Commandant Richard Somers of the United States Navy, a local boy who had risen to become the brilliant young commander of the *Intrepid*, a vessel loaded with explosives and assigned to destroy the enemy fleet at Tripoli in 1804. Young Somers, only twenty-six years old, sailed the *Intrepid* close to the fleet when suddenly his vessel exploded with a mighty roar, killing Somers and twelve others. Generally, it was said Somers lit a match to the powder magazine to avoid capture by the Turks.

Dr. Pitney, often on the beach in the pursuit of his professional duties, constantly admired its rugged beauty and its healthful air. He loved to walk along the sandy beach, and one day in 1845 as he stood on a hill watching the rolling green ocean, he turned to General Enoch Doughty and exclaimed:

"This should become the El Dorado of the Atlantic Coast, Enoch!"

By 1852 Dr. Pitney and General Doughty enlisted the enthusiasm of Richard B. Osborne, a railroad engineer, and young Samuel Richards, described as having "pleasing manners and tireless energy," qualities which have marked Atlantic City promoters ever since. They applied for a railroad charter, finally had it granted in March, 1852, mainly because powerful Camden & Amboy Railroad men never dreamed that a railroad to the shore would be successful.

Absegami Island received the name which now has meaning throughout the world on a day in the middle of January, 1853, when a group of men sat around a table to discuss plans for their "Bathing Village." They decided first to choose a name for the coming town.

Such uninspired names as "Surf", "Seabeach", and "Strand" were offered. Richard Osborne listened quietly, then suggested the board get on with his plan for the city. He unrolled his "great and well-finished map" and across the top the board saw "in large letters of gold, stretching over the waves that were delineated thereon as breaking on Absecon Beach, the words: 'ATLANTIC CITY.'"

Thus, for the ages and the unborn vacationists and souvenir labelers was the city named, and it became official on March 3, 1854, when incorporation papers were signed.

Quickly the adult males in the scattered houses along the beach organized. Only eighteen of the twenty-one eligible voters on May 1, 1854, dropped ballots through the slit in a cigar box fastened with yellow tape to insure the inviolability of the ballot. Everyone who desired an office was elected, with Chalkley S. Leeds chosen as first mayor.

They got down to business, passed regulations governing bathing and real estate taxes. Then they passed two ordinances, into which perhaps may be read lasting significance: the first was to control liquor licenses; the second, to authorize the building of a jail. That cleared the way for such things as schools.

The first Camden & Atlantic Railroad train rolled over the flat country from Camden in two and a half hours on July 1, 1854, carrying 600 dignitaries and the press. There was great rejoicing in the as yet unfinished United States Hotel, but the guests were

Ruins of the Weymouth paper mills.

Pleasant Mills Church built about 150 years ago, near center of once-thriving bog iron village.

glad to get back to the comforts of Philadelphia the same evening.

Dr. Pitney's dream grew slowly at first, hampered by both the lack of accommodations and the elements. The first excursionists amused themselves plodding through the sand among the grassy slopes, gathering seashells or clambering over the hulks of wrecked ships. Nature played a cruel hand in 1857, when the coldest winter the coast ever experienced froze ice six feet deep in the bays. A January nor'easter cast chunks of ice into 20-foot piles on the beach and stopped railroad travel for many weeks.

Even worse was the fly and mosquito plague of 1858, when greenhead flies, gnats and mosquitoes threatened to wrest the island away from the human beings. Horses covered with blood wandered through the streets; cattle waded into the ocean to escape the torture. Excursionists begged train crews to leave far before scheduled time. Hotel guests threatened owners unless screens were put up.

The Camden & Atlantic Railroad sought earnestly to improve the beach, both because of the benefits it would bring to its railroad and also because most of its promoters were in the land company which had bought on the beach for $17.50 an acre, in the hopes they might sell it someday for "as high as $500."

In 1870, Jacob Keim, tired of the sand being tracked through the rugs in his Chester House hotel, discussed the matter with Alex Boardman, conductor on the railroad. The two agreed the solution was a boardwalk on the beach. Boardman's bosses thought so much of the idea that they gave him a leave of absence to promote it. The first walk opened June 26, 1870—called "Boardman's Walk," some say—was eight feet wide and laid directly on the sands. The present permanent walk, the fifth in the line of succession, was built in 1939.

The first of the famous piers came to Atlantic City in 1882 and others followed as promoters saw the advantages of having all that space with so little boardwalk frontage. Before the turn of the century piers were both numerous and lasting.

Naturally, as business boomed in the resort city, other railroads saw the light. In 1877 the pressure for a second railroad was so great that the Narrow Gauge (with tracks spaced only three and a half feet apart) was built in the phenomenally short time of ninety-eight days. The Narrow Gauge quickly cut fares and moved in on the business.

Elsewhere the railroads through the pines brought benefits to the county. Hammond Town and Egg Harbor City—both besides the tracks—emerged as well-established communities. As a matter of fact, new life had to be found in the pines; the railroads which had nurtured Atlantic City had ruined bog iron dynasties, because ore in North Jersey became far more accessible with the advent of railroads.

The Gloucester Farm and Town Association was organized in 1854, coincidentally with the building of the C. & A. Railroad. The Association bought 36,000 acres and split them up into 30-acre divisions in the new city of Egg Harbor. The establishment of the Association also coincided with the wave of "America for Americans" feeling which swept the country in the 1850's under auspices of the Know-Nothing Party. However, the Association welcomed immigrants, and hundreds of Germans flocked to the Association to settle in Egg Harbor.

Egg Harbor's Germans were mostly cultured people who, according to an early chronicler, "abhorred whiskey but liked wine." They were delighted when John Wild found in 1858 that the surrounding soil was suitable for the growing of grapes. H. T. Dewey and Sons opened a commercial winery in 1867, but oddly enough (in that very German section) it was a Frenchman who founded the greatest winery.

He was Louis N. Renault, stranded in this country by the Franco-Prussian War in 1870 while serving as an emissary for the Duc De Montebello. Seeking to establish himself, Renault started the Egg Harbor winery which since has grown to nation-wide prominence.

Out on the western strip of the county one of South Jersey's greatest promoters, Charles K. Landis, interested Judge Richard J. Byrnes in 1858 in the possibility of a city rising in the Hammonton area where William Coffin's glassworks once prospered. Landis was a master publicist. He flooded the country with vivid word pictures of the glories of Hammonton.

Scores of New Englanders, lured by Landis's prose, headed for Hammonton. Years later most of them still remembered the shock when their train stopped at Hammonton and they stepped down. There wasn't even a station—the only marker was a lime hogshead on which "Hammonton" was crudely lettered.

Yet they stayed. They found the soil ideal for fruits and berries and they found the Landis-Byrnes

Everything ceases in Hammonton on July 16 for annual Our Lady of Mt. Carmel fete.

Boat basin at Pleasantville, suburb of Atlantic City.

idea of small lots for people of limited means highly attractive. By 1868 they were shipping seven carloads of strawberries daily to Philadelphia. Landis moved farther afield, went abroad to Italy to tell Italians of Hammonton.

At first the Italians stayed on the edge of town, making the soil yield returns which astounded the New Englanders. By 1876 they had started their annual July 16 celebration of the Feast of Our Lady of Mount Carmel. That feast, with its colorful parade, still draws many thousands of people to Hammonton each summer.

Egg Harbor had grown into a city of 4,000 by 1950, and Hammonton into a town of 8,400 the same year, with the German element clinging to Egg Harbor region and the Italians clustered along the western strip of the county just beyond the pines. Mays Landing grew slowly and quietly into a bustling county seat with a population of 2,300, still surrounded by thick forests, broken only by the remarkably straight and well-kept highways and the "Atlantic City" Race Track at McKee City, a pleasure spot literally carved out of the pines.

Close to Atlantic City, Pleasantville grew too, at-

tracting many residents across Lake's Bay to the region which William Lake, Long Island whaler, had first settled in 1702. Two of William's descendants are still honored in aptly named Pleasantville—Simon Lake, inventor of the Lake Submarine, and Jesse Lake, inventor of the self-track-laying car. All countries now use Simon Lake's patents in their submarines. Jesse Lake's self-track machine was invented to aid in building the first highway between the mainland and Atlantic City in the 1860's. The self-track car carried sand and gravel and other materials across the soft meadows and tiny streams. Today the principle is used on farm tractors and on lethal tanks.

Pleasantville was incorporated as a borough in 1888 and adopted the city form of government in 1914. Within the very shadow of the world's greatest amusement area, it is now home to more than 14,000 people.

Yet, Atlantic City obviously dominates the county. Its 1950 population of 61,642 was almost half the total county population of 132,879, and another 40,000 people live within immediately-surrounding communities. In addition, the roads annually lead 4,500,000 cars straight through the wilderness to the city; the railroad owes its existence to the city. The 16,000,000 annual visitors generally don't stop to learn about Hammonton or Pleasant Mills or Weymouth or Mays Landing—they head for the boardwalk to be, as one writer put it, "sated, tanned and loaded with souvenirs."

Obviously nearly all of Atlantic County has been resort-conscious for three-quarters of a century. For more than thirty years the county inhabitants have absorbed some of the luster of the Miss American pageants. Ever since the 1890's they have been reading and believing what the public-relations men have to say. But some of them remember what happened during the depression to the city with all its eggs in only a recreation basket.

Atlantic City was at its prosperous peak when Wall Street collapsed. The tremendous Convention Hall opened May 31, 1929, celebrating the city's seventy-fifth birthday. Hotel building went on apace. Money rolled in.

Then came the crash and Atlantic City was hard hit. Banks, twenty-eight of them, collapsed in the city. Business fell flat; the city suffered during the depression. World War II brought a resurgence of trade, and hundreds of thousands of soldiers to take over the hotels. Naturally Atlantic City has found lush times in postwar spending for rest and relaxation. In 1952, for the first time since 1929, new buildings started going up on the boardwalk.

This time, however, there are forces working to find other means of support—not that there is the slightest fear that Americans will stop seeking recreation, come war or high water.

Particularly interested in acquainting the outside world with Atlantic County are the municipalities in the western part, where thousands of acres of land stretch uninhabited and unused. Towns like Hammonton, for example, proud of its beautiful streets, its Peach Blossom Festival and its position as "The Hub of South Jersey," are offering industry every inducement to come and look around. The Southern New Jersey Development Council is pushing energetically to unite all of the southern counties in seeking industry. Even Atlantic City would welcome some industry—provided there are no smoking chimneys, of course—to help ease seasonal unemployment.

So has Dr. Pitney's child grown. Today there is no difficulty in getting medical indorsement for the city. It is established that this is "the El Dorado of the Atlantic Coast"—and more. Inland, the bog-iron forges have long since fallen to ruin, but new ventures bid fare to eclipse the long-ago prosperity.

It is not likely that 15 of the 15,000,000 visitors to Atlantic City ever heard of Dr. Pitney. It is certain, though, that few would be other than glad that the Mendham physician "aimed to stay" that day in May, 1820.

MORE ABOUT ATLANTIC

Atlantic County Historical Association, *Early History of Atlantic County*. Kutztown, Pennsylvania, Kutztown Publishing Co., 1915.

Carnesworth, pseud., *Atlantic City: Its Early and Modern History*. Philadelphia, Pennsylvania, W. C. Harris and Co., 1868.

English, A. L., *History of Atlantic City*. Philadelphia, Pennsylvania, Dickson and Gilling, 1884.

Hall, John F., *Daily Union History of Atlantic City and County, N. J.* Atlantic City, New Jersey, Daily Union Press Co., 1900.

Heston, Alfred, *Heston's Handbooks or Queen of the Coast, 1887-1908*. New York.

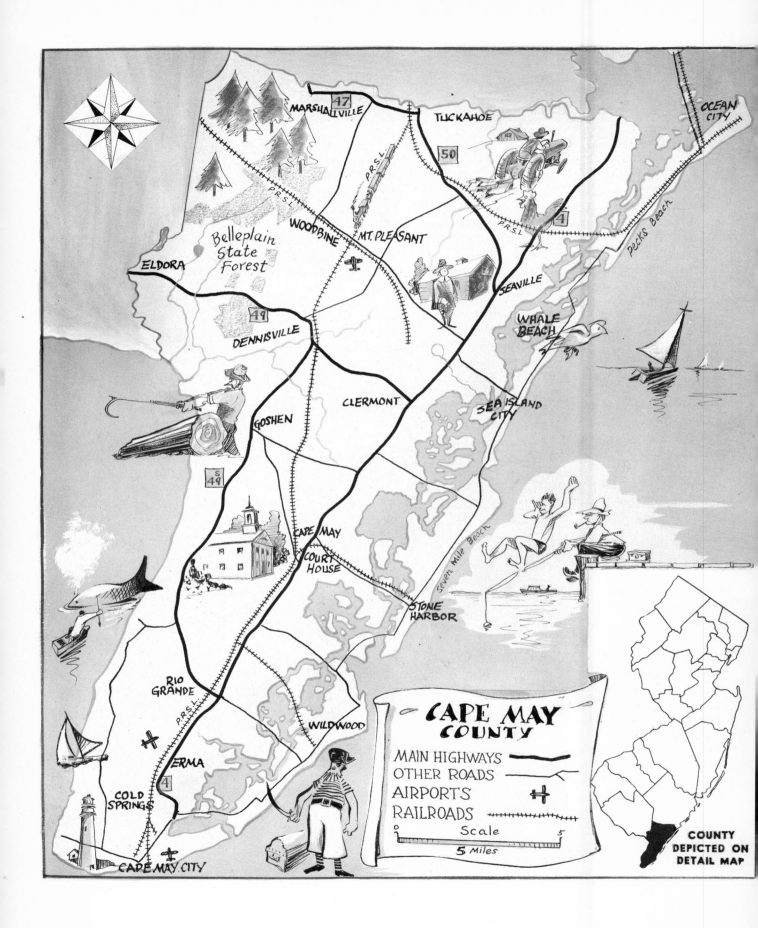

CAPE MAY COUNTY

MAIN HIGHWAYS ————
OTHER ROADS ————
AIRPORTS
RAILROADS

Scale
5 Miles

COUNTY
DEPICTED ON
DETAIL MAP

MARSHALLVILLE
TUCKAHOE
OCEAN CITY
WOODBINE
MT. PLEASANT
ELDORA
Belleplain State Forest
SEAVILLE
WHALE BEACH
DENNISVILLE
SEA ISLAND CITY
CLERMONT
GOSHEN
CAPE MAY COURT HOUSE
STONE HARBOR
RIO GRANDE
WILDWOOD
ERMA
COLD SPRINGS
CAPE MAY CITY

Pecks Beach
Seven Mile Beach

P.R.S.L.

CAPE MAY

Two Cape May County traditions quickly tell the stranger how deep are the roots of those who live on the Jersey cape. The first declares there are more *Mayflower* descendants in Cape May County than in Plymouth County, Massachusetts; the second declares that once a person "gets sand in his shoes" he'll never leave Cape May.

Walking down the shaded streets of Cape May Court House, where eighteenth- and nineteenth-century homes spread outward from the old white courthouse, it is easy to understand why sand gets in the shoes. Down on the Cape itself, meandering streets and old hotels bespeak the heritage of one of the nation's oldest "watering places." Cape May County bears the quiet 260-year-old pride of the Townsends and the Hands, the Leamings and the Ludlams, the Corsons and the Spicers—families whose ancestry can be traced back to the beginning.

However, the county name derives from the ubiquitous Dutch captain, Cornelius Jacobsen Mey, who paid extensive attention to the coast as he maneuvered his ship *Glad Tidings* around the cape in 1620. Captain Mey found the climate charming—"like Holland" (which to a Hollander is the ultimate compliment)—and named the land for himself.

The Dutch made desultory attempts to colonize the land, and a few adventurers fished for whales in Delaware Bay as early as 1633, but it took English colonists from New England (including *Mayflower* descendants) and Long Island to make Cape May whaling profitable.

On a high bluff overlooking Delaware Bay the English whalers built thirteen houses and called their village "Town Bank." They sallied into the bay in small boats to battle whales weighing up to 250 tons. Life was simple, if dangerous. If no whales were captured the one-industry town faced certain collapse. More personally, a harpooned whale had to be dispatched quickly in the elemental kill-or-be-killed struggle, since his lashing tail could bring death with a single flip.

The whalers immediately beached their quarry and stripped them, turning blubber and bones into saleable products worth up to $4,000 a whale. William Penn wrote of the lucrative Cape May whaling, and a 1698 writer told of the "prodigious—nay, vast—quantities" of Cape May "oyle and whalebone."

Whaling understandably had an impermanancy about it, and even the establishment in 1685 of

Cedar Mining near Dennis Creek, in 1850's.

219

Sea gulls and fishermen along one of barren stretches of the coast of Cape May County.

Cape May courthouse, built in 1849.

loosely defined county boundaries failed to give the Cape solidity. Dr. Daniel Coxe of London consolidated things with his 1688 purchase, sight unseen, of 95,000 Cape May acres. He never came to America, but his manorial ideas for his vast real estate holdings included two-story Coxe Hall, built by his agents and used for church meetings and for local government.

No settlers obtained land titles until Dr. Coxe sold most of his holdings to the West Jersey Society in 1692, the year the county was officially established. Shamgar Hand, first of a long Cape May line, bought 1,000 acres at Rummey Marsh (now Cape May Court House) in 1690; Thomas Leaming, who came in 1692 at the age of 18 to "go a-whaling," got sand in his shoes and stayed. John Townsend located land in the upper part of the county in 1690 and drove his team of oxen single file along the narrow forest path to his homestead.

It was a difficult land to colonize. Just behind the beaches on the ocean side, vast marshlands, up to three miles in width, extended the length of the county. Out in the west and north, impenetrable cedar forests walled Cape May off from the rest of the state. The building of the road between Egg Harbor and Cold Spring in 1706 helped immensely, but the first census in 1726 showed only 668 inhabitants in the entire county.

Pirates cruising off the coasts sometimes stopped for water from the Cape's cool springs or (if the folklorists are right) to bury treasure. Cattle herders along the coast occasionally saw the buccaneers out where grassy meadows covered the ocean side of the county. There cattle roamed free, identifiable by the unique Cape May "ear marks" (like that described in Anthony Ludlam's 1737 will, which described his ear mark as being "an El on ye underside of left ear and a slit in ye top of ye right ear").

Farms replaced the whaling villages early in the eighteenth century. Fishermen, oystermen and clam diggers eked out an uncertain living in the bay and ocean. Up in the forests woodsmen began to convert the great cedars into timber.

Such was the land of Aaron Leaming, II (born 1715) and Jacob Spicer, II (born 1716), Cape May's most prominent early citizens. Sons of county founders, both were respected for their intelligent contributions as Cape May's representatives in the Assembly. They worked together to produce in 1758 a noted compendium of the state's early laws and concessions.

Spicer's Cape May popularity diminished considerably in 1756, when he purchased from the West Jersey Society all unsold lands and privileges. The purchase disturbed residents of the Cape, since it also included rights to "hawking, fishing, hunting and fowling." In 1752 an association had been formed to buy the rights, but the association dallied while Spicer bought. The most bitter of the disappointed residents charged that Spicer's purchase price of £300 was set "at a time when the influence of the wine bottle usurped the place of reason." Nevertheless, Spicer had the rights.

Internal warring over "rights" faded in the common fight against the British, although the Revolutionary War mainly stayed out to sea as far as Cape May was concerned. Before the fighting started, Cape May pilots refused to guide tea-laden British vessels up the Delaware River. John Hatton, possessed of "an unhappy, violent temper," arrived in Cold Spring in November, 1770, to put an end to coastal smuggling. Hatton's enthusiasm for his work caused him untold grief—and in no way stopped the smuggling.

Wartime found Cape May pilots striking at British coastwise shipping, while other residents stayed ashore to act as anti-British spies, relaying information by pony express riders who galloped through the pinelands to Philadelphia.

Cape May's most important year may well have been 1801, when Ellis Hughes, proprietor of the Hotel Atlantic, placed his much-quoted advertisement in *The Philadelphia Daily Aurora:*

"The public are respectfully informed that the subscriber has prepared himself for entertaining company who use sea bathing."

Hughes was not the first to proclaim the virtues of Cape May as a "watering place," nevertheless. Reverend Samuel Finley, pastor of the Cold Spring Presbyterian Church from 1740 to 1742, spoke often of the merits of Cape May bathing, even after he became president of Princeton College in 1761. Many physicians lauded the Cape's health-giving potentialities before Hughes. The difference was that Hughes aimed to be a host.

Others took in visitors, too, so that by 1812 local citizens counted on summer dollars from Philadelphia guests. Already the Cape was far different from what the whalers had known; Town Bank was

completely gone, washed away by the relentless sea (which by known measurement cut 169 feet from the Cape May beaches between 1804 and 1822).

The War of 1812 interrupted the summer visiting, and residents at Cape May Point laboriously dug a huge ditch from the ocean to prevent the British getting fresh water from Lilly Lake. The salt water flowed into the lake through ditches cut through 16-foot-high sand dunes.

A sloop started regular service between the island and Philadelphia in 1815, the year before Thomas H. Hughes, son of Ellis, built the original Congress Hall. People laughed at "Tommy's Folly," but big, hearty Tommy replied:

"The day will come when you'll have to cover every square inch here with a silver dollar to get enough land to put up a house!"

Tommy's prediction stood up as visitors began to arrive from Philadelphia, Baltimore, Washington and the South—"as many as 3,000 in a single summer," according to an 1844 historian. In 1853, work was begun on the Mount Vernon, largest hotel in

Congress Hall Hotel, at Cape May, one of typical hotels of the old resort town.

Fishing fleet basin at Sea Isle City called the "Venice of America."

the world at the time. Builder Philip Cain startled the resort by erecting Mount Vernon's front section 300 feet wide and four stories high, then added a wing 500 feet long and three stories high. Proprietor Cain's dream of a third 500-foot wing and accommodations for 2,100 guests vanished in a fire on September 5, 1855. Cain and five others died in the blaze.

Cape May town was the most famous resort in the nation in the 1850's, local promoters said, ignoring the claims of Saratoga and Long Branch. Southern planters and the elite of the North exchanged discreet and genteel opinions in the glittering hotels. Visiting plantation owners whiled away their time and whittled away their fortunes in such gambling houses as Henry Cleveland's "Blue Pig."

Famous people came, too, such as President Franklin Pierce in 1855 and President James Buchanan in 1858. And an obscure Illinois politician named Abe Lincoln slept in the Mansion House in 1849.

Never, however, was there a Cape May visitor like Henry Clay. Summer crowds had started to disappear from the Cape in August, 1847, when "Harry of the West" asked for reservations at the Mansion House to spend a quiet week in mourning for his son killed in the Mexican War. Word leaked out, much to the satisfaction of the local bonifaces, and the outward-bound streamed back to greet Clay on his arrival from Philadelphia on August 16.

Golden-voiced Henry went swimming twice a day and possibly enjoyed it despite the vigorous ladies who chased him with scissors to clip off locks of his hair. ("When he returned to Washington," said one writer, "his hair was short indeed!") A New York delegation waited on Clay with an invitation but he refused in a moving declaration of grief for his son which made his until-then griefless audience weep openly.

Inland, Cape May County grew, too, albeit slowly. The County had no physician until 1786, when Dr. John Dickinson moved down from Salem. Education consisted of itinerant tutors on horseback until 1830, when the first crude schoolhouses were built. Religious groups had solid foundations, the Baptists having been established at Cape May Court House in 1712, the Presbyterians at Cold

Spring in 1714, and the Quakers at Seaville in the early 1700's.

Cape May Court House, named county seat in 1745, rightfully took pride in its handsome new courthouse built in 1849 (at a cost of $6,284, including a 333-pound bell cast for $99.33). The ferry at Beasley's Point, established in 1692, flourished. Nearby, Tuckahoe had a busy shipbuilding background. Out in western cedar lands, Dennis Creek prospered from shipbuilding, timber cutting, and from cedar shingles "mined" from the swamps. And Dennis Creek could boast that its 1802 post office was the county's first, and that its shingles were used on the roof of Philadelphia's Independence Hall.

On the verandas in Cape May in the summer of 1860, discussion centered on the Breckinridge-Lincoln Presidential campaign. As the Southerners returned to their plantations in August the wiser of the Cape May residents knew an era had passed. The wiser were right. The assault on Fort Sumter shattered forever the veranda quietude.

Despite its position well below the Mason-Dixon Line and its annual seasonal influx of Southern blood, Cape May quickly supported the Union cause. Off to war went its young men, including Lieutenant Henry W. Sawyer, who rose rapidly and on the morning of June 9, 1863, went into battle with his newly-won captain's commission.

Rebel troops captured Sawyer that day and sent him to the infamous Libby Prison. There, on July 6, he was called into the prison yard with other imprisoned captains and told that within a few days two of them must die in retaliation for the execution of two Confederate captains within Union lines. Sawyer and Captain John M. Flynn

Quaker Meeting House, established 1702, Seaville.

A stretch of the eight miles of beach at Ocean City.

of Indiana drew the grim assignment. Immediately the North's Secretary of War informed the South that if Sawyer and Flynn died the North would execute General William Fitzhugh Lee (son of General Robert E. Lee) and Captain Richard B. Winder, Union prisoners. The South readily exchanged the Union captains for the two Confederate generals.

Union veterans returned to a changed Cape May in 1865. A railroad had been built down the Cape in 1863. County population had jumped to nearly 7,500, but five-sevenths of the Cape remained undeveloped. More than 50,000 visitors came in 1866, the year *The New York Herald* declared:

"If they (vacationists) want a fast place, let them go to Saratoga; if they want a place where people 'are content to dwell in decencies forever' let them go to Cape May."

New Stockton Hall was opened in 1869, the year President Grant visited Cape May. Mrs. Grant set the ladies of the resort to sewing madly on red and blue flannel bathing suits, imitations of those Mrs. Grant bought from a local tailor. President Grant shook hands, of course (but not nearly as many as

the 2,500 hands President Arthur shook in a single evening during his 1883 stay).

Old Cape May town perished in the decade from 1869 to 1879. First, an 1869 fire ruined a quarter of the business section, including several old hotels. Then, on November 9, 1878, flames swept through thirty-five acres of buildings in the heart of the city, leveling most of the best hotels and private cottages. Many secretly expressed the belief, however, that the fire was a blessing in horrible disguise since it permitted rebuilding with some planning for the future.

Varying industries sought to exploit Cape May's natural advantages in the years after the Civil War. The Porpoise Fishing Company opened a factory on Pond Creek in 1868 to make porpoise skins into leather, refine porpoise fat into oil, and make "dolphin steaks" from the flesh. Commercial fishing of all kinds reached such proportions in the 1880's that local residents protested violently (sometimes reinforcing their vocal protests by shooting at commercial vessels).

Up county at Rio Grande a group of Philadelphia promoters planted 2,000 acres of sugar cane, their initiative strengthened by state bounties of a dollar a ton for all cane grown and a cent a pound for all sugar refined. The Rio Grande Sugar Company made 76,000 pounds of sugar and 87,000 gallons of syrup in 1884, but termination of the state bounty in 1885 doomed the venture. Cape May's southern exposure, by the way, has tempted various other agricultural experiments, ranging from licorice-growing to mulberry-tree-culture and the use of sea lavender for honey.

More important, however, was the interest shown in the 1880's in the extensive pasture lands along the entire ocean front, where the rolling summer surf on the best beaches in the state served only to cool herds of free-roaming cattle.

Ocean City grew from the temperance colony and Methodist summer resort started on Peck's Beach in 1880 by three minister brothers named Lake. Just to the south, Charles K. Landis (founder of Vineland and Hammonton) in 1880 laid out Sea Isle City, which by 1893 had thirty hotels and was widely known for its brilliant electric lighting.

Philip Pontius Baker of Vineland founded Wildwood in 1890 on Five Mile Beach, a spot known for its natural magnificence. Just back from the beach, tremendously tall cedars cooled visitors, and gigantic grape vines and festoons of moss hanging from the trees delighted the eye.

John Wanamaker, Philadelphia merchant, took such pride in Cape May Point (founded in 1875 as Sea Grove) that he invited President and Mrs. Harrison to visit him there. Friends built a $10,000 cottage and presented it to the Harrisons when they arrived in 1890.

Contrasting with down-Cape gaiety was the establishment in 1891 of the Jewish colony at Woodbine, where 62 farms of 30 acres each were laid out for refugees who had fled Russian persecution. The new colonists bought farms, complete with farmhouse, outbuildings and stock, for $1,200 apiece. Woodbine prospered and within a year had 700 inhabitants.

A few miles south of Woodbine young Eugene G. Grace left his birthplace in Goshen in June, 1899, for a job with the Bethlehem Steel Corporation. Fourteen years later the village heard with pride that young Gene had been named president of the tremendous company.

Another young man of eventual fortune, Henry Ford, brought a racing car to the Cape in 1903 to enter the automobile races on the flat, hardpacked beach. He tried to sell stock in his automobile company but most of the Cape's canny farmers refused to buy. Ford lost the races and had to sell one of his cars to Daniel Focer in town in order to get funds to return home. Later Focer gained the nation's first Ford franchise and many years later James Couzens (who became a U. S. senator from Michigan) sold at tremendous profit the $5,000 in stock he had bought from Ford at Cape May.

County leaders sought at the turn-of-the-century to start a much-needed ferry to the State of Delaware. In 1900 a sidewheeler made several unsatisfactory runs and in 1903 the 200-foot steamer *Caroline* tried unsuccessfully to establish service. Through the years abortive attempts have been made to link the states by ferry, including the 1926 effort which saw "Colonel" Jesse Rosenfeld of Baltimore sink an old concrete ship off Cape May Point as the anchor for a ferry terminal. The old ship still rests in the water (and a proposed ferry is still on the planning charts).

Today Cape May County has as close a tie to the past as any county in New Jersey. Descendants of old families are numerous and proud of their heritage. Cape May's streets show their derivation from the unplanned growth of the eighteenth century. Old houses are numerous and well kept (and the magnet for an annual summer historical pilgrimage). The old Cape May Point lighthouse tells of the county's former dependence on the sea.

Silent reminder of 1926 plans for Cape May Point ferry.

Industry has come in, notably a multimillion-dollar magnesite plant on Cape May Point and the industries clustered about the modern county airport. Yet fishing, farming and catering to visitors remain the Cape's principal occupations. Commercial fishermen frequent the off-Cape waters, particularly the spring mackerel fleets, and sport fishing is an important source of income. Farm lands extend all the way up the western edge of the county and through the northern part, many of them producing on contract for Seabrook Farms in Cumberland County.

Cape May County remains a "watering place" of much dignity, however, particularly in the older resort towns. Each year more than 350,000 visitors come to stay in the hotels and cottages and to relax on the long, sloping beaches. Nevertheless, visitors following "the flight from the gull" on the Ocean highway from Ocean City to Cape May are struck by the great areas of as yet undeveloped oceanfront. The Cape's uninhabited stretches of land continue to attract birds (and bird watchers) as the Cape maintains its status as a bird haven.

Sometimes visitors get sand in their shoes, and then they stay on. There's plenty of room, since only 37,131 people were counted in the 1950 census.

Quickly the newcomers absorb the traditions of Cape May and cherish them. It's easy to do.

MORE ABOUT CAPE MAY

Beesley, Maurice, M.D., *Geological Survey of New Jersey (Cape May County)*. Trenton, New Jersey, The True American, 1857.

Hand, Albert, Co., *A Book of Cape May, New Jersey*. Cape May, New Jersey, The Albert Hand Co., 1937.

Howe, Paul S., *Mayflower Pilgrim Descendants in Cape May County, New Jersey*. Cape May, New Jersey, Albert R. Hand, 1921.

Stevens, Lewis Townsend, *Cape May County, New Jersey*. Cape May City, New Jersey, L. T. Stevens, 1897.

Wheeler, Edward S., *Scheyichbi and the Strand, or Early Days Along the Delaware*. Philadelphia, Pennsylvania, J. B. Lippincott Co., 1876.

Variety Is the Secret

There you have New Jersey—as small as its 8,224 square miles, as unbounded as the world-wide markets it serves. It's as old as Henry Hudson's *Half Moon,* as new as research in scores of modern laboratories; as gay as the white sand beaches in the summer sun, as somber as the sooty Newark Meadows in winter's twilight.

Variety is the secret of Jersey. In a state which in size a Texan might consider merely an overgrown ranch, there are mountains, cities, farms and beaches—each of them well-defined and nationally-known. Few states crowd such diversity into 166 airline miles (166 miles—that's all—from High Point to Cape May).

Obviously New Jersey is progressive. A state forty-fifth in size can't rank sixth in the nation in industrial output without being alert to twentieth-century demands and techniques. Nevertheless, much of the state's fame derives from its exceptional role in the Revolutionary War.

New Jersey is scenic, too, although that's hard to prove to the millions who each year see the state only through the window of a speeding train or through the windshield of an automobile tearing over a turnpike at 60 miles an hour. Even the Grand Canyon wouldn't look good at 60 miles an hour.

But that's fate for you; the very highways and railroads which speed through the scenically-poor parts of the state also have brought to little Jersey its tremendous industrial might. New Jersey's industrial performance is fabulous, and that appraisal is provable by statistics.

Possibly the most astounding thing about New Jersey industry is its concentration within a relatively narrow corridor stretched between Philadelphia and New York. That accounts for the figures which show that New Jersey is still only 14 per cent urbanized, with the remaining 86 per cent in forest-land or farmland.

That 86 per cent is where New Jersey's future rests, and in many places that future is closing in on the trees and the furrows.

Take North Jersey, for example, where research laboratories and handsome new factories have begun to grow on the hills west of Jersey City, Newark and Elizabeth. Housing developments have mushroomed since World War II on North Jersey land that since the beginning of colonization has been considered agriculture's domain.

South Jersey, saddled for 150 years with a million acres of virtual wilderness in the noted Pine Barrens, has begun to stir. Research teams are busy in the pines, seeking to discover its natural secrets. Scattered communities like Lakewood and Hammonton and Vineland have proved that the Pines offer opportunity—in the hands of those with courage, vision and drive.

New Jersey's future may well rest in those pines, known to millions who roll through them each summer, bound from Wilmington or Philadelphia to the Jersey Shore. Known to millions, yet understood and appreciated by all too few. Long ago the Pines buzzed with the activity and prosperity of dozens of ironworks and glass manufactories. Since those collapsed in the nineteenth century, the brooding barrens have waited—and waited—for men of character to turn the land to use.

Down along the lower Delaware River valley, Burlington, Gloucester and Salem counties are set to share in the industrial boom which has overwhelmed that valley in the past decade. That part of New Jersey is on the threshold of riverfront industrial development which may alter forever the traditional agricultural set of the area.

So, New Jersey has a rich heritage, a pleasant today and the possibility of an exciting tomorrow. These are the elements which intrigue and please anyone who sets about understanding the state lodged between New York and Philadelphia.

Unfortunately, too many of New Jersey's own fail to open their eyes and ears and hearts to that which is close at hand. They philosophize, perhaps, along the line that after all, Jersey "is like a barrel, tapped at both ends." There is some justice in that, of course, but the pity is that more don't stop to sample the brew still in the barrel.

It's heady stuff!

More About New Jersey

This list is to be considered as selected readings on the State of New Jersey rather than a full bibliography of materials used in preparing *This Is New Jersey*. Not listed are the primary sources consulted, many other books on the state's history and development, and the many anniversary editions published by local newspapers. These books, as well as those in each chapter, are offered because they are generally authentic, generally available—and, above all, of interest to the general reader.

Barber, John, and Howe, Ward Henry, *Historical Collections of the State of New Jersey*. New York, S. Tuttle, 1844.

Beck, Henry C., *Forgotten Towns of Southern New Jersey*. New York, E. P. Dutton and Co., 1936.

Beck, Henry C., *More Forgotten Towns of Southern New Jersey*. New York, E. P. Dutton and Co., 1937.

Boyer, Charles S., *Early Forges and Furnaces in New Jersey*. Philadelphia, Pennsylvania, University of Pennsylvania Press, 1931.

Cawley, James and Margaret, *Exploring the Little Rivers of New Jersey*. Princeton, New Jersey, Princeton University Press, 1942.

Chambers, Theodore Frelinghuysen, *The Early Germans of New Jersey*. Dover, New Jersey, The Dover Printing Co., 1895.

Federal Writers' Project, *New Jersey: A Guide to Its Present and Past*. New York, The Viking Press, 1939.

Federal Writers' Project, *Stories of New Jersey*. New York, M. Barrows and Co., 1939.

Garber, John Palmer, *The Valley of the Delaware*. Philadelphia, Pennsylvania, John C. Winston Co., 1934.

Gordon, Thomas F., *The History and Gazeteer of New Jersey*. Trenton, New Jersey, Daniel Penton, 1834.

Hankins, Grace C., *True Stories of New Jersey*. Philadelphia, Pennsylvania, John C. Winston Co., 1938.

Harshberger, J. W., *The Vegetation of the New Jersey Pine Barrens*. Philadelphia, Pennsylvania, Christopher Sower Co., 1916.

Heston, Alfred M. *South Jersey: A History*. New York, Lewis Historical Publishing Co., 1924. 4 vols.

Honeyman, Abraham Van Doren, Ed., *Northwestern New Jersey: A History of Somerset, Morris, Hunterdon, Warren and Sussex Counties*. New York, Lewis Historical Pub., 1927. 4 vols.

Kobbé, Gustav, *Jersey Central*, New York, Gustave Kobbé, 1890.

Kobbé, Gustav, *The New Jersey Coast and Pines*. Short Hills, N. J. Gustav Kobbé, 1889.

Kull, Irving S., *New Jersey: A History*. New York, American Historical Society, 1930. 4 vols.

Lane, Wheaton J., *From Indian Trail to Iron Horse, 1620-1860*. Princeton, New Jersey, Princeton University Press, 1939.

Lee, Francis B., *New Jersey as a Colony and as a State*. New York, The Publishing Society of New Jersey, 1902. 4 vols.

Lundin, Leonard, *Cockpit of the Revolution*. Princeton, New Jersey, Princeton University Press, 1940.

Myers, William Starr, *The Story of New Jersey*. New York, Lewis Publishing Co., 1945; 5 vols.

Nelson, William, *New Jersey Coast in Three Centuries*. New York, 1902. 3 vols.

New Jersey Department of Agriculture, *New Jersey Agriculture: Historical Facts and Figures*. Trenton, New Jersey, 1943.

Parsons, Floyd W., *New Jersey: Life, Industries and Resources of a Great State*. Trenton, New Jersey, New Jersey State Chamber of Commerce, 1928.

Schmidt, Hubert G., *Lesser Crossroads (Story of an Old Farm)*. New Brunswick, New Jersey, Rutgers University Press, 1948.

Stockton, Frank R., *Stories of New Jersey*. New York, American Book Co., 1896.

Torrey, R. H., Place, Frank, and Dickinson, A. L., *New York Walk Book*. New York, Dodd, Mead and Co., 1934.

Van Sickle, Emogene, *The Old York Road and Stage Coach Days*. Flemington, New Jersey, Hunterdon County Democrat, 1936.

Weygandt, Cornelius, *Down New Jersey*. Appleton-Century Co., 1940.